TRAILS GUIDE

TO

PIKES PEAK
COUNTRY

by

ZOLTAN
MALOCSAY

SQUEEZY PRESS

Library of Congress Catalog Card Number
91-061067

ISBN: 0-9629250-0-4

Cover photograph by Charles Lamoreaux

Colorado Trail map courtesy of the Colorado Trail Foundation. Jefferson County Open Space maps courtesy of Jefferson County. Thomas Trail map courtesty of Dick Bratton. Cougar print courtesy Division of Wildlife.

Fourth Edition
Printed in the United States of America. Text printed on recycled paper.

Published by Squeezy Press
P.O. Box 60412
Colorado Springs, CO 80906-2455

to Dolores, my love

Pikes Peak Country Vicinity Map
By Chapter

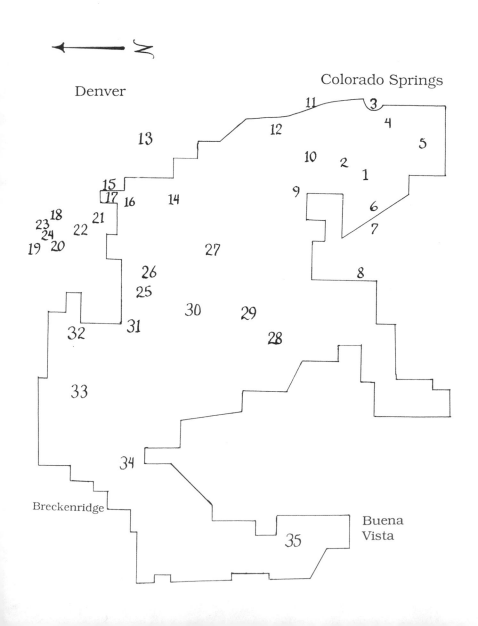

N

Denver

Colorado Springs

11
3
12
4
13
5
10
2
1
9
15
6
17 16
14
7
18 21
23 22
24
19 20
27
26
25
8
30 29
31
32
28
33
34
Breckenridge
Buena Vista
35

TABLE OF CONTENTS

5

TRAIL DESCRIPTIONS

6

9

FOREWORD--A MESSAGE FROM THE GOVERNOR

It may seem like a small world when we travel by car or plane, but if you put on a pair of hiking boots or cross-country skis, if you climb on a horse or a mountain bike, then Colorado itself becomes a vast world of its own. All those magnificent post-cards and stunning roadside views give us only a sample. If you want to know why Colorado has become so famous for scenic beauty and outdoor recreation, then you'll have to get out and see it for yourself by experiencing it first-hand. Get out and see it from the trail. These mountains offer more inspiration and more fun than can be described. Indeed, there is more to see and do today than ever before--more trails, more public lands, more ways to have fun. It's all right here, close by, and so inexpensive that we often take it all for granted--or just forget to take advantage of it.

Sometimes we see the calendar slipping past summer and wish that we had gone to the mountains more often, but most public lands don't close. Even your favorite spot looks very different in its fall glory or sparkling with winter snow. And if you cross the next ridge, you'll probably find a new favorite. There is so much to see, so much to do, that you could spend a lifetime trying to see it all and do it all, without ever leaving the state. As Governor, that makes me very proud. And as a citizen, that makes me very lucky.

Roy Romer
Governor

ACKNOWLEDGMENTS

Many people, both in and out of government, helped to make this book so accurate, not as a favor to the author, but as a public service to all those who enjoy the trails of Pikes Peak Country.

Federal Level--For the Pike National Forest: Jim Montoya, Marlin Sutton, Grady McMahon, Rick Ellsworth, Glenn McNitt, Len Newton, Henry Goehle, Lois Bachensky, Sharon Kyhl, Mike Hester, Jerry Davis and Wayne Baker. For the National Park Service: Kathy Brown, Richard Compton and Jo Beckwith. For the U.S. Air Force Academy: Staff Sergeant Gary Cunningham, Airman Don Kusturin and Charlotte Bond.

State Level--Governor Roy Romer and Jane Nelson. For the Division of Wildlife: Eric Lundberg, Doug Krieger, John Torres, Greg Policky, Phil Goebel, Susan Werner, Ron Zaccagnini,.Clete Nolde. For Parks and Recreation: Bob Finch, Susan Trumble, Terry Gimbel, Cheryl Galvin, Greg Nootbar, Harry Downer, and Annie Carter. For the Health Department: Dan Bowlds. And State Trails Coordinator Stuart MacDonald.

County Level--El Paso: Micky Carter and Ken Pals. Jefferson: Mark Hearon, Frank Kunze and Bryan Pritchett. Special thanks go to the staff of the Pikes Peak Area Council of Governments and former Executive Director Roland Gow, who published the first edition in 1980.

City Level--Colorado Springs: Bill Stookey, Fred Mais, Rick Severson and Tom Gayler. Colorado Springs Utilities: Vic Ecklund, Don Mulligan, Chet Holbrook and Mike Madonna. Denver Water Board: Bob Taylor and Michele Radice. Denver Mountain Parks: Lee Gylling and Neil Sperandeo. Manitou Springs: Chris Daly, Jim Pratt, John Shada, Cheryl Massaro, Larry Manning and Johnnie Price. Woodland Park: Sally Riley. Palmer Lake: Dale T. Smith.

Individuals--Dolores Arnold, Robert Houdek, Robert Ormes, Monty and Terri Barrett, Carl Wiese, Marvin Kershaw, Ken Jordan, Diane Russelavage, Brian Gravestock, Skye Ridley, Russ Weaver, Jan Petit, Rick Romero, Dick Bratton, Mark and Anna Ouellette, Charles Lamoreaux, Randy Jacobs, Julia Wright.

ABOUT THE AUTHOR

Zoltan Malocsay is an artist and author who lives in Colorado Springs. He grew up on the outskirts of Miami, Oklahoma, flying airplanes and riding horses. Zoltan put himself through college by working as a daily newspaper reporter and by selling Western history articles to magazines. After graduating Phi Beta Kappa from the University of Oklahoma's School of Professional Writing, he did graduate work at the University of Iowa's Writer's Workshop. He also served as a technical writer and research proposals editor for the University of Oklahoma's Research Institute.

While traveling as a magazine correspondent, Zoltan and his English wife Dolores backpacked in Canada, the United States and Mexico, following the seasons and virtually living in a mountain tent for three years.

BOY'S LIFE magazine has published 14 of the author's outdoor adventure short stories, and many of these have been reprinted in textbooks. His first novel, *Galloping Wind*, has been published in hardback by Putnam and is now a Dell Western paperback.

Working as a citizen go-between, Malocsay has worked with various government agencies to negotiate the opening of public lands that have remained closed for generations.

Zoltan is also a fine jewelry artist whose designer line of 14k earrings, earring jackets and pendant jackets are sold to fine stores throughout most of the United States.

WHAT YOU SHOULD KNOW BEFORE YOU GO

Colorado is world famous for its natural beauty and outdoor recreation, but where can you go this weekend? How do you get there, and what's it like? What can you do there and what do you need to take along? This hand-made guide is designed to answer all those questions and more.

Pikes Peak Country is a vast playground sprawling across five counties: El Paso, Teller, Park, Douglas and Jefferson. At its heart is the Pike National Forest, itself over a million acres of renowned scenery, plus a patchwork of other public lands administered by federal, state, county and city governments. It extends west to Georgia Pass, beyond Fairplay, and stretches north to the summit of Mount Evans, west of Denver. Best of all, these public lands belong to you!

The trails of Pikes Peak Country exist for your enjoyment, so the purpose of this book is to help you enjoy them as much as possible. We'll try to show you all the little things that a walking, talking human guide would show you. We'll show you where to camp and fish, the best places for cross-country skiing and mountain biking, great places to ride a horse or take the family for a hike. We'll give you road directions and trail descriptions, tell you a little about the plants and wildlife, about the history and geology, and we'll show you how to preserve and protect these delicate areas so that you and your family and friends can enjoy them--as they are--for years to come.

Our guide covers virtually all of the public trails that are marked, maintained and closed to motorized vehicles. It would take another such guide to describe all of the routes open to motorcyclists and four-wheelers. There are other trails that we could not mention because they have become so obscure that no written guide could lead you there. Others have trespass problems. The trails in this guide are legal and officially open to everyone. Where ever private property is involved, legal work has been done to guarantee your right-of-way. And just to make sure that everything is as accurate as possible, two dozen government offices have worked to verify our trail descriptions.

Rules differ greatly from area to area, so always check our guide before heading out. Trails that receive the heaviest use always have the most no-nos. But for those who wish to walk or ride a ways, the National Forest offers all of the freedoms and responsibilities of backcountry. In the most remote areas, the Forest Service offers virtually no facilities, only paths and a very few signs. You are very much on your own. **Outdoor recreation always involves an element of risk, and no guide can be a substitute for sound judgement. Your comfort and safety are your own responsibility.**

But there are other responsibilities also. The Forest Service could never clean up after all those who use the trails, so visitors themselves must watch over the land and protect it by careful use. We'll also show you the art of "minimum impact," how to enjoy the mountains without changing anything. But don't be afraid to do more than your share. If someone in your party is not behaving, then clean up after them; they might catch on. And if you see other visitors abusing your forest, be cordial but don't be shy about correcting them. Many greenhorns just don't know any better or don't believe that anyone cares.

Right now there are only a few rules for those trails marked with a Forest Service trail number. You may not pick or dig up wildflowers or other plants, may not cut on living trees or plants, may not remove moss or take souvenirs. You are welcome to look and touch and take photographs, but you are asked to leave everything in its place, to treat the forest as a living museum.

HIKING WITH OUR GUIDE

There is an old song that talks about going "a-wandering with a knapsack on my back." Now **that** is the proper attitude! Just go a-wandering. Don't go on a forced march to see how much you can take.

Our guide offers every kind of trail, so always plan an expedition around the weakest member of your party. Try not to take friends and loved ones on a hike that is so difficult that they will never want to go again.

And when you find yourself grunting uphill, stop and take a few deep breaths and look around. Try not to miss the far-off scenery or the close-up wonders around you. Then wander up to the next switchback and see how the view changes. Keep that up and you can wander for miles, having fun all the way, appreciating everything and growing stronger every time.

Always tell someone where you're going and when you expect to be back. Estimating hiking time is very tricky. A lot depends upon the terrain, the condition of the trail, the weight of your pack, even your mood. As a rule of thumb, realize that many backpackers figure on making only one mile per hour packing uphill, but twice that on the downhill.

Dayhikers need to watch the time and start back with plenty of daylight. We recommend carrying a small disposable flashlight in case some delay should leave you in the dark, but we have a whole section on what to take along--and why. A small item can make the difference between fun and misery, between safety and danger.

You must have good boots or sturdy shoes with a lug sole. We've seen grown-ups in sneakers fall flat on their faces because steep trails are lubricated with fine gravel. You need lug soles to bite down through that to grip the mountain. Modern light hikers come ready to wear, unlike the heavy hikers that used to take a lot of breaking in.

Buy a pair big enough to accommodate two pairs of socks, a thick wool outer pair and a thin soft inner pair. That's still the best way to prevent blisters. Take the socks with you when you buy the boots and always use the same kinds. If the ensemble doesn't feel like heaven, keep shopping.

You can prevent blisters by paying attention to your feet and stopping immediately if you feel a hot spot. Put Moleskin on that spot soon enough and a blister won't form. If the blister has already formed, never put Moleskin directly on it. Instead, cut a hole in the Moleskin the same size as the blister. That will keep your boot from rubbing the blister.

No joke: It is important to cut your toenails because your foot will scoot farther forward than you might imagine on a downhill, bumping the ends of your toenails so gently that you won't feel it, yet bruising the quick. Then your toenails turn blue and later may fall off!

No matter how great the weather seems, take along some warm clothes and a poncho to keep you dry. Read up on hypothermia, discussed later, because it is truly more deadly than bears.

And please take municipal water from home, perhaps half frozen in a plastic canteen. But don't drink from streams or spring pools. Read our section on water parasites before you scoff. This author got very sick researching the first edition.

Pack the night before and be sure to get an early start with a good breakfast. With a little preparation, you can almost guarantee a great time.

MOUNTAIN BIKING

Mountain bicycling is the fastest growing sport on the Front Range. Indeed, bikers now outnumber hikers on many trails. If you've never tried it, consider this: Just as mechanical advantage helps you jack up a car, mechanical advantage can help boost you over mountains. If you get puffed trying to pedal up a hill in your neighborhood, you can still mountain bicycle. You'll just have to push it more than others do, but you'll get stronger--and probably have a good time doing it!

It is no disgrace to dismount and push your bike uphill, no matter what my wife says. You'll soon find a gentler stretch where you can pedal again, and downhill is always a breeze. If you're really out of shape, a little preconditioning would be wise, but our guide describes many trails where the pedaling is easy. All trails are rated.

Biking allows you to cover more distance than you could on foot, but this also means that it will take you farther from your car, which brings up a safety point. Mountain biking is really more like hiking than many purists would like to think. You need most of the same gear--warm clothing, rain protection, food, drinking water, the stuff that day hikers carry for comfort and safety.

Don't use a backpack; it'll spoil your balance. Paniers tend to snag rocks and trees, but there are packs made to Velcro to a rack atop the back wheel. These have no snagging problems, they come on and off in a flash and don't flop around.

Even if you never fall down riding street bikes, you can expect to fall while riding mountain bikes, and since falls occur among rocks and stumps, if not downhill, then no one should have to convince you to wear a helmet.

Some biking footwear is entirely too slick. When you dismount on a steep trail, you don't want your feet sliding out from under you. Your feet need tread just as your tires do.

The greatest danger to the sport itself is lack of sportsmanship. Bikes are banned in some areas and may be banned in more areas because of bikers speeding downhill, riding out of control, spooking horses, chasing hikers off trail, shortcutting switchbacks, rutting soft ground or tearing up tundra.

Always yield the right-of-way, even when it is inconvenient. This means that biking is not much fun wherever there are crowds of people because you end up walking the bike more than riding. There are lots of better places.

Pass with care. Sometimes people don't hear you coming, so let them know with a friendly greeting. If you wind up overtaking people, you often have to wait until there's a good place where they can let you by. In any case, hikers and horses have right-of-way. Be especially careful around horses; wait for a nod from the rider.

Safe speed depends on terrain. At one speed, you have enough control to stay on the trail, but that isn't good enough. You need to be able to stop, if you encounter the unexpected.

Most of the trails in our guide are open to bikes, but there are scattered exceptions, so be sure to check. Have fun!

Horseback Riding

If grunting up a mountain makes you stop and pant, ever consider a horse? They stop and pant, too, but Indians and mountain men found them pretty handy--and so will you.

No need to own one. You can rent horses a number of places, even outside some parks. Check the yellow pages. We had a great time with Marvin Kershaw of Old Country Rides between Divide and Cripple Creek

Indeed, visitors to our area should consider using local horses rather than bringing horses from lower altitudes because mounts have to be conditioned for the high country, just as people do. Even mounts raised at 6,000 feet will find the air thin at 11,000 feet, so take it easy. When going uphill, you have to stop frequently and rest your horse with the head pointing downhill to help circulation.

An anxious horse can expend so much energy in the first hour that it may never be able to recover for the rest of the day, so it is especially important to hold back for the first hour or so. Horses allowed to travel at their own pace may collapse and die. Be especially careful above timberline, of course, where the air is thinnest. Some horses get frisky when they break out of the trees and want to run in the open. Above timberline, that could be deadly.

Never carry your wallet in your back pocket; they tend to squirm out of your hip pocket as you ride.

All the stuff that you would normally carry in a daypack is still necessary on a trailride, except that you've got saddlebags to carry it. But if you should need to reach for a poncho or a jacket, remember to stop and dismount so the horse won't spook.

The average horse would just as soon go back to the trailer without you, so you really do need to keep your mount under control every second. Always be willing to have someone hold your horse while you make some adjustment. Never try to tie it by the reins. Don't give a strange horse the chance to slip away. Davy Crockett's diary has a story about following a loose horse day after day without being able to lay hands on it. The horse was simply going home!

Horse manure is no problem in backcountry, but very popular trails can turn into manure troughs, creating a nuisance for all those who hike or bike. So when you ride in popular areas, please dismount and move manure off the trail. That way its nutrients can do some good. No need to bury it. It would take too big a hole anyway. Before now, this has never been a part of trail etiquette in these parts, but this comes with heavy use. Your consideration will be appreciated and may prevent future restrictions.

We did some of our longest trails on horseback, some with the Cavalier Riding Club. It's a great way to see the mountains.

Cross-Country Skiing

Imagine skiing without lift lines, without crowds, without lift tickets, without bumper-to-bumper traffic on the way home. No wonder cross-country skiing is such a fast growing sport! Colorado has only two problems when it comes to cross-country skiing--too little snow and too much snow. Many areas are only skiable after major storms because our sunny weather soon melts it all away. And in higher country, the problem may be getting there. The Crags area, for example, offers wonderful tour skiing, but the road leading there is seldom plowed and creates a lot of business for tow truck operators. Lost Park is likewise a beautiful area, but the road has the same problem.

Which brings up the subject of emergency gear for your car and for your pack. Tour skiing is generally safer than downhill because you don't go as fast or fall as hard, but then again, there is no ski patrol on our trails, and an accident in backcountry can turn into a survival situation. It is most important that you don't go alone, that you tell someone where your party is headed, and that you take the food and clothing that dayhikers normally carry. See What To Take Along--And Why.

Fishing

Imagine an airplane flying over a mountain peak, then diving over the other side, swooping down to a lake hidden in a glacier-gouged pocket. The airplane bombs the lake with native cutthroat trout, then flies out the valley.

That's your State Division of Wildlife making sure that Colorado fishermen have plenty to brag about. The numbers show that Colorado's fishing just gets better and better, year by year, through scientific management funded by fishing licenses. Indeed, some waters featured in this book have just about all the fish they could possibly support.

Our guide will show you all the hidden places that can only be reached by those who hike or ride. No roads go there All you need is a valid Colorado fishing license, some gear and an understanding of the rules.

Regulations have become a little more complicated in recent years because biologists are trying to fine-tune fishing to maximize each particular situation. So **watch for changes in the literature provided with your license each year.** The rules are meant to improve your fun in the long run.

Only poaching can ruin this effort. If you see a violation, try to make note of the vehicle description, license plate, direction of travel, clothing, anything possible, and call Operation Game Thief at 1-800-332-4145 or 295-0164 in the Denver area. You need not reveal your name or testify in court, but you may receive a reward Even if you don't have enough informaton to catch them this time, a pattern of reports may lead to future arrests.

One of our trails is for catch-and-release fishing only. Returning fish immediately to the water may not appeal to some, but at least this means you can fish for wild trout, not stockers, of a size that is generally seen only on walls. Besides, you'll have just as much fun catching that one again next time. Some of the biggest have been caught many times and are wary enough to be a real test of skill.

Biologists no longer recommend handling fish with wet hands; people have to squeeze too hard to get a good grip. It's best to become practiced with a pair of surgical hemostats, which can pluck out a hook without your having to touch the fish at all.

Be careful about over-playing fish in warmer lake waters because a fish can die of exhaustion. If a fish appears weak, revive it by holding it gently and pushing it through the water, making figure eights so that water runs through the gills.

Non-motorized trails lead to many lakes, streams and beaver ponds for stand-up fishing, but don't ignore the many smaller streams where you can sneak up on brook trout. They can be a lot of fun, and the more you fish them, the better they do. Brookies grow to 18 inches in Pikes Peak Country (honest), but tend to stunt themselves through overpopulation, so the state allows you eight extra brookies under eight inches so you can help out by eating plenty.

Every trail that offers fishing is marked with a symbol in our table of contents, and our trail descriptions will tell you about the kind of fishing there, the types of fish and other information that might be useful. For example, we've seen people hike in with a big tackle box (when all the gear they really needed could have fitted in pockets) and then start back early because they didn't bring a flashlight. So just when the fish started to bite at dusk, they were forced to leave. If you're going to be hiking at night, however, be sure to familiarize yourself with the trail in daylight. Night hiking is always risky.

In some waters lake trout are not getting big enough to reproduce because anglers mistake them for other trout and remove them. The special limit of one laker over 20 inches (at Jefferson Lake and Rampart Reservoir) is vigorously enforced, and mistakes are no excuse, so watch for the deeply indented tail fin that characterizes the laker.

Don't miss out. The best trout we ever tasted was cooked within minutes of leaving the water, so if you've never experienced hike-in fishing, you're missing a lot of what Colorado has to offer.

Camping

The National Forest operates a large number of pay campgrounds throughout Pikes Peak Country, some on a reservation basis and some not, some with handicap access and some not, some for groups only. Many tourists feel they need the convenience, the services (potable water, trash haul-out, etc.) and the knowledge that other folks are nearby. But if you'd rather get away from it all, away from everybody, and take care of yourself, then you have just opened the right book!

What you have in Pikes Peak Country is over a million acres of free camping on a first-come basis with no services. Again, your comfort and safety are strictly your own responsibility. With few exceptions, you may camp along any of the National Forest trails, but the Forest Service would like you to camp with ecology in mind.

Camping at the edge of water, for example, may pollute the

water as well as expose you to the danger of flashflood. Above timberline you will damage tundra by simply walking around, so try to avoid making camp above timberline. You'll find more protection in the trees anyway.

Cutting green boughs for bedding is illegal, it damages the forest and it makes a lumpy bed for your effort. Light foam pads will serve both you and the forest better.

Trenching your tent may be necessary in other parts of the country, but Colorado soil is so porous that water tends to sink straight down instead of gathering around your tent. Trenching makes ugly scars that encourage erosion.

All camp cleaning should be done with biodegradable soaps. The same soap will wash you and your clothes and the dishes, but even biodegradable soap should never be used near streams or lakes. Nobody likes to drink your wash water.

If you use minimum impact camping skills, the Forest Service allows you to camp in one spot for two weeks at a time, if you like. But eventually, even minimum impact takes a toll, so after two weeks, you must move to another area to give your old campsite a chance to recover. In return for this stewardship, you may camp all you want.

There are other things you should know about minimum impact camping, things about campfires and sanitation and drinking water, and we'll cover these items in detail, but the point of all this is to enjoy the forest without leaving a mark, without changing the beauty you came to admire. If you do it right, you should be able to look back and see nothing but some bent grass where your tent was.

Building Campfires

Campfires are an outdoor tradition that may be going the way of the buffalo robe. They are becoming illegal in more and more areas and are banned in other areas when fire danger becomes high. They scar the land, encourage vandals to cut living trees when deadwood becomes scarce; they burn up wood used for homes and food by wildlife—and sometimes they burn down the whole forest.

If you like to cook in backcountry, better get used to carrying a lightweight backpacker stove. Once you have tried one on a wet and cold morning, you won't begrudge carrying the extra 18 ounces or so. They are clean, fast, efficient and they work when open fires won't. But most of all, they protect the forest, and that is why they are becoming required in more and more areas.

If you do make a fire, make it small. A small fire makes less smoke, and you won't have to strip the woods to keep it going. Pots are easier to handle on a little fire, and wind won't blow so many sparks from it. A small campfire is safer in case someone stumbles and falls, is much easier to put out and is much less likely to rekindle itself somehow. You'll also find that small fires are much easier to erase. You can hide all traces. No need to leave a fire ring.

All that said, never make even the tiniest fire when fire danger is high. Remember that Smoky the Bear was named after a real bear cub orphaned by a forest fire.

Trail Etiquette

A great many people can share a wilderness with a sense of privacy, if everyone shows a little consideration. Good manners are essential to the kindly and relaxed atmosphere that visitors are seeking. Try to keep your party from becoming a loud party. Loud radios and shouting are not appreciated by others, and shouting may be taken as a signal for help.

Always share information with anyone who asks, and if you are being overtaken by a faster group, move aside and let them pass. If you should meet horses on the trail, remember that they always have the right-of-way. When horses are coming toward you, move off to the side, preferably downhill, and talk among yourselves in order to make sure that the horses know that you are there and won't be startled.

Never allow members of your party to roll or throw rocks from the trail. You cannot be certain that no one is below because well-mannered hikers don't make much noise. If it should happen that a rock or log or any other object falls away, yell the word

"Rock!"--even if it is not a rock. This word can be yelled faster than "Look Out!" and is meant to warn that some kind of object is falling.

Never allow anyone in your party to short-cut down slopes whether barriers exist or not. It may not seem to do any harm at the time, but the first hard rainstorm will start making a gully out of your short-cut. This kind of erosion has erased hundreds of miles of interesting trails in our region. Whenever you leave the trail for any reason, pick the gentlest route and tread carefully.

And please pack **out your garbage. Anything that you try to hide or bury will only be dug up by animals and scattered around,** so please carry out your garbage and as much of anyone else's garbage that you can. Disposable diapers must also be carried out for the same reason; animals dig them up and then rains wash them into streams. Which leads us to an essential subject, sanitation.

Sanitation

All nature requires is a little cooperation. There are no restrooms anywhere near most of these trails. So, select an area at least 50 to 100 feet from any open water or spring. With your heel, scrape out a hole no deeper than several inches. That's because the first several inches--the biological layer--contains a system of disposers that will I break down the wastes. If you go deeper, you spoil this effect.

If there is any sod, try to keep it intact and replace it after covering the hole with dirt. Sprinkle on some needles and such. Nature does the rest.

Taking Dogs Along

Division of Wildlife officers are legally empowered to shoot dogs chasing wildlife and to arrest their owners. Both civil and criminal penalties apply. And not having your dog on a leash can cost you $400 anywhere in Jefferson County, not just in the parks.

These are a sample of the serious considerations involved in taking a dog to the woods.

You do have the right to take your dog with you on most of the trails in this book, but everyone who enjoys this freedom is in danger of losing it because of problems caused by some dogs and their masters. Dogs used to be allowed in the Florissant Fossil Beds, but they ran the elk, chased other critters and gobbled the ground-nesting birds, so now they are totally banned. There are a number of such places listed in our guide (so always check) and the number is increasing. Dog owners can help protect their freedoms by making sure their pets don't become the cause of new regulations--and by encouraging others to be just as considerate. Don't fool yourself into believing that your pet cannot catch the critters it chases: Persistence pays.

When considering whether or not to take a dog along, a lot depends upon the personality of your pet, its training and your willingness to control it every second. So treat it like a member of the family. If you had a member of the family who threatened other visitors, picked fights with their dogs, went after horses and llamas, jumped into water where others were trying to fish or fill a canteen, you might well leave such a brat at home next time.

And if your child pooped on the trail, you would stop and clean it up, so do the same for the four-legged member of your family. Seriously, it does the environment no good left on the trail. It creates a nuisance and resentment (and ultimately more regulations). But when buried off-trail, it becomes fertilizer that nature can use.

Besides all this, keeping your dog strictly under control may prevent your trip from being ruined by an encounter with a porcupine, a skunk or something meaner that was only trying to hide from you both. Your consideration will help protect your dog and your right to take a dog onto trails.

Meeting Cattle

Parts of the National Forest are leased to ranchers as pasture, so you are bound to encounter herds of cattle on some of our trails. Cattle rarely hassle people who know how to handle them, but bulls or cows with calves can be very protective, so don't assume that such powerful animals will always run away from you. Even a cow may charge if she feels that you are endangering her calf.

Cattle will usually be found directly in your path because it is really their path. In such areas cattle make more trails than the Forest Service does, and you will have to navigate carefully. The best thing to do is to keep your distance and hike quietly around them. If you climb high enough and keep enough distance, they will probably be too lazy to move, and you can pass them.

Carrying a large stick may make you feel more secure, but you must be careful not to spook cattle. If you do, they will start off along the trail ahead of you. They will not be anxious to leave their trail or to climb uphill, so they will continue to block your way, stopping when you stop, moving when you move, and you could be left following in their dust for miles.

Don't assume that you can scatter them because cattle have a herding instinct that makes them tend to huddle together when frightened. And the rancher won't appreciate your running precious pounds off his cattle. So the best thing to do is leave them where you find them, and try to pass at a distance.

Meeting Mountain Lions and Bears

Colorado's wildlife boom means that mountain lions and bears are becoming more common also, and since a teenage jogger was killed by a mountain lion in Idaho Springs in 1991, everyone should be aware of the possibility of meeting a mountain lion or bear.

Also called cougars or puma, mountain lions generally prowl at night and are often seen near dawn or dusk. If you see one in daylight, he might be hungry. They are generally shy and will try to flee, but if you should surprise one, the Division of Wildlife has this advice: Don't try to bend down to pick up something to throw. Don't crouch or run or act threatening. Instead, face the cat (but don't make eye contact; they feel threatened by eye contact) and slowly back away with your arms raised above your head to make you seem as large as possible. Talk to it calmly as you go. In the extremely unlikely event of attack, fight back as fiercely as you can and try to keep the cougar from getting behind you. They generally kill with a bite below the base of the skull.

There are no grizzlies reported in Pikes Peak country, but the black bear population seems to be on the rise. Bears try to avoid you, but if you should meet one, follow the same procedure outlined above. If you are wearing a pack, get ready to shrug it off, and if he should charge, throw your backpack toward him as hard as you can and run. Typically, that distraction works to make the bear maul the pack, giving you a chance to get away. Only 10% of a bear's diet is meat, so they are not as likely to be hunting something to kill. Sows with cubs can be especially dangerous, however. If you find a cub, chances are mom is close by and will come back soon. If a sow thinks she is being separated from her cub, you can bet she'll attack.

Maintain a clean camp. If you pour grease on the ground, for example, take it a long way from camp. Don't sleep with food in your tent. Lock it in the trunk of your car or suspend it at least 10 feet off the ground. Avoid cooking foods that give off strong odors and burn all tins and food scraps. But don't bury garbage; pack it out.

Evidence indicates that bears may be more aggressive toward those wearing scented cosmetics, hair spray, deodorant and toward women during their menstrual period.

DOW authorities estimate that if you have been on dozen hikes, you have probably been observed by a cougar or bear or both. That may seem creepy, but it should be reassuring because the pattern is clear: They don't want to bother you.

Getting Lost With Map And Compass

We were two days deep in the Lost Creek Wilderness, backpacking with map and compass, when suddenly we came to a stream that was flowing the wrong direction! We were not where we thought, and it was not a good feeling.

So we backtracked, carefully exploring to see where we went wrong. As it turned out, we were on the right trail, but the government had drawn it wrong on the map, which only goes to show that even the U.S. Geological Survey can get mixed up in the woods. That should never have happened, of course, but that's the problem with getting lost: It should never happen, but it does happen sometimes for odd and unexpected reasons.

We corrected our guide's map, but no guide, no map can guarantee that you won't get lost. So it is best to learn how to protect yourself. First of all, never strike out alone; someone should always know where you are going and when you expect to be back. And your party must stay together. Don't let individuals race ahead or straggle behind or stray off on other routes, planning to meet up later. And never ignore your own backtrail. Keep turning and looking back so you know what the trail looks like in reverse. The same piece of trail can look far different from another angle. Follow your progress on the map and use a compass to help orient yourself. If you think you've gone wrong, hug that trail and carefully go back the way you came. Continuing ahead could take you anywhere, and leaving the trail could take you nowhere!

You'll generally find it easy to keep your bearings by following your progress on a topo. Especially important is keeping track of which drainage you are in: Water is your best compass! If you are hiking up a trail that follows a stream, you cannot change streams unless you climb over a ridge that leads to a whole new drainage. However, that mistake is easier to make at higher altitudes where one side of a bump may lead to one creek and the other side to a different creek, so be careful on such finger ridges.

A compass will not keep you from getting lost, especially if you don't know how to use it. It can show that a trail is going the wrong direction, for example, but may not tell you where you went wrong. Don't strike out "as the crow flies," following a compass bearing. Stay on trail and backtrack.

When you use a compass, remember that the needle does not point to true north in Pikes Peak country, but instead points to magnetic north, which is about 14 degrees east of true north. There is a diagram at the bottom of USGS maps showing the difference between the two. Read a book on orienteering if you're confused, then go out and practice in a fairly safe place.

That's how you keep from getting lost, but suppose you get lost anyway. Suppose you have lost the trail entirely. The first thing to do is sit down and think and relax. There is a great temptation to panic, to run, to wear yourself out in a frantic search, so beware of that and try to remember that your first responsibility is to take good care of yourself. Virtually all people who get lost are eventually found, either alive or dead, so the idea is to stay alive no matter how long you have to stay lost.

But think for now. Which way did you come? Getting lost in the mountains isn't like being lost on a flats where you might wander any direction at all. In the mountains your routes are restricted by the lay of the land. Trails tend to follow water or ridges or hillsides, so what kind of trail was it? By looking around and by using process of elimination, you may be able to discover which way you came simply because there aren't that many choices.

But suppose that doesn't work. Well, you have to make some cool and logical decisions. How much time do you have? Estimate how long it has been since you left camp and realize that it will take even longer to get back. If the weather is turning sour or nightfall is coming on, you may not be able to make it, so use your precious daylight to prepare for night. Hole up somewhere in the most sheltered spot you can find. Collect firewood, but don't let your pack out of your sight; if you lose that pack, you're in much worse trouble. Build a tiny fire that won't use up all your firewood, the kind you can huddle over. Try to make yourself as safe and comfortable as possible.

Never try to travel at night or in the rain or in fog. Sit it out. The wilderness SOS consists of three signals of any kind repeated at regular intervals, three flashes of a mirror or shiny knife, three shouts, three whistles.

But let's suppose that you are on a high lookout and still can't fathom which way to turn. In that case, the best way to go is the safest way, for the only thing worse than being lost is being hurt and lost. Never start down into a canyon or gorge that seems to be at your feet; you may trap yourself in a treacherous spot. Instead, follow the gentlest route, no matter which way it leads. Follow a ridge down to the timber, then look for any kind of game trail that leads downhill. That will take you to water. Once you have found a stream, you have found a route to civilization. The only exception in our area is the Lost Creek Wilderness, where Lost Creek disappears into box canyons, running under cliffs and reappearing from caves in rocks beyond. This is very unusual geology and is cause for extra caution when hiking the trails near Lost Creek.

Another exception might be the Rampart Range, where most roads are on ridges and where water drains down some very woolly gulches. Once you find a road, you can generally tell if you're going toward civilization by changes in the road's condition. Backcountry roads are like bull whips, increasingly narrow and nasty toward the uncivilized end, growing wider and nicer toward toward civilization.

If you are injured and lost, try to make it to a clear area or for a promontory of some kind where you can build a signal fire in daylight with wood and green boughs. Above all, remember that you will be found, either alive or dead, so concentrate on staying alive, no matter how long you have to stay lost

What Non-Hunters Should Know

All forest visitors should be aware of hunting season and should wear the same orange reflective clothing that hunters are required to wear. There is no such legal requirement for non-hunters, but the safety advantage is obvious.

Non-hunters should also be aware of hunting regulations because the Division of Wildlife needs the vigilance of all visitors to protect wildlife from poachers. Colorado's Operation Game Thief even pays rewards, almost $47,000 in its first four years. You do not have to reveal your name or testify in court. Just call 1-800-332-4155 toll-free or 295-0164 in the Denver area and provide as much information as you can about the vehicle, direction of travel, clothing, any descriptive details. Anything might help.

Contrary to popular belief, putting food on the table is one of the least common motives for poaching. Thrills and profit are the common motives, and poachers use vehicles, spotlights, radios, nets, traps, the cruelest and most unsporting methods imaginable.

Poachers represent the same greed that once nearly wiped out Colorado's wildlife. Early in this century, when Colorado Springs financier Spencer Penrose wanted to take a maharajah elk hunting, they planned to go to Wyoming because earlier settlers had virtually killed off Colorado's elk! Penrose imported 55 elk from

Yellowstone in 1915, the beginnings of the Pikes Peak herd. Today, thanks to generations of scientific game management--based on carefully regulated sport hunting--Colorado has about 170,000 elk, more than any other state. Deer populations have exploded from only 5,000 statewide in 1910 to three quarters of a million today. All sorts of other wildlife have experienced similar booms, so today we see far more wildlife of all kinds.

For many, the idea that sport hunting could somehow increase wildlife populations seems absurd, but it works for the same reasons that ranching works. Every ranch works by harvesting excess males in order to leave more food for the very young and those needed for breeding, and that's what the hunting license system is designed to do by designating which categories of animals will be taken in each area. And like a ranch, the profits from this harvest (license fees) are used to improve and acquire habitat and sometimes buy food to help the herd survive the worst winter storms. The result is a healthier herd with more young surviving in the spring. Despite the killing involved, this system is restoring Colorado's wildlife to levels not seen since pioneer days.

Certainly, you don't have to become a hunter to support this effort. By checking the wildlife **donation** box on your Colorado Income Tax Form or by making a direct donation to the DOW, you can help pay for managing non-game species, protecting endangered species and reintroducing species that Colorado lost, such as the peregrin falcon and the moose. **The DOW does not use state taxes.**

What To Take Along--And Why

On our first visit to Devil's Head, we saw lots of people starting up the trail with no equipment, just as if they were going to stroll out to a roadside overlook. And the sign said it was only a little more than a mile. But an elderly couple in the parking lot gave us a warning: "That's a real hike," the old man said. "If you've got hiking stuff, take it along."

That proved to be wonderful advice! We saw visitors in sneakers and sandals slipping and sliding, but our lug soles gripped the mountain. That steep trail was sweaty work for awhile, so we were happy to have our icy canteens. And then a cloud came over, so we were glad to have long trousers and long-sleeved shirts in our packs. When the wind blew, we had jackets to wear. Our lunch was the envy of other visitors, and when it started to rain, we were snug in our ponchos, enjoying the storm that drove others off the mountain. Yet we could hardly feel smug about all this because we had nearly left everything in the car!

We hope to pass on that old man's advice so that you and yours can have a great time on these trails. You don't want to lug a heavy load, but you do want to take along a few things than can make the difference between comfort and misery, between safety and danger. So here's a list of handy items for day trips, plus another list of things to add for overnighters. Hikers, bikers, equestrians and cross-country skiers all need essentially the same gear to have fun in the woods.

Day Trips:

Take drinking water (see Water Parasites for an explanation), lunch, rain protection (see Hypothermia), light long trousers (though you may start out in shorts in summer), a long-sleeved shirt, a jacket or vest, a bandanna to use as washcloth, handkerchief, bandage or sling; Swiss army knife, wristwatch so you'll know when to start back, toilet paper, sunglasses, SPF-15 or better sun lotion, lip balm with sunscreen (remember that sunlight has more dangerous UV the higher you go in the mountains), extra plastic bag for carrying out trash, a map or guide book, a compass (see Map and Compass), a small disposable flashlight in case you get caught on the trail after dark, a little whistle for signalling and an emergency kit.

Your emergency kit need not be heavy or bulky. For example, you don't need a bottle of ibuprofen, just a couple of tablets wrapped in foil or plastic. And things such as tweezers, scissors and a surgical blade that are usually mentioned in such kits may already exist on your Swiss army knife. But you should have: Moleskin for blisters (see Hiking), two bandaids, safety pins, a lighter or waterproof matches, ibuprofen (like Advil) for pain, antiseptic cream in tiny tube, insect repellent in tiny container, an antihistamine for runny nose or insect stings and bites, one gauze dressing (sealed), a bit of adhesive tape wrapped around a sealed bottle of water purification tablets, Imodium A-D caplets (anti-diarrheal) and an antacid. Be sure the seal on your water purifiction tablets remains unbroken because they quickly start losing potency once the bottle has been opened. They are for emergencies only because you probably won't like the taste of the stuff (See Water Parasites).

In addition, we carry a steel Sierra cup with instant soup mix in case of hypothermia. Building a tiny fire to make hot soup in that cup is also a pleasant way to sit out a storm. And in chilly seasons or at high altitude, a stocking cap and gloves are also handy.

Overnight Trips:

Take everything listed for day trips, plus more food, a second flashlight (the new disposables are very powerful and lightweight), a second lighter, some biodegradable soap, a scouring pad, cook kit, tent, sleeping bag, foam pad and a bigger pack to carry it all.

Your pack must fit properly or it can hurt your back. A tent is necessary because rain generally comes with a windy storm. Fiber-filled sleeping bags are cheaper than down and have the advantage of drying out quickly if they get wet. Down is still the lightest and most compressible for the warmth provided, but if your down sleeping bag gets wet, you may as well start for home.

Food is the big limiting factor in a multi-day pack trip. Freeze dried food may not win prizes for taste, but the weight savings make it wonderful. For example, fruit dried to a crisp is much lighter than fruit dried to a leathery consistency.

The old rule of thumb was: The heavier your pack, the heavier your boots should be. The new lightweight hikers have changed that slightly. You need only look for a stiffer sole, which does weigh more, but not a lot more.

REAL DANGERS OF THE MOUNTAINS

There are some real dangers in the mountains, but not the ones you might imagine. You have little to fear from wild animals, but you have more chance of being stricken by hypothermia, heat prostration, altitude sickness, water parasites, or even lightning.

For example, many visitors fear Rocky Mountain spotted fever, yet the State Health Department reports that Colorado averages only one case per year and that no deaths have resulted in recent years. Your chances of contracting this rare disease are much greater in flatland states such as the Carolinas, Oklahoma, or even New York, where ticks are more common. In fairness to the Rockies, this disease is now being called "New World Tick Fever" or "Tickborne Typhus Fever."

The State Health Dept. believes that the public is safer knowing what they should really worry about. The point is not to convince you that some danger isn't dangerous, but to give you a realistic perspective so you may take proper precautions.

The Great Killer--Hypothermia

Too many people don't realize that you can freeze to death in 50-degree weather, and that is why hypothermia has become such a common killer. Even worse, this condition affects the brain, so victims show poor judgement about saving themselves.

Hypothermia--also called "exposure"--begins when the body starts losing more heat than it generates, and two things contribute to this--inadequate food and lack of warm, dry clothing. The explorer who skips breakfast or who eats lightly on the trail soon loses the nourishment that it takes to produce heat, and after that, even sweat can dampen clothing enough to begin the chilling process. No blizzard is required. A little wind, a little overcast, especially with a sudden rain to dampen clothing, and conditions are right for another fatal mishap.

Warm sunny mornings fool many a greenhorn into believing that the Rockies are a paradise where all you need are a pair of sneakers and shorts and sunglasses, and that may be true for awhile, but rain showers occur often and suddenly, especially in summer. The weatherman may say that no storm systems are moving into the area, but the mountains create their own local weather, and the summer forecast will still read "Clear to partly cloudy with chance of isolated thunderstorms." And that is precisely what happens all too often--clear, then cloudy, then rainy, then clear again.

As heat radiates from hands and feet and elsewhere, the body tries to conserve warmth by concentrating circulation among the vital organs and by restricting circulation to the extremities, including the brain! Our victim may be shivering constantly, but may also insist that everything is all right. Coordination gets bad as well. When the shivers start coming in violent waves, the victim's thinking becomes even more confused, disoriented, apathetic. The victim may lose the sense or the will power to zip up a jacket, so you must watch your friends and yourself and be ready to help.

If you suspect that a friend is coming down with hypothermia, stop at once to change out of damp clothing and to eat. Make hot soup or cocoa, but do not let your friend out of your sight, even to answer a call from nature, because victims sometimes wander off into the bush and never come back.

Near the end, the victim may become even more convinced that everything is all right, for the shivering stops, though arms and legs feel strangely stiff. Coordination is so bad that victims often stumble and hurt themselves; sometimes they walk off cliffs or just keep plodding along until the earth rushes up and hits them in the face. The victim faints, and without aid, never wakes up again.

All this may happen in as little as 30 minutes, though usually it takes longer, and recovery with hot soup and everything may take six or eight hours, so be prepared for a long wait.

Make the victim eat while changing out of wet clothing. If you have a sleeping bag along, prewarm it with someone else's body and have the victim climb in. Better yet, double up in the bag so the patient shares body heat with one or two healthy persons. You may actually rescue the rescuers this way, for other members of the party may be ready to come down with hypothermia as well.

Of course, dayhikers, mountain bikers, trailriders and tour skiers generally don't carry sleeping bags or much in the way of cooking gear, yet run the same risk of getting hypothermia, so prevention is the key. You must stay warm and dry and well nourished, which means that you must take along the minimal day trip gear that we recommend, even if the weather seems warm and sunny when you start, even if members of your party complain.

Hypothermia has also been known to strike the exhausted camper who climbs into a sleeping bag without eating and without changing out of sweaty underclothes. It can also strike motorists who are stranded on a cold night, even if clothing is dry, so beware of this slow killer and take along the stuff you need to survive.

Water Parasites--Why You Must Not Drink From Streams

No matter what you have read or heard, our mountain water is not safe to drink without careful treatment. No matter how beautiful it looks, no matter how cold, no matter how high the altitude, no matter how remote, no matter how far it tumbles, wild water may carry cysts that spread giardia, a single-celled parasite that attacks both people and animals worldwide.

Giardia infests the intestinal tract, causing diarrhea, gas, vomiting, loss of appetite and loss of weight. Symptoms may come and go, returning with greater strength later, and some people contract the disease but never show symptoms, thus becoming carriers.

Other types of disease can also be contracted by drinking wild water, but giardia may be the most difficult to avoid because its cysts are so difficult to kill, and the State Heath Dept. warns that all surface water supplies must be suspected of containing giardia.

For day trips, always carry water processed by municipal filtration plants. We fill plastic canteens about a quarter full, then freeze them overnight and top them off with sparkling water before starting out. The result is cold water that tastes as good as the streams. But since it is not possible to carry enough safe water for longer trips, campers must either boil or treat water with chemicals or use one of the new filter devices made for backpackers. At present, filter devices yield fairly small amounts of water and offer no protection against any virus that might be present.

Lab studies show that both virus and giardia cysts die quickly in boiling water, but experiments have not been done at very high altitudes. Many guidebooks recommend boiling for 20 minutes, but most cook kits will boil dry in less time than that. Still, boiling seems to offer the best all-around protection against all sorts of critters, both viral and bacterial, and surely produces good tasting water. Be sure that your water achieves a rolling boil, however, and maintain that for a number of minutes. Then fill your canteen, cool it in a stream, and you have good tasting water.

If you choose to use pills to treat water, beware that Giardia cysts are especially hard to kill in very cold water, so directions must be followed carefully. Notice, for example, that two hydroperiodide tablets are required for each quart, if the water is to remain cold during the waiting time, but only one tablet is required if the water is warmed. The water will taste better, of course, if you warm it during the waiting time--so you can use less disinfectant--and then rechill the water for drinking after the waiting time is over. Be sure tablets are fresh. Both Halazone and hydroperiodide pills quickly lose strength when exposed to air, moisture or heat.

When using chemicals, be sure to wait the proper amount of time. Lemonade crystals, for example, may improve taste, but do not add any product until the waiting time is over; otherwise, the product may react with your disinfectant, nullifying its effect before the cysts are dead.

Heat Prostration and Heat Stroke

Weakness, dizziness, cramps and rapid pulse are signs of heat prostration, and the victim who is not helped at this stage may faint with heat stroke. This can be fatal, so get the victim out of direct sunlight, give plenty of water and apply moist cloth to face and back of neck.

You may prevent this from happening, however, by drinking plenty of water as you go and by adjusting clothing to the rapid changes of temperature.

Altitude Sickness

Hiking burns up so much oxygen that visitors from lower altitudes sometimes become ill from the thinner air at high altitude. Symptoms include headache, dizziness, weakness, poor appetite, nausea, impaired judgment and--in extreme cases--severe shortness of breath caused by pulmonary edema. The only real treatment is retreat to lower altitude. Do not hyperventilate: Short, shallow breathing can make you pass out.

Lightning

Trees split and charred by lightning mark almost every ridge, so let these remind you to watch the clouds overhead, especially as you cross ridges or wide meadows. You will never be entirely safe, but lightning usually strikes the highest point or peak, lone trees, cliff edges, caves high in cliffs or simply the largest object in a flat area. Obviously, pitching a tent above timberline is asking for it.

Retreat from high or open ground if a storm threatens and wait until it passes. If you find yourself trapped in an exposed area, crouch down with your poncho forming a tent around you and wait it out.

Rattlesnakes

The rattlesnake is the only poisonous snake naturally occurring in Colorado. Rattlers have been known to climb to timberline, but are rarely seen except at lower altitudes (under 8,000 feet). Listen and watch for them, especially in the rocks and bluffs of the foothills. The Air Force Academy, Castlewood Canyon and Roxborough State Park are among the areas that report rattlers most often. Generally they try to get away, if they can, but they will fight if cornered or if they are protecting their young. You are more likely to see one if you travel in small groups because they seem to sense ground vibrations from larger groups and hide.

Health authorities no longer recommend tight bindings or cutting and sucking bites. Instead, wash the wound with soap and water or mild antiseptic, then wrap above the bite firmly with cloth, but do not cut off circulation. Immobilize the limb with a splint. Ice packs are recommended, though you aren't likely to have one. Watch for signs of shock while monitoring vital signs, and get medical attention.

Rattler fangs make one or two puncture wounds. A bite that looks like a horseshoe is non-poisonous. The bull snake does a good imitation of a rattler, but they generally overact, being more aggressive, puffing their neck out and spitting or even barking. But they don't have rattles or poison.

Rare Problems

Prevention of any disease is better than treatment, and some diseases--especially the rarest ones--are most dangerous if you don't know about them. So the State Health Department would like you to be aware of some odd problems that are generally associated with the outdoors.

A number of diseases arc passed on by insect bites. In considering these, remember that Colorado has far fewer bugs than most areas. For example, encephalitis is contracted from mosquito bites, but Colorado doesn't have the great swarms of mosquitos so common elsewhere. Still, a repellent is recommended for your emergency kit.

Plague, the Black Death, once wiped out a third of Europe, but today is treatable and so rare that some doctors fail to recognize it. The Health Dept. would like everyone to remember that fleas on skunks or rock squirrels, for example, may pass on this disease, so don't try to hand-feed wildlife.

Ticks can transmit a number of diseases. Unlike the disease that used to be called Rocky Mountain Spotted Fever, mentioned earlier, Colorado Tick Fever is common (100-300 cases per year) and is usually a mild infection, but may be serious in children, with acute fever, headache, muscle ache, and loss of energy. Tick-borne Relapsing Fever has similar symptoms, but may come back perhaps 10 times. It can be treated with antibiotics. Lyme Disease, named after Lyme, Conn., is serious but rare in Colorado (three cases in 1988, one in 89). It is characterized by a donut or bullseye rash that develops around the bite days or weeks later.

Again, Colorado does not have as many ticks as most states, and they are generally a spring time problem. Oldtimers say the tick season is generally over at any given altitude when you see the columbine blooming (usually sometime in June). They are most common on south-facing slopes exposed to the sun. Check every several hours to see if you have picked up any. Often you can find them before they have attached themselves, but if you find one too late, health officials say you should remove it immediately by slowly and gently tugging until it gets too tired to hang on. The best tool is something like the edge of your Driver's License. If you should get sick days or weeks later, remember to tell your doctor about the tick bite.

Tularemia is a disease generally associated with skinning and dressing infected rabbits, but it can be transmitted by eating insufficiently cooked rabbit meat, by drinking contaminated water or by inhaling contaminated dust. There are generally only several cases per year in Colorado.

Avoid any animal that is behaving strangely: It might have rabies. If you are bitten by any animal, even a neighborhood dog, rabies must to be considered. Prompt and proper treatment is vital.

The Health Dept. would like to remind you to discuss your travel and outdoor experiences with doctors, if you should experience any puzzling symptoms.

This one should be saved until mid-June or later because the trail skirts a shady ridge that keeps its snow for a long time. An ice ax and gaiters may be necessary for earlier attempts.

The trail crosses an area called "windfall" because so many large trees were once flattened here by a windstorm. From there it climbs to timberline and dead-ends in a pocket where granite walls rise up to 3,000 feet around you on three sides. Many rock wall and ice climbers try their skill here, and it is a spectacular, if somewhat forbidding landscape with many waterfalls spouting from the cliffs. This flow decreases in late summer. Be sure to fill your canteen at Cabin Creek near the turnoff from Barr because there is no reliable water between here and the Pit.

MOUNTAIN VIEW TRAIL, Forest Service #671, 1.2 miles one way, elevation gain 220 ft., rated easy. Features campsites and link with Cog Railway.

This short and gentle trail provides access to campsites along Cabin and Sheep Creeks. To find the trailhead, watch for a metal sign on Barr Trail 0.58 miles below Barr Camp, with the trail leading off to the south (left as you go up Barr Trail).

This trail has changed coarse slightly, no longer going past the roofless log cabin at Cabin Creek. Instead, it crosses Cabin Creek higher up, then crosses Sheep Creek, ending at the Cog Railway's Mountain View Station. Hikers with one-way space-available tickets often disembark here.

You may not cross the tracks into watershed country without a free permit from the City of Colorado Springs Department of Public Utilities. Call 719-636-5616.

MANITOU RESERVOIR TRAIL, Forest Service #638, 3.3 miles one way, elevation gain 275 ft, loss 900 ft.; rated difficult. Features scenic vistas and camping, though not near the reservoir.

A metal sign marks the turnoff 1.75 miles below Barr Camp. This dead-end trail offers many beautiful campsites along the streams it crosses, but it is steep going as it washboards over a series of ridges. It starts by diving toward South French Creek. There you find a meadow with large aspens and a stream. Your trail switchbacks up the opposite ridge, then drops again toward another drainage which has no name, and so it goes until you find yourself standing above the watershed for Manitou Reservoir, which is closed to the public. This is drinking water for the City of Manitou Springs. **Do not approach the lake.** As soon as you see the lake ahead, you must turn around and backtrack to Barr Trail because the area surrounding the lake is closed to all recreation, and there is no public access to that end of the trail. A caretaker lives at the reservoir, and the area is vigorously patrolled with trained security dogs..

FREMONT EXPERIMENTAL FOREST TRAIL, Forest Service #669,0.5 miles one way to end of Experimental Forest or 1.5 miles as part of loop; elevation gain 380 feet, rated moderate. Features campsites and ruins of experimental station.

A brook crosses Barr Trail at a complex intersection 8.9 miles down from the summit. Here the upper Incline Trail, a single track, comes down to join Barr at the stream crossing. If you follow the brook upstream, you will be traveling an old road into the Fremont Experimental Forest, where the Forest Service once planted exotic evergreens to see which varieties would do well in this area. Only the foundations of the station buildings remain now.

When hiking Barr Trail from the bottom, this area offers the first good campsites, so it receives a lot of use. This route has been used as a road to haul fencing for Barr Trail, so it is wide and leads to Long Ranch Road. Keep to the right as the brook you were following curves away to the left. You climb a short, steep section and arrive at a ridgetop where Fremont T-junctions against Long Ranch Road. This is the end of Fremont Trail itself, but if you turn left onto Long Ranch Road (#329), you can make a 1.5-mile loop going up to Barr.

Note: The rest of Long Ranch Road may be opened as part of the proposed Barr-Ute Indian Loop going back to Manitou Springs. See Barr-Ute Indian Loop.

INCLINE TRAIL, Forest Service #623, 0.5 miles one way, elevation gain 120 feet, rated easy. Features gentle trails to old Incline station.

There are actually two Incline Trails, but since they parallel each other closely, they share a common trail number. The upper trail is a single track that passes beneath a huge boulder that spans the trail, an excellent shelter on rainy days. The lower trail is a continuation of the Fremont Experimental Forest Trail-road, and it leaves Barr Trail just below the stream crossing. Both meet up higher up and continue to the closed Incline Railway station.

The Incline Railway was built in 1906 to haul men and equipment to build the Manitou pipeline and it operated as a tourist attraction for many years with a perfect safety record, but has now been closed to make more parking available for the Cog.

EAGLES NEST AND MT. CREST CRAGS, Forest Service # 623, 0.1 mile to Eagles Nest and about 0.5 mile to Mt. Crest Crags; elevation gain 650 ft., rated easy to moderate. Features climb to overlook.

This trail is also called Rocky Mountain. As you climb the path behind the Manitou Incline's upper station, it turns right toward Eagle's Nest and Mt. Crest Crags. The path heads north, but a side trail soon branches off and heads uphill toward the clump of rocks that overlooks the station. This is called the Eagle's Nest. The main trail wraps around the mountain and begins a series of switchbacks to a higher set of rocks known as Mt. Crest Crags. From there you can see the white bluffs of Williams Canyon, the Rampart Range beyond, and even portions of the Ute Indian Trail that runs between Manitou and Cascade.

ELK PARK TRAIL, Forest Service #652, 5.2 miles one way, elevation gain 200 ft., loss 1,680 ft. from Elk Park Knoll, rated easy from Elk Park Knoll, more difficult from Barr. Features tiny ghost town and large spring flowing from mine tunnel, access to Barr Camp .

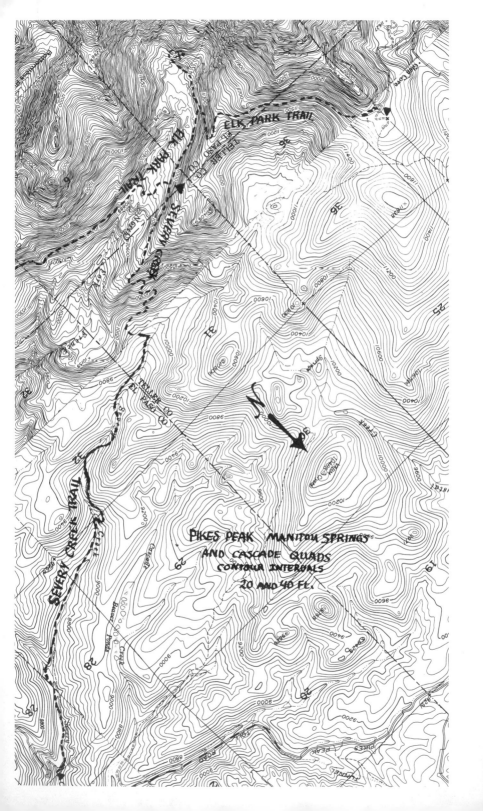

ELK PARK TRAIL

SEVERY CREEK TRAIL

PIKES PEAK MANITOU SPRINGS
AND CASCADE QUADS
CONTOUR INTERVALS
20 AND 40 FT.

This is the back way, leading downhill from Elk Park Knoll off the Pikes Peak Toll Road to Barr Camp, and it goes to an area romantically called Ghost Town Hollow. The so-called ghost town was a tiny mining and lumber camp, something like a half dozen cabins. Just above is the Cincinnati mine, which struck water instead of gold. The headwaters of North French Creek pour out of this tunnel in the granite, providing part of the drinking water for the City of Manitou Springs.

Note: New rules from the City of Manitou may ban horses and overnight camping from the North French Creek-Ghost Town Hollow area. However, camping is available in other drainages. Do not follow North French Creek downstream toward Manitou Reservoir, which is closed and vigorously patrolled with security dogs. Stay on trail through this sensitive area.

Starting at Elk Park (see road directions), you follow a badly washed roadway that curves down from timberline through forest to North French Creek. At the bottom, you find a fork with a sign pointing left, or down creek, toward Barr Camp (4 miles), and straight ahead toward the Oil Creek Tunnel (1/4 mile).

To see the mine, you walk up a gentle valley that is heavily forested. Soon you pass a few crumbling log cabins. The roofs are gone, the walls collapsing, and wildflowers bloom from the floor spaces. Visitors have carried away everything but the most uninteresting rusted garbage.

The mine is just above, still producing a valuable flow of water. In the winter, this produces weird ice sculptures. All of the mine timbers have rotted away, so exploration would be very dangerous. A huge iron boiler stand s outside .

Backtrack to the trail fork. From here, Elk Park heads downstream for a short distance, but actually climbs slightly, following a sunny ridge above the stream. Then your trail forks again. Elk Park Trail turns right to cross the creek, while the trail ahead (Severy Creek Trail) leads over the ridge.

After crossing North French Creek, Elk Park switchbacks up the opposite ridge. This climb is fairly gentle and soon the trail almost levels out, skirting the end of the ridge with Manitou Reservoir visible below. Next you cross a high park meadow, then drop down into the South French Creek watershed.

Your trail follows the creek downhill a short way, with the creek is just out of sight to your right, and then you find a shallow crossing. On the other side, climb to the left and find yourself walking a ledge on a cliff's side with the creek roaring below. Your trail goes past a prospect hole, over a rise, then descends to the cabins of Barr Camp. You arrive just a few yards above the cabins themselves.

SEVERY CREEK TRAIL, Forest Service #661, 4 miles one way, elevation gain 2,550 ft., rated moderate. Features beautiful trail along high mountain stream, linking with Elk Park Trail.

Long considered one of the region's most beautiful trails, Severy Creek remained closed to the public since 1913, chiefly to help protect the water supply for the community of Cascade, which lacked a modern filtration facility. Yet in the fall of 1990, Cascade switched to municipal water from Colorado Springs, and in the spring of 1991, the City of Manitou Springs, in cooperation with Colorado Springs, began a legal process which may result in the reopening of this Forest Service Trail. If you have not seen this opening advertised through the media, call authorities before attempting Severy.

Severy Creek is best approached via the Pikes Peak Toll Road, which means you must pay the toll. The only other route is up Barr Trail to Barr Camp, then Elk Park Trail to Ghost Town Hollow, then down Severy Creek and back again.

The creek itself originates below Elk Park Knoll off the Pikes Peak Toll Road, but please do not spoil the tundra by bushwhacking down from there. If you want to take Severy as a downhill, it is just as easy (no altitude gain!) to start at Elk Park Knoll and go down the Elk Park Trail to North French Creek, where you will find the upper trailhead for Severy. Of course, taking Severy as a downhill means a long climb back up to your car at the end of the afternoon when the Toll Road closes. (You may not park at Elk Park overnight and may be ticketed if you are late exiting the mountain). Be sure to check the closing time for that day, and remember that bad weather sometimes closes the road early

The best way to see Severy is from the bottom. (see ROAD

DIRECTIONS). That way you can explore up as far as you like and have an easy downhill to your car, which will be parked less than two miles from the Toll Gate. Less chance of being late and getting a ticket. Be sure not to block this important access road.

From the parking lot, go up the road about 50 yards beyond where the creek passes beneath the road. The trail starts as a short gap in the willows to your right. A tributary joins Severy right at the trailhead, so the first few yards of trail are permanently flooded with an inch or two of water, but is firm gravel beneath. Volunteer work may relocate this trailhead to avoid the wet.

Beyond the willows, you enter the world of mossy evergreens. Cross Severy on a plank bridge and start up its far side. Rated as moderate, the trail has many easy stretches mixed with short steep sections. The creek is often in sight, tumbling between boulders, forming a number of charming cascades. You pass through aspen glades, crossing and recrossing the creek. As you mount one group of giant boulders, Pikes Peak suddenly shows itself towering above.

In a broad meadow just below 10,000 feet, the trail leaves the creek and switchbacks up the ridge separating Severy from the North Fork of French Creek. Rounding that ridge, you continue above French Creek to link up with Elk Park Trail below Ghost Town Hollow.

Overnight camping may be allowed along Severy Creek itself, but may **not be allowed** in Manitou's North French Creek (Ghost Town Hollow) watershed at the upper end of Severy Trail. Remember that you may not leave a car overnight anywhere off the Pikes Peak Toll Road, not even at the lower Severy trailhead.

Horses will probably have no access to Severy because horses and trailers are not permitted on the Toll Road and horses may not be allowed in the North French Creek watershed.

UTE INDIAN TRAIL, Ute Pass Historical Society Trail, 3.2 miles one way; elevation gain 1,040 feet, loss 340 feet; rated moderate. Features historic foothill and mountain route.

The Ute Indians believed that the gods lived below the springs at Manitou, that their breathing caused the bubbles in those mineral waters. So the Utes made pilgrimages to these springs over an ancient trail that extended from Utah. This trail was used by trappers, by mountain men, and later it carried wagons toward the mining areas in the mountains.

Our description begins at the southern trailhead directly below the Manitou Incline station on Ruxton Avenue. You hike up and around the base of the mountain, following a road-like path up Rattlesnake Gulch. Your trail washboards over a series of ridges where the land is somewhat arid at first, dominated by Gambel's oak and yucca, and then the evergreens close in.

A metal sign marks the point where the Ute Wagon Trail joined the Ute Indian Trail, and further on you pass under a pipeline that crosses the trail on a steel trestle. Several utility lines follow this trail toward Cascade, and much of the right-of-way belongs to the City of Colorado Springs Utilities Department. As you walk by steel pipes that jut from ridges, listen for gurgling caused by pressure changes in the water pipelines.

You pass by the remains of Long's Ranch, one of the oldest ranches in the area. Nearby is a spring, but it is sporadic and small, so we advise bringing your own water.

Cross-country skiers often turn back just before the last downhill section that takes you into the French Creek watershed. .The trail ends near Highway 24, one-half mile east of Cascade.

This trail was built through the efforts and cooperation of the Chipita Park-Cascade Bicentennial Association, the Ute Pass Historical Society, the National Hiking and Ski Touring Association, Boy Scout Troop 18 and Explorer Post 24 the Lions and Kiwanis Clubs, the Colorado Springs Utilities Department, the Fourth Infantry Division of Fort Carson, and of course, private land owners.

Horses are not allowed on Ute Indian Trail.

BARR--UTE INDIAN LOOP, Forest Service and Ute Pass Historical Society Trail, 11.2-mile loop, elevation gain-loss 3,820 ft., rated difficult and then easy   Features one-way uphill-only bicycle access to Barr Trail, forming a loop by coming down Long Ranch Road and then down Ute Indian Trail to Incline station near Barr trailhead.

Not just for mountain bicycles, this trail is being designed with bikes in mind for increased safety and fun. If approved, the Barr--Ute Indian Loop should eliminate the danger of bikes coming down steep switchbacks on lower Barr Trail and legally open a scenic back route. If you have not seen media reports of this trail opening, check with authorities before starting out.

Park at the Barr trailhead on Ruxton Ave. and climb Barr Trail. About 1.3 miles past the Experimental Forest turnoff (mile 4.5 from the bottom trailhead), where the trail is fairly flat, Pikes Peak comes into view and a single track takes off to your right, turning into a double track within about a third of a mile. This is Long Ranch Road, built by Fred Barr and R.A. Long to haul timber from this area. The top of Experimental Forest Trail (also a road) comes up from your right and T-junctions against Long at mile 5.3 from the bottom, but stay on Long (straight ahead). You pass between Rocky Mountain and Mount Manitou and then begin a long descent toward Ute Pass. Near the bottom (mile 8.1 from the lower Barr Trailhead) you will come to a gated fence.

Continue down the road, but do not go all the way to Hwy. 24. At mile 8.3 you will come to an intersection where a gated road is on your left and Ute Indian Trail is on your right (see Ute Indian Trail). Take the Ute Indian Trail back to Manitou. The most difficult part of the trail is at the bottom, but future trail work may improve this very steep section. Then go up Ruxton Avenue to the Barr trailhead.

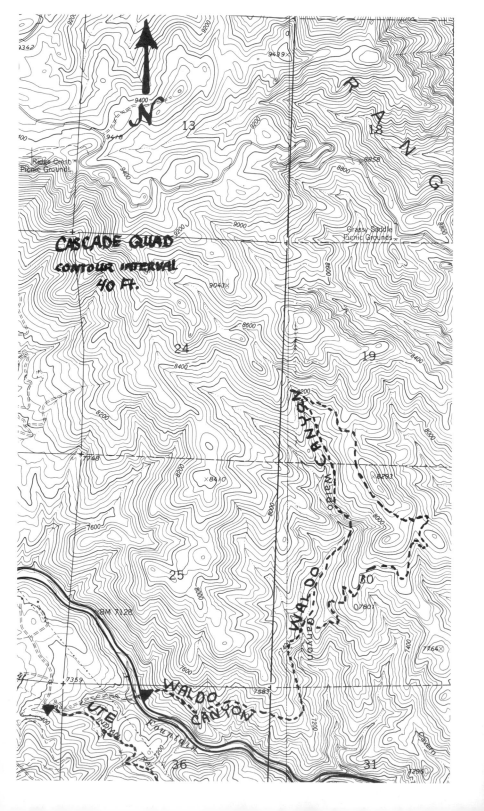

UTE PASS AREA

Waldo Canyon Trail
Thomas Trail

Ute Pass itself is one of the region's oldest trails, first serving the Ute Indians from Utah, then trappers, mountain men, soldiers, miners, lumberjacks and ranchers. And today it is still one of the most important routes to the mountains. Many old trails in the Ute Pass area have gone out of use, but there is a new movement to restore them, so this is one chapter that will doubtless grow in future editions. Waldo Canyon is located on USGS Cascade quad, and Thomas Trail is on the Woodland Park quad.

ROAD DIRECTIONS: To find the trailhead for WALDO CANYON TRAIL, drive 2.2 miles west of the Cave of the Winds exit at Manitou Springs on Hwy. 24 and watch for the large parking lot on your right.
To find the THOMAS TRAIL, continue on Hwy. 24 west and take either exit for Green Mountain Falls. Park on the west side of the town lake (Lake St.) near the gazebo. Do not park in residential areas.

WALDO CANYON TRAIL, Forest Service #640, 6.8--mile balloon loop, including about 2 miles to beginning of 3-mile loop, then 2 miles return; elevation gain 1,280 ft., rated steep at first, then easier. Features scenic route through wooded canyon.

According to trails researcher Gwen Pratt, Waldo Canyon used to be the site of Waldo Hog Ranch, and Waldo used to haul garbage from Manitou to feed his stock. The mortgage was owned by a man named Jones, and one day the two men had a falling out. Waldo demanded to see the mortgage document, but when Jones handed it to him, Waldo ate it!

Such is the history of this scenic canyon that now features one of the region's most popular trails. Indeed, it's popularity is its major protection and its major problem. So far, its popularity has helped prevent the threatened expansion of a nearby gravel strip

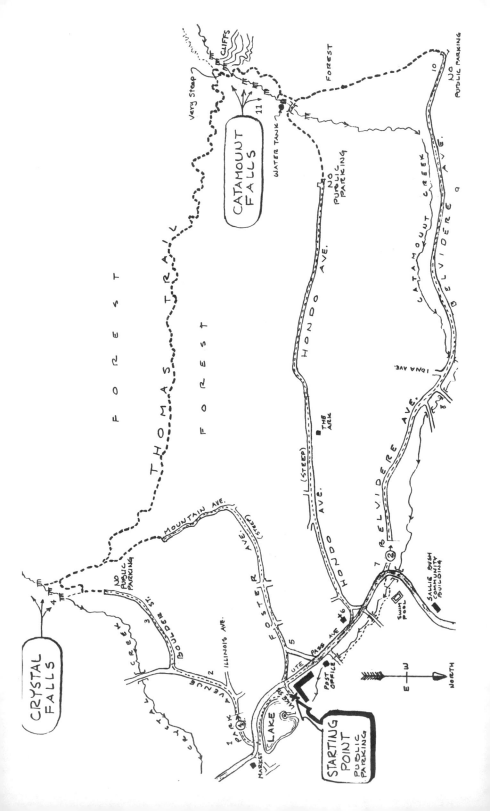

mine, but the notoriety and its prominent situation on a busy tourist highway has resulted in large numbers of people visiting Waldo. This trail is generally crowded! Knowing that, you can plan your own visit accordingly. Weekdays, early mornings, especially off season, offer the best chance of beating the rush. It is also fair to say that many people visit Waldo Canyon over and over again simply because they simply don't know anywhere else to go, and it is our hope that this guide will help solve that problem by offering more choices.

Waldo used to begin with a long flight of concrete stairs, but so many mountain bikers were bushwhacking down the steep hillside to avoid the stairs that erosion began taking a toll. So the Forest Service replaced the stairs with a conventional set of switchbacks, yet the abuse continues, so the FS may be forced to ban bikes from Waldo.

Frankly, mountain biking is more fun on less traveled trails because constantly yielding the right-of-way amid a crowd of people means that you walk more than you ride. There are better places.

After the switchbacks, the first couple of miles are arid, but this "string" leads to a "balloon loop" within a moist canyon. The canyon loop is three miles in itself, a beautiful route through ponderosa pine with a brook along the west side. The loop is more gradual if hiked clockwise because the opposite way begins with a set of switchbacks.

THOMAS TRAIL, 3 miles one way including street access, elevation gain 737 ft., rated moderate. Features forest hike between two sets of falls.

Back in the 1890s, when hiking was the major recreation for tourists in Pikes Peak Country, men used to sprinkle pine needles on trails so ladies wouldn't soil the hems of their long dresses. Green Mountain Falls is now working to rebuild its historic trail system.

Using the Pikes Peak Atlas, local architect Dick Bratton discovered traces of Felton's old trail above his home and spearheaded a community effort to rebuild the route. Renamed the Thomas

Trail in honor of the present owners of the land it crosses, this historic path (along with two short urban trails) was dedicated in 1990 at the town's centennial celebration.

The two shorter loops, Crystal Falls and Catamount Falls, are mostly gravel street routes, leading directly to the Thomas Trail and the falls at each end of town. These are popular walks for those unable to do strenuous hiking. Crystal Falls Loop is one mile long; Catamount Falls Loop is two miles long.

The Thomas Trail, on the other hand, is no urban trail, as you'll see. Bikes and horses are not allowed because the trail is too rough and narrow to be appropriate.

Please do not try to shortcut by parking in residential areas. Besides, the shady gravel roadways which form the two loops that lead to Thomas Trail are pleasant walks with a dozen points of interest. For example, the House of Fortune is a quaint Victorian home where miners came to weigh their gold. And the owner of Tanglewood, an historic log home, is restoring the Iron Spring Gazebo just for the comfort of passing hikers. Ask any merchant for a free map listing points of interest.

If you've ever wondered, "Where are the falls in Green Mountain Falls?" you're about to find out. Leaving Lake St., hike back along Ute Pass Ave. and turn right onto Park Ave., then right again on Boulder to find the Thomas trailhead at the end of Boulder. Right away your single track is climbing up along the tumbling waters of Crystal Falls (pretty steep here). Farther along, the middle portion of the trail levels out, contouring along a steep wooded hillside. A small cave niche along the way has been a traditional shelter during rains. Your path rolls along, studded with rocks and roots, fairly gentle until it finds Catamount Falls cascading down a high-walled gorge. Here the path is at its steepest, crossing the creek and climbing down along it to a plank bridge that gives you a choice. You can recross the creek and head back along Hondo Avenue or you can keep to the west of the creek and take a longer trail down to Belvidere Ave. Either way, you will return along the urban Catamount Falls Loop.

COLORADO SPRINGS AREA

Palmer Park
Garden of the Gods
White House Ranch Historic Site
Bear Creek Regional Park

Colorado Springs has the rare honor of having been founded as a resort community. An Easterner was fascinated by its beauty and climate and came back years later, after the Civil War, bringing with him a railroad to help share this place with the world. General William Jackson Palmer laid out streets wide enough for his wagon to turn around in a circle, he set aside what is now Palmer Park and he planted 10,000 trees, as well as the seeds of many people's dreams.

ROAD DIRECTIONS: Palmer Park is located in northeastern Colorado Springs and may be approached by Templeton Gap Road or Paseo Road. To find the main Gateway entrance to the Garden of the Gods, take the Garden of the Gods Exit west off I-25 and follow signs. The White House Ranch Historic Site is located near the Gateway entrance. Bear Creek Regional Park is located on 26th St. south of Hwy. 24, and the Bear Creek Nature Center is at 26th and Lower Gold Camp Road.

PALMER PARK TRAILS, City of Colorado Springs Parks and Recreation Dept., four different trails up to 2 miles long, rated moderate. Features interesting nature trails and horse rental from nearby stable.

Palmer Park is a sprawling mesa area with evergreens and sandstone formations. A maze of gravel and paved roads lead to picnic areas scattered through the rocks, some on overlooks with views of the city and mountains and plains. Nature trails lace the area. Mountain bikers will find some very technical riding, but

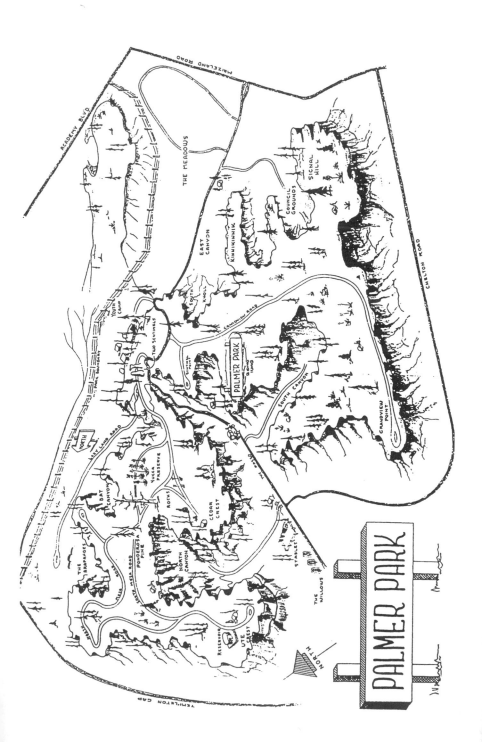

please stay on designated trails and roads to minimize environmental impact. Horses can be rented from a nearby stable.

Geologic oddities include sandstone boulders weathered into odd shapes, some resembling mushrooms, and ball-shaped rocks called mud rollers that were created by material rolling downhill through mud and sand during prehistoric storms. The top of the mesa is a botanical reserve called the Yucca Area, where thousands of yuccas blossom each June.

Palmer Park opens at 5 a.m.and closes at 11 p.m. (May 1 to Nov. 1) and at 9 p.m.otherwise. Dogs must be on leash. No open fires (grates only and charcoal only--no wood), no firearms or fireworks, no alcoholic beverages, no overnight camping. The Lazy Land, Council Grounds Youth Camp and Meadows Picnic Areas are open by reservation. Call 719-578-6640.

GARDEN OF THE GODS, City of Colorado Springs Park and Recreation Department, short nature trails, features colorful and majestic geologic formations.

Millions of years ago, ancient seas and rivers laid down sediment layers that turned to sandstone. Then Pikes Peak rose from below, pushed upward by the buckling of the earth's crust. And at the edge of this upheaval, giant sandstone slabs were broken and tilted up on end to form the Garden of the Gods.

This exotic garden was fully appreciated by Indians of both the mountains and plains. The Utes visited here as part of their pilgrimage to the sacred springs at Manitou, and the plains Indians made a trail that led to the Garden from the east. Today the City of Colorado Springs owns and takes care of the Garden.

This park receives such heavy use that hiking and horse riding are limited to designated trails in order to allow delicate plant life to recover. All trails are closed to mountain bikes, though bikers can still enjoy the roads. Horses are available from nearby stables, but horses are not permitted in the heart of the park where rock formations are largest. Dogs must be on leash, and no alcoholic beverages are allowed.

The Garden of the Gods Park opens at 5 a.m. daily, but closes at 11 p.m. in summer and at 9 p.m. Nov. 1--April 30. No camping, no hunting, no collecting, no open fires (grates only and charcoal only--no wood), no firearms or fireworks. Visitor Center hours are 9 a.m. to 5 p.m., June through Labor Day, and 10 a.m. to 4 p.m., September through May.

Daily nature hikes are led by naturalists throughout the summer (no reservations required), and the Visitors Center has information, publications, exhibits and slide programs. Group nature tours can be arranged. Call 719-578-6933.

Photographers will find the colors most vivid near sunrise or sunset. In late winter or early spring, watch for bighorn sheep that graze on the hogback ridge immediately north of the Garden.

WHITE HOUSE RANCH HISTORIC SITE, Colorado Springs Parks and Recreation Dept. Features short Living History Trail and wheelchair accessible nature trail with raised lettering on signs.

You can step back in time at the White House Ranch, where life still goes on much as it did in the late 1800s. The interpreters dress in period clothing and illustrate the historical development of the Pikes Peak region by interpreting an 1868 homestead, an 1895 working ranch and a 1901 country estate.

Walter C. Galloway first homesteaded the Ranch in the 1860s, and his cabin has now been rebuilt in the old ways, using square nails and fittings made by the resident blacksmith. Robert Chambers operated his Rock Ledge Ranch here in the 1890s, growing vegetables for the plush Antlers Hotel. His asparagus now grows wild along the Living History Trail, and the Chambers garden is still being tilled by hand, though now the vegetables are sold to the public in the Ranch's general store.

Yet the Ranch is named after the elegant "white house" (actually called the Orchard House) built in 1907 by General Palmer for Mrs. Palmer's half-sister. The house is now open for public tours during the summer and at Christmas.

In the working ranch you can see ranch animals and a working blacksmith. A 1/4-mile Nature Trail is paved and has signs with raised lettering, describing the plant life surrounding a picturesque pond.

White House Ranch Historic Site is operated with assistance

from the White House Ranch Living History Association. The Ranch is open Tuesday through Sunday, 10 a.m. to 4 p.m. from early June through Labor Day and weekends from September through December. There is an admission fee to the historic area.

BEAR CREEK REGIONAL PARK NATURE CENTER, El Paso County Park Dept. Features Nature Center with interpretive trails, plus regional trail linking the Equestrian Center and National Forest.

Located in southwest Colorado Springs, this Nature Center offers exhibits and interpretive displays about animals, insects, birds and fish, plus special programs, guided nature tours and a lot more.

If you have a hard time getting used to topographic maps, you might compare maps with the large model of Pikes Peak, which is complete with trees and rocks and roads and trails all laid out from an eagle's eye view.

The nature trails are well marked and have station signs describing flora and fauna. These are not described here separately because future changes are being planned, but at least one is handicapped accessible. Bicycles, horses and dogs are prohibited from the nature trails, but other paths used by equestrians and bikers extend from the Penrose Stadium Equestrian Center through the park to access Bear Creek Canyon Trail, El Paso County's Section 16 Palmer-Redrock Loop and the new Intemann Trail. Trailriders should park trailers at the Equestrian Center's north lot or at the creekside lot on 21st St.

Groups of 15 or more may make advanced reservations for tours led by naturalists. Call 719-520-6387. The Center is open from 8 a.m. to 5 p.m. Tuesdays through Saturdays year round, except holidays.

Playfields and group facilities for picnics can be reserved by calling 719-520-6375. The park itself is open from 5 a.m. to 11 p.m. No hunting, no firearms or fireworks, no open fires (grates only), no camping, no picking of flowers or collecting of artifacts or other souvenirs. Dogs must be on a leash in those areas where they are allowed.

71

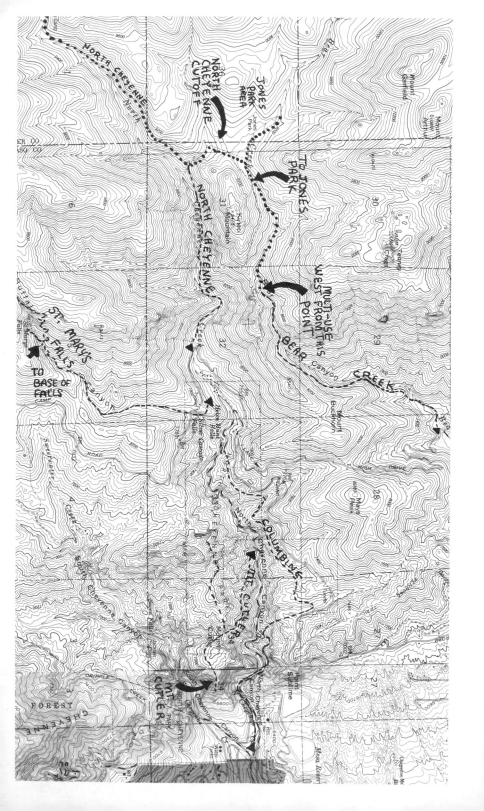

CHEYENNE CAÑON--HIGH DRIVE AREA

Columbine Trail
Mount Cutler Trail
North Cheyenne Cañon Trail
North Cheyenne Cutoff
St. Mary's Trail
Bear Creek Trail
Palmer-Redrock Loop
Intemann Trail

Located on the southwestern edge of Colorado Springs, the Cheyenne Cañon--High Drive area offers a variety of beautiful mountain trails under the jurisdiction of city, county and federal governments. Closure of the St. Mary's Tunnel has also closed eight miles of the Upper Gold Camp Road, so that section of the gentle old railroad grade has now become popular with mountain bikers, horse riders and cross-country skiers, though it is recommended that you climb over the damaged tunnel instead of going through. Still, the additional road walk has not discouraged use of St. Mary's and North Cheyenne Canyon Trails.

Cheyenne Cañon is a famous practice area for technical rock climbers and has signs showing the best routes up the cliffs, but **climbing is prohibited without full equipment.** Unfortunately, visitors sometimes disobey this rule with bloody or fatal results, risking their lives, a $500 fine and up to 90 days in jail. The same is true of the slippery rocks beside Silver Cascade (Spoon) Falls above Helen Hunt Falls. The short path leading there needs no description, but violating its warning sign may carry the death penalty. It has in the past. Please obey the signs.

ROAD DIRECTIONS: Take West Cheyenne Road off Nevada to an intersection where you can turn left into South Cheyenne Cañon (where Seven Falls is located) or right to enter North Cheyenne Cañon. Take the right fork. Columbine Trail now begins at the Discovery

Center here at the canyon mouth. To find its mid-point trailhead, drive along the city picnic grounds that line the creek for 0.9 miles. The trailhead is on your right. Mount Cutler is 0.5 miles farther and is on your left. Helen Hunt Falls is another 1.2 miles distant, and there you find the short path leading up above Helen Hunt Falls to Silver Cascade Falls. The western end of Columbine meets the road on a switchback above Helen Hunt Falls.

Continue up another 0.6 miles and you come to a large intersection where you join the High Drive and the closed portion of the Gold Camp Road. To find trailheads for North Cheyenne and St. Mary's Falls, park here and start up the Gold Camp on foot or bike or horseback. North Cheyenne Cañon trailhead is on your right 0.6 miles from this intersection, where the first creek crosses. St. Mary's has two lower trailheads on either side of the tunnel, which is 1.2 miles from the intersection. Entering the damaged tunnel is not recommended, so please use the first trailhead, which takes you up and over the tunnel itself. For directions to St. Mary's upper trailhead, see GOLD CAMP ROAD AREA.

To find the trailheads for BEAR CREEK and PALMER-REDROCK LOOP, start at the intersection above Helen Hunt Falls and take the one-way High Drive (closed in winter). One mile up you find the trailhead for Mount Buckhorn, a motorized trail not described here, but sometimes used as a loop with BEAR CREEK. BEAR CREEK'S trailhead is located on the left at a metal gate 2.4 miles from the start of the High Drive. Only roadside parking is available, but the caretaker's parking lot at the base of the High Drive has space for another 10 cars.

The upper trailhead for Palmer-Redrock is 2.7 miles from the High Drive start, roadside parking only. To find the lower trailhead, continue downhill on the paved portion known as Bear Creek Road and turn left at its intersection with the Lower Gold Camp Road. Proceed 0.2 miles and watch for it on your left.

Intemann Trailhead is located on the lower Palmer-Redrock, about half a mile up from the Section 16 trailhead. Intemann has another trailhead on Crystal Park Road. Find the entrance to Crystal Park Road across from the Manitou Springs Swimming Pool. Drive up 1.5 miles and park beyond the Kangaroo Campground.

COLUMBINE TRAIL, City of Colorado Springs trail, 3 miles one way, elevation gain 800 ft., loss 200 ft.; rated moderate. Features an overlook of canyon and falls.

The columbine is the Colorado State Flower and grows in the moist shade of evergreens near Columbine Spring. Look for them blooming in late June and early July. It is illegal to disturb them.

Columbine has been extended clear to the canyon mouth, so now the main trailhead is at the Discovery Center where North and South Cheyenne Cañons meet. The trail follows the creek upstream, crosses the road, then switchbacks up a scree slope for three quarters of a mile. This is a good winter hike because sunny exposure helps keep it clear of snow. Higher up you will find Columbine Spring flowing except in the driest times. The trail follows the slope with only glimpses of the road below.

The final mile is the most beautiful, with views of Silver Cascade and Helen Hunt Falls. The trail ends on the road just above Helen Hunt Falls. This trail is so narrow, steep and popular that it is fairly unsuitable for mountain bikes.

Columbine was built as part of a Civil Works Administration project in 1934, and the work was so difficult that a blacksmith labored under the evergreens, resharpening 100 picks a day.

MOUNT CUTLER TRAIL, City of Colorado Springs trail, 0.8 mile one way, plus 0.2 mile for Broadmoor overlook; elevation gain 600 ft., rated moderate. Features overlooks of Colorado Springs and Seven Falls.

This is one of the few trails that we recommend for a night walk because it is short and wide and has no confusing points--and because it offers a view of Colorado Springs that looks like a carpet of jewels. In the summer, Seven Falls is illuminated with colored lights as well, so this can be a fine place to hike with good flashlights. Keep your small children close at hand for the trail does climb the canyon rim and the overlooks have steep drop-offs.

Near the top, the trail forks. The right fork climbs Mount Muscoco for a view of the seven distinct cascades in South Cheyenne Cañon. Seven Falls is a private tourist attraction

The left fork wraps around Mount Cutler itself, passes a white quartz outcropping and dead-ends at an overlook where the Broadmoor lies 900 feet below.

75

NORTH CHEYENNE CAÑON TRAIL, Forest Service #622,
about two miles one way; elevation gain 1,800 ft., rated mod-
erate to difficult. Features streamside walk over numerous
bridges, 25-foot cascade.

Nobody quite knows what to call this one, for its name has
changed so many times. It used to be called Lovely Corners after
John Lovely, a Frenchman who lived in a tent in this canyon and
who homesteaded several acres there in1902. Later it was called
Six Bridges but then another bridge was added, so it was called
Seven Bridges for awhile. Perhaps the current name will stick.

These bridges (logs mostly) give you close views of the creek
as it pours and splashes over polished stones. Near what we call
the end of this trail, the stream slides down a steep granite face for
25 feet or more, forming Undine Falls. As you climb the trail
overlooking the cascade, however, beware of a dangerous spot
where a slab lubricated with gravel slants toward a drop-off.

There are campsites farther up near a tributary that joins from
the north. Your trail leaves the creek here and skirts the base of
Kineo Mountain, heading up that tributary toward a trail called
North Cheyenne Cutoff that links with Bear Creek at Jones Park.
As you climb the tributary,however, you see another trail coming
down to join the tributary from your left.

That other trail leads back toward the headwaters of North
Cheyenne Creek, but this is a motorcycle trail. It climbs a steep
section called "the ladders" that used to have wooden steps leading toward Nelson's Camp. Nelson's cabin, built in the late 1800s,
remained intact with bunk beds and metal stove until vandals
destroyed it in the early 1970s.

If you use two vehicles, you can make a long circuit by going
up North Cheyenne to the Cheyenne Cutoff and take that to Bear
Creek and down again. See North Cheyenne Cutoff.

NORTH CHEYENNE CUTOFF, Forest Service #668, 0.5 mile,
elevation gain 200 ft.; rated easy. Features saddle walk link-
ing North Cheyenne and Bear Creek Trails.

At the upper end of North Cheyenne Canyon Trail, you find a
distinct path leaving the creek and climbing past the north slope of

Kineo Mountain. The path follows a tributary that joins North Cheyenne from the north. As you continue upwards, another trail comes down to parallel the brook on the other side, but keep to the Kineo side of the brook. The other trail leads to Nelson's Camp on a motorcycle trail, though a sign may mention Rosemont.

Soon you find a grassy area with scattered evergreens. Look for a distinct path that cuts away to the right, leading away from the tributary and up into the trees. Now you are crossing the saddle between Kineo and the high ground to the west, dropping down into another watershed. This is Jones Park, a high grassy area dotted with evergreens and wildflowers. You share this area with motorcycles. Your trail ends where it crosses Bear Creek.

ST. MARY'S FALLS TRAIL, Forest Service #624, 1.6 miles one way to the falls, plus 1.2-mile road walk; elevation gain 1,200 ft.; rated moderately difficult. Features large cascade and view of Broadmoor.

St. Mary's Falls is a water slide that churns for about 40 feet down the side of Stove Mountain. The trail that leads there from the Gold Camp climbs 1,200 feet in 1.6 miles, but starts out fairly gently, so the last section to the falls is quite steep.

This trail is changing at both ends. The closure of the tunnel adds 1.2 miles to your journey, but the top part is so confusing and in such bad shape that for 1991 the Forest Service is considering the falls to be destination of St. Mary's Falls Trail. The route to Frosty Park is still technically open for those who wish to explore, but plans call for rerouting that section to use the higher Nelson Trail, which also leads to Frosty Park. Volunteer work is needed.

Starting at the tunnel, the trail follows Buffalo Creek upstream through pines and blue spruce. Higher up there are some small campsites. Eventually the trail leaves the creek and switchbacks up the hillside. A metal sign says "Base of Falls 500 feet," pointing left and "Top of Falls 0.2 mile," pointing right.

Both the base and top of the falls share an overlook of the pine and blue spruce valley that slants toward the Broadmoor. Be especially careful of falling rock, for anything dislodged from the top would hit just about where people stand at the bottom.

For those who wish to explore higher, the Pikes Peak Atlas is the best map. The traditional route continues up Buffalo Creek, then switchbacks up to a road called FS-381 and follows the road before branching away toward Frosty Park. For road directions to Frosty Park (FS-379), see GOLD CAMP ROAD AREA.

When the Nelson Trail route is completed, St. Mary's Falls Trail will measure about 6.4 miles to Frosty Park with an elevation gain of 2,300 feet and a loss of 700 feet.

BEAR CREEK TRAIL, Forest Service #666, 2 miles one way from High Drive, but add one mile for winter trailhead below High Drive; elevation gain 1,980 ft., rated moderate to difficult. Features historic climb through a scenic canyon.

In 1873 the U.S. Army Signal Corps built the highest signal station in the world atop Pikes Peak, and the trail to the top led through Bear Creek Canyon. This trail began at Manitou and wound 17 miles up through Jones Park and the Seven Lakes Area, but the popular Lake House Hotel at Lake Moraine burned down long ago. Bear Creek Trail is all that remains of this historic route.

As you leave the summer trailhead on the High Drive (winter users must hike up to this point from where the road is closed below), you follow the creek bottom for a short way, then begin climbing a steady path up the side of a ridge. Soon the creek is nothing but a sound below. Raspberries, dog roses and juniper grow in the loose rock beside the trail.

Another trail on the opposite slope provides a side trip to the area just below Josephine Falls, where it is necessary to cross over to the main trail to continue on.

Above you and to the right stands Specimen Rock, a natural breeding area for peregrin falcons. This high area is closed until July 15 each year to protect nesting, so please stay on trail.

All this climbing leads you to a high overlook where the falls roar below you--barely in sight, unfortunately. From this high ledge you can see all the way to the Black Forest.

Now the canyon narrows and you return to streamside. You pass the remains of an old toll road bridge built in 1891 to carry wagons and workers on their way to build reservoirs in the Seven Lakes area. Higher up the Buckhorn Motorized Trail crosses the creek to join Bear Creek, so expect to share the path with motorcycles traveling to Jones Park.

Still higher, you pass a mine tunnel immediately beside the trail. All the supporting timbers have now rotted away, so beware. Bear Creek Trail ends at Jones Park, but there it links with North Cheyenne Cutoff to North Cheyenne Creek.

PALMER-REDROCK LOOP (SECTION 16), El Paso County Park Dept., 4.7 miles one way (from winter trailhead, add 0.7 mile); elevation gain 620 feet, loss 1,140 feet; rated moderate. Features forest route through area of geologic interest.

This is not a true loop trail because it does not return to the same trailhead, but since the road does connect the two trailheads, it can be hiked as a loop by traveling part way on the road. Private property has now cut off the access to Crystal Park, so hikers are urged to stay on the route we show in order to avoid trespassing.

Because the lower part of this trail is steep, most hikers begin at the higher trailhead and walk the lower part downhill. The trail is much more difficult if hiked the other way around. Mountain bikers find it especially challenging.

Starting at the trailhead on the High Drive, you enter an aspen grove and soon find a place where the main trail doubles back to the right and begins climbing. If you continue in the meadow instead of climbing, you will find a chimney from an old Boy Scout Camp and a dead-end below Sentinel Rock.

Your path gains altitude, snaking through evergreens, then curves west through a mossy forest, keeping high on the mountainside to maintain altitude. You cross an intermittent brook called Hunter's Run that drips off a large rock near the trail. You climb very gently from here and find an intersection on a small saddle ridge. The left fork leads 0.3 mile up and around some rocks to a small natural overlook. From there you can see the Garden of the Gods, the Rampart Range, etc. Do not explore farther because soon you run into private property.

Return to the intersection and the main trail that now heads east along a ridge saddle. This trail soon begins to angle downward and then dives along an old four-wheel track to end on the

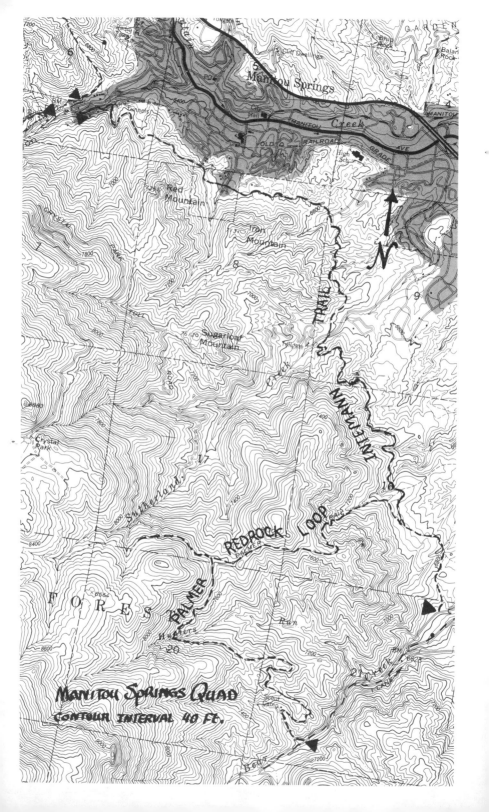

Lower Gold Camp Road at the trailhead called Section 16. On the way, you pass the trailhead for Intemann.

INTEMANN TRAIL (partially completed), eventually five miles one way, elevation gain-loss depends upon exact route, rated easy. Features scenic link between Section 16 of the Palmer Redrock Loop and Pikes Peak Barr Trail in Manitou Springs.

Paul Intemann dreamed of linking the many unstructured paths following the contours of Red Mountain and Iron Mountain, creating a wild trail near urban centers. Tragically, this Manitou Springs city planner died in 1986, yet now hundreds of volunteers are working to fulfill his dream. And thus the formal name is Paul Intemann Memorial Nature Trail.

When completed, this path will connect Section 16 of the Palmer-Redrock Loop and the Pikes Peak Barr Trailhead in Manitou Springs, a distance of about five miles. Low altitude (about 6,700 ft.) and sunny exposures make this a pleasant outing on any but the hottest days. Intemann receives considerable winter use. Except for two relatively short switchback sections, the trail rolls along mountain contours. It repeatedly ducks into forest, then returns to hillside brush, passing red sandstone formations like those in the Garden of the Gods. There are many views of the city, making it a pretty night hike.

Though the trail is not steep, there are narrow portions, so its builders recommend Intemann for more experienced mountain bikers and horse riders.

The unusually flat area downhill is an old landfill, now reclaimed. Locals have their own paths leading up to this trail, so be sure to stay on the main trail, because those other paths quickly take you into trespass situations. Above Crystal Park, the trail switchbacks down steeply to the Crystal Park Road.

At the time of this publication, the southern end (more than two miles) had been constructed as far as Crystal Park Road, but volunteers were beginning to work from the Manitou end. The middle will be completed last.

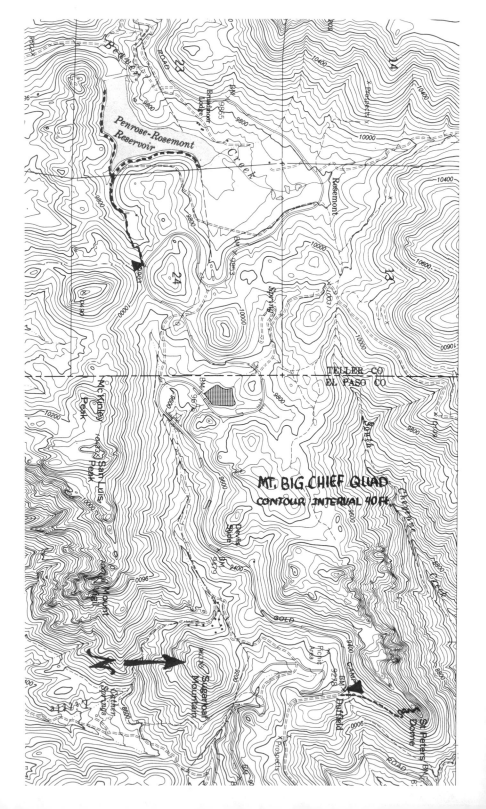

Penrose-Rosemont
Reservoir

MT. BIG CHIEF QUAD
CONTOUR INTERVAL 40 Ft.

TELLER CO
EL PASO CO

McKinley Peak

San Luis Peak

Devils Slide

Sugarloaf Mountain

St. Peters Dome

GOLD CAMP ROAD AREA

St. Peter's Dome Trail
Penrose-Rosemont Reservoir Trail

Teddy Roosevelt called the Gold Camp Road the route that "bankrupt the English language," simply too beautiful for words. This was the route of a narrow-gauge railroad hauling gold ore from Cripple Creek to the smelter in Colorado Springs. You can still see the smelter smokestack from Highway 24 near 21st Street. Gold Hill is made of its tailings and Van Briggle Art Pottery was the railroad round house. As you drive the Gold Camp, sometimes you'll see railroad timbers showing in the roadway where tall trestles were filled with rocks and dirt to make the road.

Unfortunately, the St. Mary's Tunnel has suffered a cave-in, closing eight miles of the Gold Camp above Helen Hunt Falls. The closed section is enjoyed by mountain bikers, equestrians and cross-country skiers, but it also means that you must park farther from the trailheads for North Cheyenne Canyon and St. Mary's Falls. See CHEYENNE CANYON--HIGH DRIVE AREA.

The closure also means that you must take the Old Stage Road to access the Gold Camp and its trails higher up. The Old Stage Road is much steeper than the Gold Camp because harness horses could climb a steeper grade than slick-wheeled locomotives. Both roads must be driven with caution because they are very narrow, have many blind turns and are crowded with folks who are naturally distracted by scenery.

ROAD DIRECTIONS: Old Stage Road is located at one corner of the Broadmoor Golf Course at the intersection of Cheyenne Mountain Blvd. and Penrose Blvd. on the way to the Cheyenne Mountain Zoo. Starting at that intersection, drive up Old Stage for 6.5 miles, where you will pick up the Gold Camp. About a mile farther you reach ST. PETER'S DOME TRAILHEAD at the popular roadside lookout. Set odometer here. Continue for another 2.6 miles and find FS-381 at the Wye Campground; this four-wheel drive route leads to the (future) midpoint of ST. MARY'S FALLS TRAIL. At mile 3.5 from St. Peter's Dome,

you'll find a parking lot on the right for Penrose-Rosemont Reservoir
Fishing Trail. Go another 1.3 miles (4.8 miles from the Dome) to find
FS-379, which leads to the (future) Frosty Park trailhead for Sт.
Mary's Falls Trail.

ST. PETER'S DOME TRAIL, Forest Service #621, 0.7 miles one way; elevation gain 400 ft., rated easy and then moderate. Features scenic overlook of Colorado Springs.

Future improvements may restore this trail to its picture post-card glory, but the iron stairway leading to the top section was destroyed by vandals a number of years ago, so visitors have no safe way to reach the lookout that made this trail famous.

The path begins at the St. Peter's Dome overlook on the Gold Camp Road and gently wraps around the wooded hillside before reaching the short cliff where the stairway once stood. Oddly enough there are no views of the city from this wooded trail because the lookout view featured in picture books is only visible from atop the rocks above. The elevation gain and moderate rating refer to this upper section atop the rocks.

Incidentally, a dead-end side road from the overlook leads back to a Division of Wildlife shooting range.

PENROSE-ROSEMONT RESERVOIR TRAIL, Colorado Springs Dept. of Public Utilities, Colorado Division of Wildlife and Pike National Forest, less than one half mile one way, elevation loss 100 ft., rated easy. Features walk-in fishing access to mountain lake, where no other recreation is permitted.

Almost every tourist who has ever driven the Gold Camp Road has taken snapshots of Penrose-Rosemont Reservoir. This mountain lake was once the private fishing hole for Broadmoor Hotel guests: Celebrities such as Boxing Champ Jack Dempsey were photographed fishing there. After becoming part of the Colorado Springs water system, it was closed for many years, then experienced a dam leak after the City of Colorado Springs Department of Public Utilities opened it to fishing once more. Yet now the dam is fixed, the lake has refilled and is scheduled to be restocked for public fishing in the fall of 1991.

Opening this lake was a cooperative effort. The city provided legal work, the Pike National Forest built the parking lot and fisherman's trail and the Colorado Division of Wildlife provided concrete vault restrooms, litter barrels and stocker trout. Public cooperation is also necessary to protect this vital resource.

All drinking water reservoirs have special rules, but this one needs extra protection because it is so small, only 83 acres. Many forms of recreation are outlawed to keep human impact down. No dogs are allowed, no horses, no mountain bikes, no skiing, no camping, no open fires, no wading, swimming or water-body contact of any kind; no boating, no floatation devices of any kind, no firearms or fireworks, no alcohol, no ice fishing and no picnicking. Indeed, fishing is just about the only recreation allowed at this picturesque lake. That's why the trailhead sign says, "Trail for Use of Fishermen Only."

Another reason for the special regulations is that all improvements are paid for by fishing license fees, so you pay your way by buying a fishing license. For example, no picnic facilities are provided, and picnicking is actually forbidden by legal agreement. The only legal way to picnic there would be to go fishing. **Every member of your party over the age of 16 must have a valid Colorado fishing license and a rod.**

The trail leading down to the lake is short and easy, and the trail along shore is almost flat. It is an exceptionally beautiful stroll, but remember that you may not even hike here without fishing. Do not approach the dam, the caretaker's house or private property on the north side of the lake. A fence and sign about halfway along the northwest edge mark where you must stop. The trail on the southeast side goes almost all the way to the dam.

This is a day-use area only, open from 5:30 a.m. to 9 p.m. Due to icing, the lake is open only during the warmer months, May 11 to October 31. Fishing is by flies and artificial lures only. The area is well patrolled by a resident caretaker and DOW officers. Report any violations. Your cooperation and care may help to open other such areas in the future.

Catchable rainbow trout is the mainstay of the DOW stocking effort at Penrose-Rosemont, but future plans include the addition of lake trout.

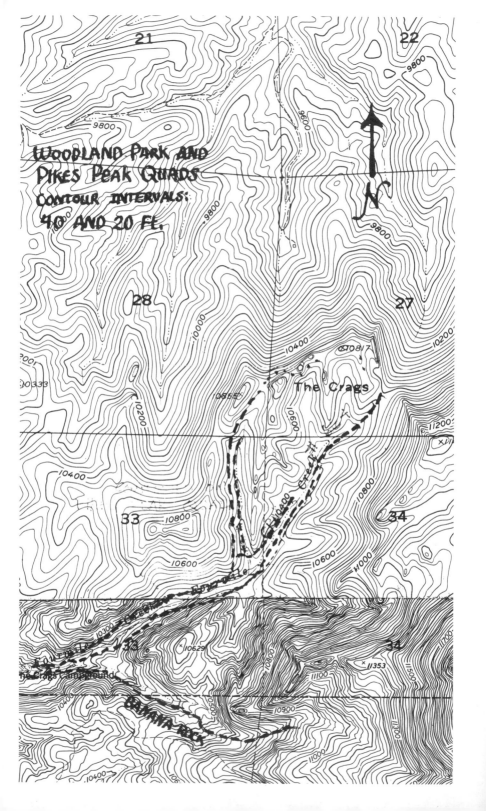

WOODLAND PARK AND
PIKES PEAK QUADS
CONTOUR INTERVALS:
40 AND 20 Ft.

The Crags

The Crags Campground

BANANA ROCK

CRIPPLE CREEK AREA

The Crags Trails
The Crags--Banana Rock Trail
Horsethief Park Trail
Horsethief to Pancake Rocks Trail
Horsethief Falls Trail

The second "Pikes Peak or Bust" gold rush was actually focused on the diggings around Cripple Creek and Victor on the backside of Pikes Peak. This colorful area has some very beautiful trails and is the scene of new trailbuilding and trail changes, as you'll see.

ROAD DIRECTIONS: Starting at the community of Divide on Hwy. 24, turn south on 67 toward Cripple Creek. The turnoff for the CRAGS trail system is located 4.2 miles from that intersection. Watch for a bridge on your left. A sign mentions Rocky Mountain Camp, and this refers to the Mennonite Camp that is located along this road. Another 1.5 miles past the Mennonite camp, you reach a National Forest auto campground with restroom facilities and potable water. The trailhead for the twin CRAGS TRAILS is located at the backside of the campground itself. THE CRAGS--BANANA ROCK TRAIL follows another tributary. Find it by taking the path between campsites #9 and #10

To find the HORSETHIEF PARK trail system, stay on paved 67 until you pass through an old railroad tunnel. Park on the other side of the tunnel on the right. This is a popular overlook. The approach to all Horsethief Park trails leaves from here and loops back up over the tunnel to head east on the other side. You must return this way because the Oil Creek trailhead farther up the road is closed, and the published number for asking permission has been disconnected.

THE CRAGS TRAILS, Forest Service #664, 1.5 miles one way (either way), elevation gain 700 ft., rated easy to moderate. Features gentle valley route to rocky overlook.

Heavy use has created a number of paths in this scenic region, so the old Crags Trail is really two trails following the same creek, forking at a tributary higher up, but ending at the same high lookout. Here you have a 3/4 panorama that is limited only by Pikes Peak on one side. From the top of these eroded granite formations, you can see distant mountains to the north and west and the flatlands with the City of Colorado Springs to the east, as well as nearer features such as the north slope reservoirs of the Pikes Peak watershed.

Because of its high altitude (above 10,000 ft.), the Crags gets and holds snow better than other areas popular for cross-country skiing. However, the access road is not often plowed and creates a lot of business for tow trucks, so be careful.

In summer, the Crags is very popular among hikers, bikers and horse riders, so avoid weekends if you want more solitude.

Leaving the trailhead, the twin trail soon follows both sides of the stream. Ahead, the valley opens up. Near the head of the valley, an unofficial trail takes off to the right, but keep following the stream. As we mentioned, the creek forks and both tributaries lead to the Crags lookout. Taking the right fork, you go through a shady ravine and then climb steeply among jumbled boulders. As soon as you reach the ridge saddle, North and South Catamount and Crystal reservoirs come into view. The vista is even better from higher up among the big crags, but if you have small children along, this would be a good place to quit, for this impressive overlook of lakes and forest and flatlands is a rewarding sight, but does require scrambling around on rocks where children might fall.

CRAGS--BANANA ROCK TRAIL, Forest Service # pending, currently one mile one way, rated easy to moderate. Features snow-holding cross-country ski route up tributary.

Plans call for extending this trail clear through Devil's Playground on the Pikes Peak Toll Road to the summit of Pikes Peak, but at present it fades near timberline, and that is where the Forest Service wants you to stop until that extension is built. Tragically, people are damaging the tundra by seeking their own routes above timberline, creating a lacework of trails with so many cairns that it looks like a pinball machine. Even careful walking damages tundra, and it takes many years, even generations, to regrow, so do what you can to persuade others not to hike beyond the trail.

That said, the existing first mile below timberline is a charming route that follows another tributary of Fourmile Creek. It is a favorite among cross-country skiers because it gets less sun and holds snow better than the others. In 1990, an early storm made it skiable at Halloween. A number of small paths within the campground lead to this trail, but skiers can avoid a stream crossing by taking the path near campsite #9, which begins below the confluence of Fourmile Creek and this trail's tributary. Your trail stays to the right of the tributary, passing Banana Rock, before fading near timberline.

HORSETHIEF PARK TRAIL, Forest Service #708, 1.5 miles one way, elevation gain 700 ft., rated easy to moderate. Features scenic meadow trail suitable for cross-country skiing.

Once the hideout of horsethieves, this beautiful area has become a favorite among bikers and cross-country skiers, as well as hikers and equestrians. The most difficult section is the very beginning, climbing up and over the Little Ike Tunnel. Your first 3/4 mile is an old roadway that tunnels up through dense timber. As soon as the valley opens up, turn left and cross the boggy stream to pick up the old road on the other side. Beaver workings have blocked this old crossing, so look for the new one in the brush just a few yards downstream.

Your double track heads north, skirting the edge of a wide meadow lined with aspens, glorious in fall. It passes some old log ruins and forks at the head of the valley. This fork will form the basis of a triangular loop planned by the Teller County Trails Committee, but at present the right fork is especially faint as it climbs into the trees, frequently blocked by fallen timber and marked only with an occasional cairn. The planned loop will climb to the ridge top, then turn left, following the ridge to pick up the other fork, returning to the meadow.

Bikers note: There is no real trail between Horsethief Park and The Crags. There are pieces of trail in that direction, but the American Biking Association and the Forest Service oppose bush-

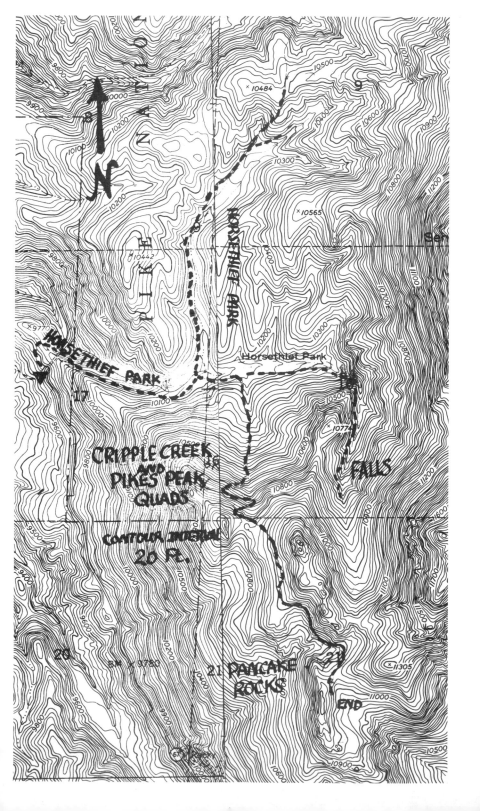

whacking with bikes because of damage to delicate flora and soggy meadows.

HORSETHIEF PARK TO PANCAKE ROCKS, Forest Service #704, 2.75 miles one way from tunnel, elevation gain 1,400 ft., rated moderate to difficult. Features spectacular lookout.

Start up from the tunnel as just explained, but do not cross the stream where the valley opens up. Instead, continue straight ahead (east) and find the intersection marked for the Falls (straight ahead) and Pancake Rocks marked two miles to the right. From here you have a steep climb up through mossy evergreens. High up, the trail seems to start downhill, and some pancake-looking rocks stand high above on the left, but this is not your destination. Keep going and the trail rises again, suddenly depositing you on a high table surrounded by rocks in the shape of stacked pancakes. The view is so grand it even seemed to impress our horses.

Remember, you may no longer descend to the Oil Creek trailhead. You must return the way you came.

HORSETHIEF FALLS TRAIL, Forest Service number pending, I.75 miles one way from the tunnel, elevation gain 900 ft., rated moderate. Features forest trail to waterfall.

Starting back at the intersection with the trail to Pancake Rocks, head east and then south, following the stream up to the falls. This is actually a long cascade tumbling down the granite, with a seven-foot fall at the bottom. Near the base is a small bathtub worn in the rock, which must be tempting on a hot day.

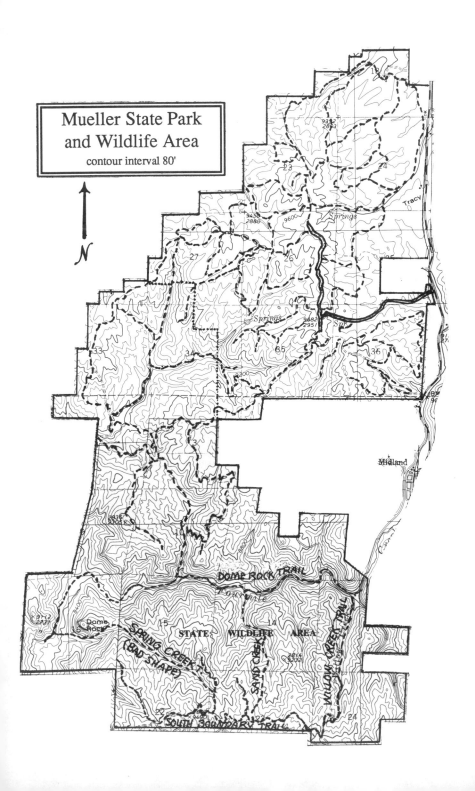

Mueller State Park
and Wildlife Area
contour interval 80'

N

MUELLER STATE PARK AND WILDLIFE AREA

Dome Rock Trail

Imagine a place of evergreens and aspens, of lofty overlooks and grassy meadows, with elk and deer and bighorn sheep, with a trout stream and 16 ponds--12,000 acres (almost 19 square miles) laced with 90 miles of non-motorized trails. Mueller State Park and Wildlife Area is all that and more.

The Wildlife Area in the southern part has been open for some time, and Dome Rock is its principal trail. The northern portion is soon opening, but its master plan is so ambitious that construction will continue for a number of years.

The vast majority of the park will remain as backcountry, but the state is developing a small portion at its heart as a full service park. For example, vehicle campers will be able to reserve pull-out, back-in or drive-through campsites with electricity, picnic tables and fire grills. Conveniently located nearby will be potable water, a sanitary sewage dump, restrooms, hot showers, vending machines and laundry facilities. Handicapped access camping and picnic facilities are under construction, and a livery concession is also being considered. The park will stay open all year, providing cross-country skiing and ice skating in winter. To find out what facilities are ready for your visit, call (719)-687-2366.

The park's trail system is being worked out by process of elimination, using old ranch roads. Some are being allowed to revegetate, some are being closed off for fire access, and the rest are being designated as non-motorized trail. Approximately five miles of paved road will remain open to public vehicles. Future plans call for a few additional link trails, an interpretive nature trail, a children's trail, some handicapped access trail and an easy trail near roadways in the developed area to provide a taste of wilderness for those who might not think of themselves as hikers and to provide an alternative to walking on paved roadway.

Rules are still being worked out. Horses will be allowed on

some trails, but not on others. Bicycles will be allowed on some, but not on others, and both will be permitted on many trails. And all trails will be open to hikers. Backpackers will be able to camp overnight in the northern portion at designated campsites, but not in the southern portion, which has special rules to help protect wildlife. In the high-use area and its loop trail, dogs may be allowed on leash only. Dogs will not be allowed in backcountry, north or south.

A day pass is required for day use in the northern region, where services are offered. At present, no pass is required for exploring the southern day-use region because there are no services.

W.E. Mueller of Colorado Springs operated a ranch and game preserve here for 25 years and wanted to see it preserved as a natural resource for public enjoyment. With the help of the Nature Conservancy, the state was able to acquire the ranch in 1978 and 1980.

Before Mueller's day, this patchwork of homesteads had a colorful history. There were horsethieves and moonshiners (ruins of over a dozen stills can be found), attempts at potato, lettuce and dairy farming, ranching and mining. Historic ruins and prospect holes are scattered through backcounty. Note: Removal of any artifact is prohibited by state law.

The park is surrounded by private development, so stay on designated trails to avoid trespassing and to protect the environment. Rules may change, so obey all signs.

ROAD DIRECTIONS: To find Mueller, take 67 from Divide toward Cripple Creek. Go 3.8 miles and turn right into park. To find DOME ROCK TRAIL, go another 1.8 miles and turn right toward Rainbow Valley. The trailhead will be on your right about two miles down.

DOME ROCK TRAIL, Division of Wildlife, about five miles one way, elevation loss 600 ft., rated easy. Features easy journey along scenic fishing stream.

After the turn of the century, coaches rolled along this trail, splashing across fords in the creek, hauling Eastern investors to the Crescent Cattle Company's private resort. At their magnificent

Jack Rabbit Lodge investors enjoyed fishing, hunting and other sports--including sporting ladies. These weren't local girls, mind you, but high-class professionals from Denver, yet the ladies weren't allowed to work inside the lodge. Their profession was restricted to some tent-cribs out back.

The lodge burned down in 1941, leaving only chimney ruins beside the trail. The property is now owned by the Division of Wildlife, and Fourmile Creek (which flows from The Crags) is stocked with Pikes Peak cutthroat trout. No dogs, fires, camping or mountain bicycles are allowed. Elk and bighorn use the area near Dome Rock itself, and this region may require further restrictions during certain seasons.

Dome Rock Trail is a streamside rollercoaster that makes a challenging cross-country ski route, but remember that it is all uphill on the return. Leaving the trailhead, the first stream crossing is easy. After that, the original coach route fords the creek numerous times, which is fine for equestrians on long-legged horses, but hikers will find it difficult and dangerous when the creek is running high. In such times, visitors have created an unofficial single track by climbing along the north side of the creek. It is not up to park standards and will be closed off if bridges are built in the future. Remember that you are very much on your own in backcountry and are expected to make prudent decisions about your own safety. If the situation looks dangerous, turn back.

Most of the time the creek is not running high, of course, and then the nine fords make it a fun trip. Follow the creek down past the lodge ruins. At the base of Dome Rock, the creek and your trail swerve south, leading to a high point with a great view of Dome Rock. This is a good place to turn around because soon after there is a gate marking private property and trail's end

There are other trails in this area also, but they are unmarked, unmeasured and in various conditions. The first is close by as you start back, though it is faint or nonexistent as it heads up a tributary to the east. Spring Creek Trail then follows a branch southeast, finally joining a more distinct trail called South Boundary, which connects with Sand Creek and then Willow Creek, making it possible to do loops on the return to Dome Rock Trailhead.

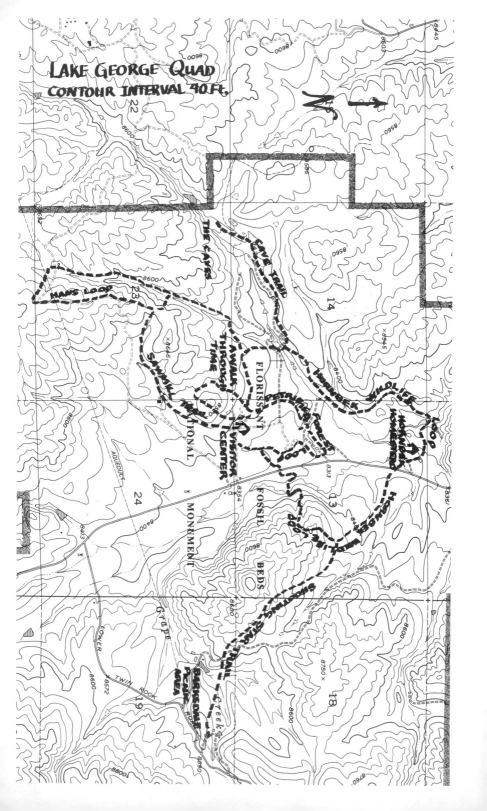

FLORISSANT FOSSIL BEDS NATIONAL MONUMENT

A Walk Through Time Trail
Petrified Forest Loop
Sawmill Trail
Cave Trail
Hornbeck Wildlife Loop
Shootin' Star Trail

Nothing in Arizona's famed Petrified Forest can match the fossils at Florissant for sheer size. Over 100 petrified stumps of giant Sequoia redwoods stand in the Florissant Fossil Beds National Monument, though some have been reburied to preserve them. The largest is 13 feet in diameter and 41.9 feet around! When alive, this redwood probably stood 300 feet high and was at least 700 years old.

This is the Pompeii of Pikes Peak Country, an area smothered by volcanic ash and mud flows millions of years ago, preserving everything from insects to animals in deadly detail. Even the hairs on the insects' legs can be seen in these fossils. Many thousands of Florissant specimens have been collected by museums around the world.

But don't you take any--not even the smallest piece--and quickly report anyone who does. Visitors have proven to be effective and zealous guardians of this national treasure. Besides, you can buy legal specimens collected from outside the park at a shop nearby.

Since its trail system blossomed from one to seven, this has become one of the finest cross-country ski areas in Pikes Peak Country. However, its high park terrain (meadows with scattered ponderosa) is so sunny that snow melts off faster than it would in dense forest. No entry fee is charged during the winter, but the

Visitors Center remains open and staffed, offering information, book sales and warm restrooms. All trails are gentle enough for skiing, but those on the east side of the highway are more challenging.

During the summer, the Visitors Center charges a small entrance fee, but the pass is good for a week and none is required for using the east side trails. Guided nature tours can also be arranged, including an unusual moonlight tour where visitors listen to the sounds of wildlife. Call 719-748-3253 for information.

Department of Interior rules forbid mountain bikes. Horses are permitted on east side trails, but on the west side horses should travel only beside trails, not on them, in order to keep trails cleaner. Remove any manure from trails.

The park opens at 8 a.m., but closing time varies with the season (4:30 or 7 p.m.). The park is home to elk and ground-nesting birds, so no dogs are allowed. No mountain bikes or snowmobiles are allowed. No camping, no hunting, no firearms, no fireworks, no open fires (grills only), no collecting of fossils, flowers, or other souvenirs. Located on USGS Lake George quad.

ROAD DIRECTIONS: The community of Florissant is located on Highway 24 between Divide and Lake George, 39 miles from Colorado Springs. At Florissant take Teller County 1 south for 2.5 miles and turn right to the Visitors Center. To find SHOOTIN' STAR trailhead, continue on Teller 1 and turn left on Lower Twin Rock Road. Go 1.6 miles and park at the Barksdale Picnic Area on your left

A WALK THROUGH TIME TRAIL, 0.5-mile loop, elevation gain nil, rated easy. Features geologic time lesson and giant fossil exhibit.

It takes some imagination, but this loop trail is designed to help you appreciate the enormity of geologic time. The first sign along the way says "4.57 Billion Years Ago, Earth Begins," and every two inches of the trail after that represents the passage of a million years, with more signs to help give you that perspective. Unfortunately, many visitors are so distracted by the giant triple stump exhibited here that they miss the time demonstration.

PETRIFIED FOREST LOOP, one-mile loop, elevation gain nil, rated easy. Features interpretive trail.

Be sure to pick up the pamphlet describing this self-guided nature loop or you won't know what the numbered posts mean. This trail covers part of the bank and bed of prehistoric Lake Florissant. Big Stump, one of the largest of the silica giants, was supposed to be cut into sections for shipment to the *Columbian Exposition* in Chicago, but the sawblades broke and can still be seen sticking out of the stump.

SAWMILL TRAIL, 2.1-mile loop, elevation gain-loss 200 feet, rated easy to moderate. Features scenic and varied terrain with sawmill ruins.

In previous editions, this was the park's only trail. Starting at the Visitors Center and going clockwise, Sawmill passes the picnic area and eventually climbs a fire road to a gravel road. The markers lead to an abandoned sawmill that operated from the late 1800s to the 1930s. From here you follow old roads and paths, over a ridge with a view of Pikes Peak, then along a stream and meadow frequented by elk.

HANS LOOP, 1.2-mile loop, elevation gain-loss 80 ft., rated moderate. Features homestead ruins.

This is a new extension of Sawmill Trail, leading down from the ridge to a meadow valley with a wetlands habitat. It passes the ruins of a rustic homestead, then follows the stream down to Sawmill.

CAVE TRAIL, 2 miles one way, elevation gain 120 ft., rated easy. Features unusual rock formation.

Cave Trail is a long branch off the Hornbeck Wildlife Trail, leading up a sunny meadow with a stream and ponds. At the park boundary, you find The Caves, actually huge boulders that have tipped together to form a cave-like place where the stream flows through. A new route under construction will lead over the ridge to Sawmill, but is not included in our figures.

HORNBECK WILDLIFE LOOP, 4-mile loop, elevation gain-loss 120 ft., rated easy to moderate. Features stroll to Hornbeck homestead.

Beginning at Sawmill Trail near the Visitor Center, Hornbeck leads through scattered trees and along broad meadows that were once the bed of prehistoric Lake Florissant. As the trail nears the road, you find the Hornbeck homestead, recreated complete with outhouse and root cellar. Then your path crosses the road, arching up through the east meadow to link with Shootin' Star before returning to the Visitors Center.

SHOOTIN' STAR TRAIL, 2 miles one way, elevation gain 80 ft., loss 120 ft., rated easy to moderate. Features scenic link with Hornbeck.

Shootin' Star Trail is named after the nearby ranch, which was named after the wildflower so common here in early summer. Its highest elevation is at the southern trailhead at Barksdale Picnic Area. From here, the trail crosses a meadow, goes over a wooded ridge and then joins Hornbeck on the grassy slope above Teller 1. Cross-country skiers may want to start from the Hornbeck homestead parking lot instead, because this would make the return trip downhill.

WOODLAND PARK AREA

Manitou Park Bicycle Trail
Painted Rocks Bike Trail
Lovell Gulch Trail

Located where Hwy. 24 intersects with 67 to Deckers, Woodland Park is a crossroads for mountain access. It is also the headquarters for the Teller County Trail Committee, whose volunteers have been busy building new trails and improving older ones throughout the county. Yet perhaps we should point out that nearby Manitou Park and its Manitou Lake are nowhere near Manitou Springs, but are owned by the city of Woodland Park.

Trails are located on the USGS Mt. Deception quad.

ROAD DIRECTIONS: The trailhead for Manitou Park Bicycle Trail is located at the South Meadows Campground, 5.9 miles north of Woodland Park on County 67. Painted Rocks Bike Trail is a short branch located just north at the Painted Rocks Campground. To find the Lovell Gulch trailhead, take the turnoff marked for the Rampart Range Road next to McDonald's in Woodland Park. Go 2.2 miles north to the Dog Pound next to the Woodland Park Maintenance Center. The Lovell Gulch parking lot is located at the Pound.

MANITOU PARK BICYCLE TRAIL, Forest Service #669.2, 2.1 miles one way, elevation gain less than 100 ft., rated easy. Features wheelchair-suitable link between campgrounds and Manitou Lake.

Not just for bicycles, Manitou Park Bicycle Trail is perfect for wheelchairs, baby strollers and families with toddlers. Wide and paved, it runs like a flat sidewalk beside County 67, linking three Forest Service pay campgrounds with the fishing lake at Manitou Park. Yet this is no urban trail: Please close the gates to keep the cattle from getting out.

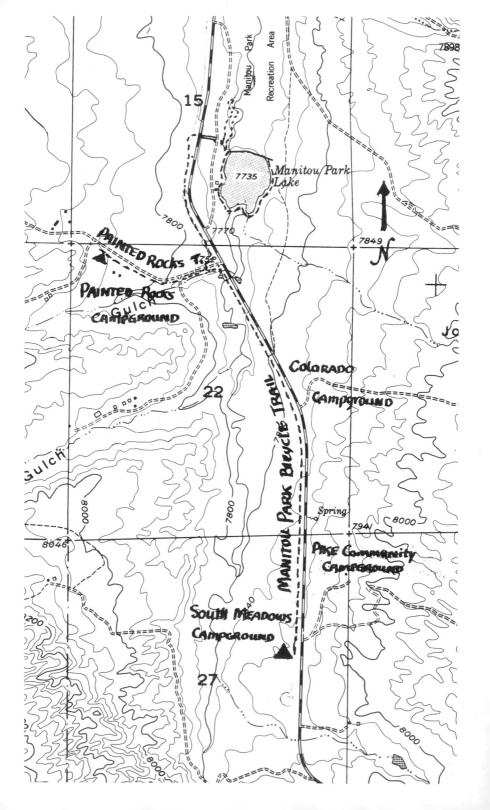

Manitou Park itself is being improved to make it accessible for wheelchair visitors. A new boardwalk and more hard-surface trail will mean that handicapped visitors will be able to fish in this scenic area. The park is a day-use area open from 6 a.m. to 10 p.m. The lake is stocked with catchable size rainbows by the Division of Wildlife.

PAINTED ROCKS BIKE TRAIL, Forest Service #669.1, 0.3 miles one way, elevation gain nil, rated easy. Features link between Painted Rocks Campground and Manitou Bicycle Trail.

This is just a short spur off the Manitou Bicycle Trail with the same hard surface and flat design, making it suitable for wheelchairs, baby strollers and toddlers. This area boasts strange red sandstone columns, some shaped like mushrooms. These were formed because softer sandstone was capped with a patch of harder rock that preserved the column while everything else weathered away around it.

LOVELL GULCH TRAIL, Forest Service number pending, 5.5-mile balloon-shaped loop, elevation gain-loss 640 ft., rated easy to moderate. Features forest walk with scenic views.

Wildflowers decorate most trails, but Lovell Gulch may be the perfect habitat. Not just the meadows, but even the forest is crowded with flowers after a rain. Gentle rolling hills capture rainfall, minimizing runoff (which allows soil depth to build), and the widely spaced evergreens provide the right mix of sun and shade (energy and moisture protection). Please remember that it is a federal violation to disturb wildflowers in the National Forest.

This "new" trail has been around for quite some time--and is very popular with local equestrians--but locals became aware that a growing lacework of trails was trampling the area. So volunteers from the Teller County Trails Committee worked in cooperation with the Forest Service to establish the trailhead, post signs, clean up and block off many extra paths with sticks. So please take the hint and stay on the posted trail. It was designated as an official FS trail in 1990.

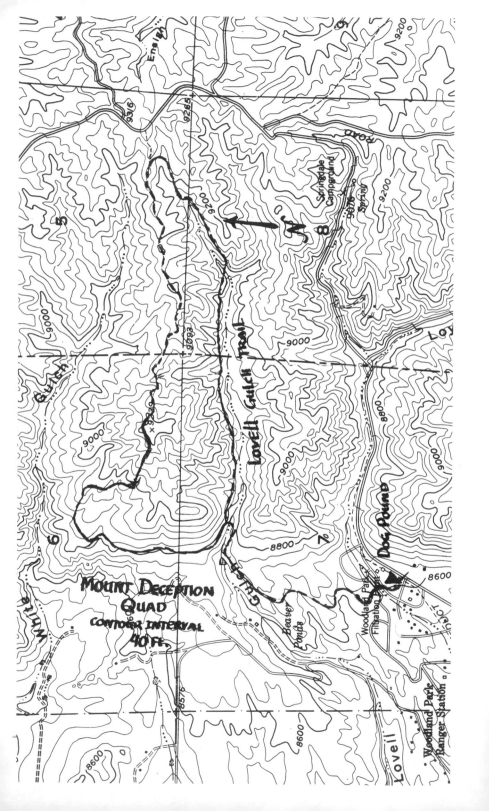

The first mile (the string of the balloon) is nearly level, leading north out of Woodland Park along the edge of timber. Then it crosses a stream and forks where a sign describes the loop ahead as being 3 3/4 miles. Cross-country skiers will probably want to ski this one counter-clockwise in order to gain altitude more gradually. So turn right and travel upstream along a narrow meadow for about 1.5 miles. Climbing to the top of a ridge, it loops back to the west along the ridge, offering spectacular views of Pikes Peak and Ute Pass. The descent from this ridge is the steepest section. Turn right at the fork and you're on your way back along the string.

Note: Very heavy animal traffic here makes it necessary to ask animal owners not to leave feces on the trail. Dog feces should be buried like human waste; horse manure should only be moved, not buried, because of the hole size necessary.

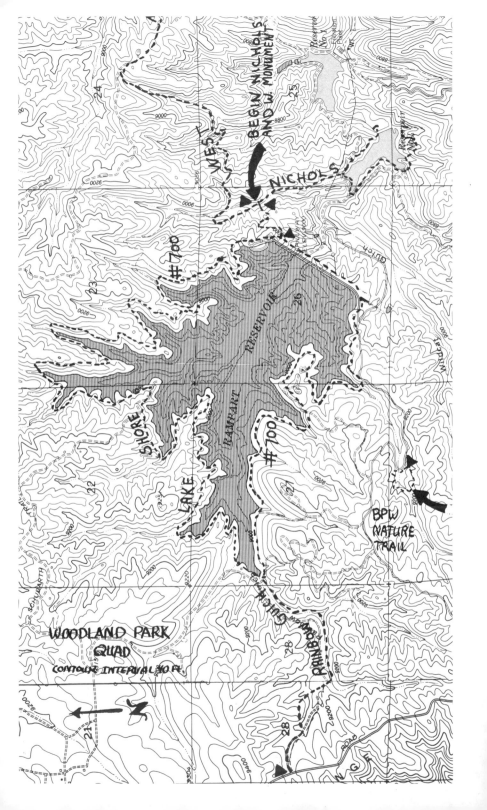

RAMPART RESERVOIR AREA

Rainbow Gulch Trail
BPW Nature Trail
Rampart Reservoir Trail (Lake Shore Trail)
Nichols Reservoir Trail
West Monument Creek Trail

Rampart Reservoir stores water piped over the Continental Divide from the Western Slope, then passes it down through Nichols and another reservoir to a Colorado Springs treatment plant located at the mouth of West Monument Canyon beside the Air Force Academy. Except for a portion of West Monument Creek Trail, all trails in this area are for day use only. This means you are not permitted to leave a vehicle overnight at Rampart Reservoir, though you may at the Air Force Academy once that trailhead is reestablished.

Rampart is stocked by the Division of Wildlife with rainbow and lake trout. The state limit of one laker over 20 inches is vigorously enforced because some anglers are spoiling reproduction by taking smaller lakers, perhaps mistaking them for other trout. Lakers have have a distinct notch in the tail fin. Rampart also has some brown and brook trout.

The Forest Service has built beautiful picnic facilities at Rampart. Groups wishing to camp overnight may do so at Springdale Campground on the Rampart Range Road. Call 1-800-283-2267 for reservations. There is no potable water.

These trails are located on the USGS Cascade quad, except for the very beginning of Rainbow Gulch, which is on the Woodland Park quad

ROAD DIRECTIONS: The Rampart Range Road may be accessed from the southern end of the Garden of the Gods in Colorado Springs or from Hwy. 24 at Woodland Park. The way is well marked. To find RAINBOW GULCH TRAIL *from Woodland Park, turn at McDonald's and go 2.9 miles to Loy Creek Road. Turn right and follow Loy to its inter-*

section with the Rampart Range Road. Turn right and set odometer. Springdale Campground is on your left. RAINBOW GULCH Trailhead will be on your left about 2.4 miles from the Loy-Rampart intersection. A sign there says "RAMPART RESERVOIR CROSS-COUNTRY SKI TRAILS."

At mile 4 you find the turnoff for Rampart Reservoir. Go 1.6 miles and look for the trailhead for the BPW NATURE TRAIL on your right at the second switchback past Promontory Picnic Ground.

Continue across the Rampart Reservoir Dam and park on the far side at Dikeside Overlook. You can see Nichols lake from the dam. The trailhead for LAKE SHORE TRAIL is near the boat ramp. The trailhead for NICHOLS IS nearer the dam. WEST MONUMENT CREEK TRAIL branches off the NICHOLS TRAIL 0.4 miles from the parking lot.

The Rampart Reservoir Road is closed in winter, but trails may be used by those who wish to hike or ski into the area.

RAINBOW GULCH TRAIL, Forest Service #714, 1.4 miles one way, elevation loss 120 ft., rated easy. Features gentle ski and bike trail to lake.

After leaving the Rampart Range Road, Rainbow Gulch Trail slopes gently downhill to join Lake Shore at the Rampart Reservoir. The trail soon leaves the ponderosa pine forest and follows a grassy meadow and tributary to the lake. A sign at roadside only mentions it as a ski trail, but it is open to hikers, bikers and equestrians

BPW NATURE TRAIL, Forest Service #712, 0.4-mile loop, elevation gain-loss 40 ft., rated easy. Features easy nature trail designed to serve everyone, including the blind and persons confined to wheelchairs.

The BPW Nature Trail is sponsored by the Colorado Federation of Business and Professional Women's Clubs and offers a wilderness experience with special facilities for blind and wheelchair visitors. The trail itself leads through three different kinds of ecosystems, including a willow bottomland, a ponderosa pine and a spruce-fir area. It has bridges, benches, and a wooden observation deck that overlooks Castaway Gulch. The path is about four feet wide and has a firm but natural tread.

This is a self-guiding nature trail with 14 stations along it.

The station signs are also translated into Braille. Restrooms suitable for use by the physically handicapped are also provided.

RAMPART RESERVOIR TRAIL, Forest Service #700, 11.6-mile loop, elevation gain-loss 40 ft., rated easy. Features easy biking, skiing, and access to shores of Rampart Reservoir (fishing permitted).

Rolling around the edge of Rampart Reservoir, this easy trail is a favorite among mountain bikers and cross-country skiers. However, in wet times it has a lot of muddy spots where drainages come down to the lake, and bikes really get messy. But it has wonderful views.

Boats and fishing are permitted, but dogs must be on a leash and no overnight camping is allowed. No firearms, no fireworks, no open fires (grates only).

Once called Lake Shore Trail, this one is a very pretty when the reservoir is full, but because the lake is a domestic water supply for the City of Colorado Springs, it is subject to considerable drawdown in dry years. This can leave Lake Shore somewhat distant from the shore.

NICHOLS TRAIL, Forest Service #709, 2.3 miles one way, elevation loss 280 ft., rated moderate. Features lake shore walk at Nichols Reservoir (fishing permitted).

Nichols Trail begins at the Dikeside Overlook on the north end of the Rampart Reservoir Dam Parking Area, and provides access to the shores of Nichols Reservoir. It goes down through a ponderosa pine forest and follows a small drainage toward the lake. The trail forks at the reservoir to follow the lake shore. It generally stays about 30 feet above the water, following contours to stay level. Some of this work was done by the Youth Conservation Corps. The trail now goes all the way around the lake, except for the dam itself, which is closed to the public.

Nichols is stocked by the DOW with catchable rainbow trout, but this drinking water reservoir has many special rules to help protect the resource: no horses, no mountain bikes, no camping, no

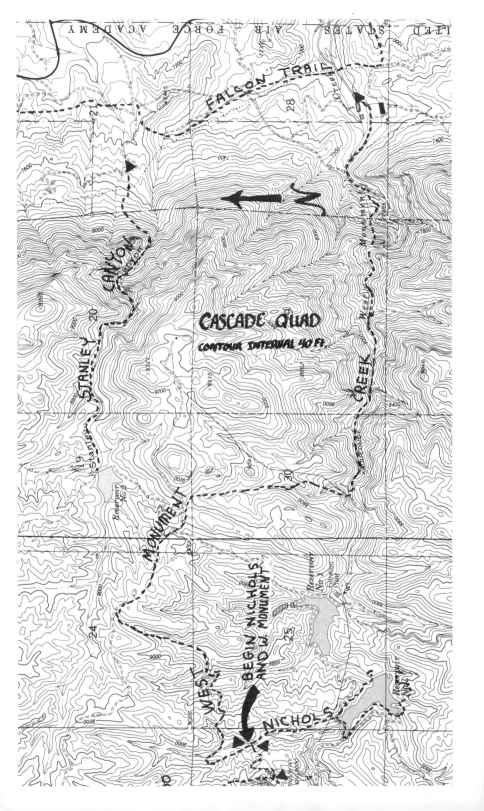

ice fishing, no boats or floatation devices of any kind, no swimming, wading or other body contact, no bait fishing--only flies and artificial lures are permitted. Dogs must be on a leash not longer than six feet and must stay 50 yards back from the water. **You must stay off the dam.** And please do not explore or fish around Reservoir #1 (Northfield), which is located downstream to the east and is closed to the public. A caretaker lives there and patrols the area. Nichols is also known as Reservoir #4 on USGS maps.

WEST MONUMENT CREEK TRAIL, Forest Service #713, 6 miles one way; elevation loss 2,000 ft., gain 60 ft., rated moderate to difficult. Features varied scenery along an old logging route.

There are still some special problems with this trail because the upper end is confusing and the lower end is temporarily closed and needs a new trailhead. In addition, the upper end is in a day-use area. You are allowed to camp in the National Forest once you leave the Rampart Reservoir vicinity, but you may **not** leave your vehicle there overnight, so it is best to be dropped off for overnight expeditions. We recommend that you scout the upper half as a day trip before being dropped off, however, because many people get lost in this area. Unfortunately, the two trailheads are more than an hour and a half apart by car, so the usual two-car system is inconvenient for one-way day trips down West Monument.

The upper trailhead branches off Nichols Trail 0.4 mile from the dam. It climbs over a ridge and washboards over three drainages before climbing to a level section on high ground. Heading southeast, it crosses more tributaries as it winds through ponderosa pine and aspen. This route is very confusing because of all the old traces in the area. Volunteer work is needed to mark this route plainly. We recommend taking along the Pikes Peak Atlas topo because it charts just about everything. If you don't go wrong, you will eventually find West Monument Creek downstream from Reservoir #1 (the reservoir is closed). Follow the creek down a steep canyon toward the Air Force Academy.

At the mouth of the canyon is a Colorado Springs water filtration plant, where a new tunnel is being bored to bypass the pipeline that runs down West Monument Canyon. Construction has temporarily closed the lower trailhead at the time of this writing, but the Forest Service plans to reestablish the trail in the canyon once the tunnel is finished. Be sure to obey all Utility Dept. signs in this sensitive area, and check with the Forest Service before heading out. Call 303-636-1602. For road directions to the lower trailhead, see AIR FORCE ACADEMY AREA.

AIR FORCE ACADEMY AREA

Falcon Trail
Stanley Canyon Trail

As the Air Force equivalent of West Point and Annapolis, the US Air Force Academy is quite a tourist attraction. Set in a beautiful foothills area, it has two public trails, one of which (Stanley) extends into the Pike National Forest. Our road directions also describe the future site of the lower West Monument Creek Trail, which is temporarily closed for utility tunnel construction. See Rampart Range Area for a description of West Monument Creek Trail.

Academy trails are located on USGS Cascade and Palmer Lake quads.

ROAD DIRECTIONS: Enter the south gate of the U.S. Air Force Academy. Proceed three miles, cross the railroad overpass and turn left onto Pine Drive. To find the trailhead for FALCON, follow Pine Drive for 3.6 miles and turn right onto Community Drive. At the top of the hill, a distance of almost a mile, you turn right and find your way back to the Youth Center, Building #5132, which is the small building on the southwestern corner of the complex. The trailhead is located behind the building and a large blue sign marks the spot.

To find the lower trailhead for WEST MONUMENT CREEK TRAIL, turn left off of Pine Drive at the Fire Station's west side and follow the gravel road to the Colorado Springs Department of Public Utilities Filtration Plant. Do not drive through the gate! Park outside the gate along the roadside. The CSDPU keeps this gate locked at night and all weekend, so your car could be trapped inside. Persons on foot find it easy to exit past this locked gate, so you may leave at any time. See RAMPART RESERVOIR AREA for a trail description of WEST MONUMENT CREEK.

To find the STANLEY CANYON trailhead, follow Pine Drive another 1.4 miles past the Community Drive turnoff. The paved road will rise on a hill until it overlooks the Academy Hospital on the right. There, on the left, is a gravel turnoff that leads back 0.9 mile to the parking area for STANLEY CANYON. Follow the markers. There is limited park-

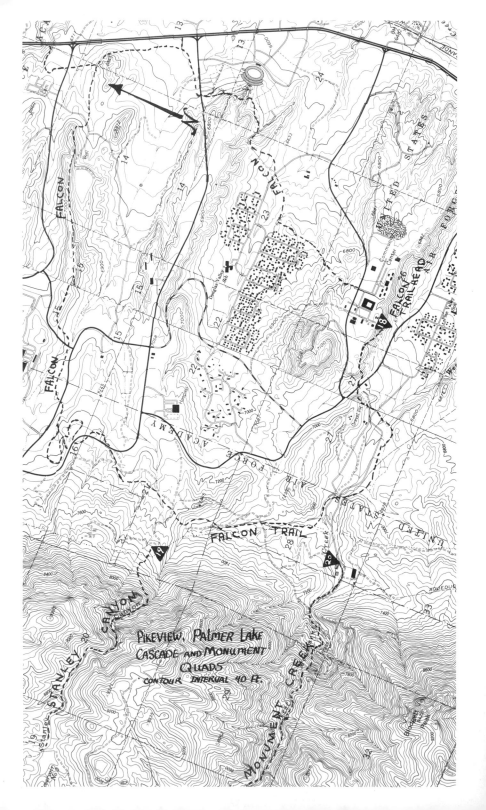

PIKEVIEW, PALMER LAKE
CASCADE AND MONUMENT
QUADS
CONTOUR INTERVAL 40 FT.

ing, but more is available at the Academy Hospital. The Hospital lot is constantly patrolled and is considered safer for overnight parking.

Remember that the public may enter Academy gates only during day hours that vary seasonally, though you may park overnight for pack trips into the National Forest. No camping is permitted on the Academy itself. You may leave the Academy at any time.

FALCON TRAIL, Air Force Academy Trail, 12 mile loop ; elevation gain 880 ft., rated easy. Features well marked nature trail with varied terrain and wildlife, plus a restored settler's cabin.

This long and varied trail is maintained by the Boy Scouts, but is open to all hikers for day use. No horses, firearms or fires are permitted. Hikers no longer need to register, but the Academy warns hikers to stay on the trail to avoid military training and construction that may be in progress nearby. The trail is marked with signs showing a white falcon against a blue background.

Falcon Trail begins on a hill at the Community Center's Youth Center Building. It first descends the wooded hillside, crosses Pine Drive and enters grassland. Then it climbs behind an arid hill with Blodgett Peak towering to the west and crosses the gravel road that leads to the filtration plant. Here you enter the trees once more, cross a stream on a wooden bridge, and join another stream, the one that flows from Stanley Canyon.

In this area Scouts have built small dams to help prevent soil erosion and to provide shelters for aquatic life. Fourteen signs point out natural and man-made features along the way, and the Academy Visitor Center provides brochures to explain the points of interest.

Your path wanders through ponderosa pine and Gambel's oak. It crosses Academy and Interior Drives and then skirts a small marsh where cattails grow. After crossing another road, the path climbs again to follow a pine-covered ridge that overlooks a reservoir, eventually leading past a pioneer cabin.

This log cabin has been so well preserved and restored that it looks almost as if the pioneer family has locked it up to go visit friends. Wooden tombstones in the yard mark the graves of family members.

The trail ends where it began at the Youth Center. Remember that rattlesnakes are among the many kinds of wildlife seen along Falcon Trail. If you visit in the fall, be aware of a limited deer hunting season and wear orange reflective clothing.

STANLEY CANYON TRAIL, Forest Service #707, 3 miles one way; elevation gain 1,500 ft., rated moderate to difficult. Features climb through spectacular canyon.

This scenic trail begins on Academy property, but quickly climbs into National Forest, following the stream that pours down Stanley Canyon. Within 1/4 mile you reach a bend in the trail where the trees open up, revealing an overlook of the surrounding country.

Higher up, where the canyon grows most narrow, you have a view of the distant prairies framed in granite. Be careful making your way up through the streambed narrows, for this can be a treacherous spot when icy or rainy. Then the canyon turns sharply, shutting off the view. Your trail grows more gentle after that, leading through forest and meadow toward Stanley Canyon Reservoir. The best camping spots are downstream from the lake; camping beside the lake is prohibited and would be unecological anyway.

This beautiful lake is owned by Colorado Springs, but fishing rights have been granted **only** to the Air Force Academy. A special Academy permit is required, and is only sold to Academy personnel and their bona fide house guests, defined as a persons who live permanently out of state and who are actually staying in the home of Academy personnel. The lake is stocked, paid for by license fees, not taxpayer money. There are special bag limits.

MONUMENT--BLACK FOREST

Monument Trail
Mount Herman Trail
FOX RUN REGIONAL PARK TRAILS:
North Loop
West Loop
What's In A Name Trail

Located north of the Air Force Academy, the Monument--Black Forest Area has seen increases in trail use, both official and unofficial. Unofficial paths used by locals are likely to receive volunteer work and official designation in the future. Meanwhile, the opening of Fox Run Regional Park in the Black Forest has added miles of trail for hiking, biking, horseback riding and cross-country skiing. Monument and Mount Herman are located on the USGS Palmer Lake quad, and Fox Run Regional Park is on the Monument quad.

ROAD DIRECTIONS: To find MONUMENT and MOUNT HERMAN, TRAILS, take I-25 to the Monument-Palmer Lake Exit #161 west and drive through the town of Monument. Cross the railroad tracks at Third St. and turn turn south on Mitchell Ave. Go past the turnoff for Monument Lake (private) and turn right on Mount Herman Road. To find MONUMENT Trailhead go 0.6 miles and turn left onto Schilling (where the pavement ends), then go another 0.6 miles to the intersection with Linberg and park as best you can near the gated fence with a stile in it. To find MOUNT HERMAN Trailhead, stay on Mount Herman Road and note your odometer when you cross the National Forest boundary. Drive 1.6 miles and turn left at the fork. Go another 2.7 miles and watch for the trailhead on your right as you make a tight curve at a drainage area leading down toward Beaver Creek. Overall distance from the National Forest boundary is 4.3 miles.

To find Fox Run Regional Park, take the next exit south of Monument-Palmer Lake, marked Baptist Road Exit #158 east from I-25. Shortly after the road curves, turn left on Becky Lane for one half mile, then turn left again on Stella Drive. Follow Stella for another 0.6

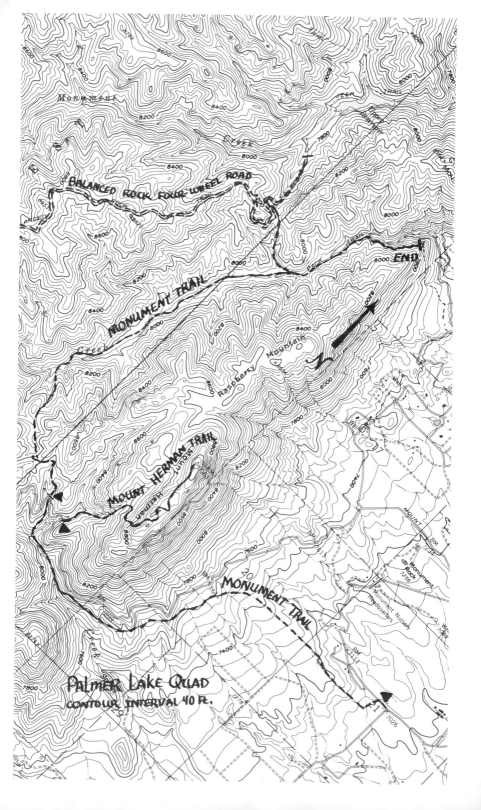

Monument Creek

Balanced Rock Four-Wheel Road

END

8000

Monument Trail

Raspberry Mountain

Mount Herman Trail

Monument Trail

Monument Rock 7256

Palmer Lake Quad
Contour Interval 40 Ft.

miles to find the main entrance to Fox Run Park. To find the north trailhead, proceed on Stella and turn left on Rollercoaster Road. Parking is on the left.

MONUMENT TRAIL, Forest Service #715, 8.2 miles one way, elevation gain 200 ft., loss 1,200 ft.; rated moderate going, more difficult coming back. Features varied scenery.

This is the same trail with the same number that used to be called officially the Mount Herman Trail, even though it never climbed Mount Herman. The new name suits it better. It begins at Memorial Grove, where a plaque and planted trees memorialize dead Forest Service personnel. Go through the stile in the fence and up the road for a very short distance before turning left (south) onto the trail. This first section is flat enough to make good cross-country skiing and is also popular among local joggers. It leads through Gambel's oak, eventually climbing steeply beside the creek that flows below Mount Herman Road.

Crossing Mount Herman Road, your trail shares a four-wheeler route for about a third of a mile and cuts northwest off the road as the road continues southwest. Now your trail narrows and wanders through aspen until it connects with Monument Creek in Limbaugh Canyon. It follows the creek through willow-brush and aspen meadows for about a mile and a half, then forks. The right fork continues downstream for 1.1 miles to the Forest Service boundary. Beyond this point is private and utility property, so the trail dead-ends here. The left fork leaves the creek and climbs up to the Balanced Rock four-wheel drive road. If you're on foot, you may turn right and go down past the gate to Palmer Lake, but horses and bikes are not allowed past the gate. The Balanced Rock road is in such poor shape that there is virtually no access to it from the Rampart Range.

MOUNT HERMAN TRAIL, Forest Service #716, about 2 miles one way, elevation gain 1,000 ft., rated moderate. Features hike to summit of Mt. Herman.

To end confusion about Mount Herman Trail the Forest Service has made a logical change. The trail that used to be called

Fox Run Regional Park

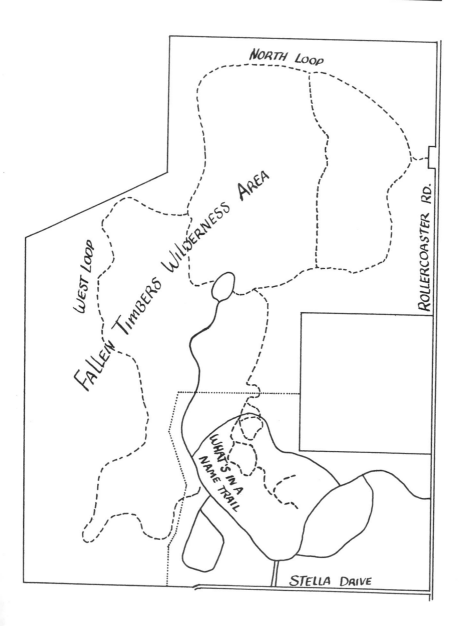

Mount Herman will now be called Monument because it starts there and leads to Monument Creek, and the trail that climbs Mount Herman will be called Mount Herman, as some locals have insisted for years.

Starting up from the Mount Herman Road, your trail follows a tiny tributary for a short way. Where it forks, taking the right fork before switchbacking up Mt. Herman. The trail is gentler on top, leading to a popular outlook where the Great Plains are laid out below you. Look for a cooler covered with a tarp. Inside is a trails register where you can record your name and impressions. This register is provided by a local citizen who replaces it each Christmas and wishes to keep doing so in order to build an historical record. Imagine how much fun it would be to look up what people had said about a trail and a view a hundred years ago.

FOX RUN REGIONAL PARK TRAILS:

Once a part of a fox ranch, Fox Run Regional Park offers gentle trails for cross-country skiing, hiking, horseback riding and mountain biking. The entrance of this El Paso County Park looks like an urban park, with flower beds and mowed lawns, pavilions for picnics and areas for games, but 90% of its 390 acres has been left in a natural state and has been designated as the Fallen Timbers Wilderness Area.

Fox Run has the best self-guided interpretive trails in Pikes Peak Country. If you don't learn something from these interpretive signs, you deserve some kind of honorary degree. All three trails have the signs.

Wide and well-marked with frequent "You are here" maps, the trails tunnel through dense ponderosa so typical of the Black Forest. Two trailheads, one in the center of the wilderness and the other on Rollercoaster Road at the north end of the park, each provide restrooms, parking, potable water, picnic sites and interpretive displays.

The usual park rules apply: no hunting, no firearms or fireworks, no open fires (grates only), no camping. Dogs must be on a leash. Bikes, horses and dogs are permitted on the loop trails, but are prohibited from What's In A Name Trail.

NORTH LOOP, 1.5-mile loop, elevation gain nil, rated easy. Features easiest wilderness route.

The North Loop is really two loops because of an extra north-south route that cuts across it. If you use that extra section to make two loops, the eastern loop measures about a mile by itself and the other half measures about 1.25 miles by itself. All of the park's trails are easy, but this one is almost flat. This kind of evergreen forest extends into the plains because of a layer of sandstone beneath the surface that traps enough water to make trees grow.

WEST LOOP, almost 2 miles, elevation gain negligible, rated easy to moderate. Features more challenging skiing and hiking.

West Loop is more hilly than North Loop, and bikers will find it sandy in spots. Still, these hills only make gentle rolling trail; there are no switchbacks. Don't miss the interpretive signs along the way.

WHAT'S IN A NAME TRAIL, 0.25 miles one way, elevation gain negligible, rated easy. Features great view of Pikes Peak across lakes.

Bikes, horses and dogs are prohibited from this short trail because of heavy use. Interpretive signs highlight aspects of history, geology and wildlife as revealed in their names. The trail circles Aspen and Spruce lakes (which are small enough to be called ponds), offering a grand view of Pikes Peak.

CASTLEWOOD CANYON STATE PARK

Inner Canyon Trail
Rim Rock Trail
Homestead Trail
Creek Bottom Trail
Lake Gulch Trail
Climbers Trail
Cave Trail

Working in a downpour, the caretaker was trying to relieve the mounting pressure on Castlewood Canyon Dam when he heard a rumbling noise. He ran to a phone and gave the alarm as the dam burst. The 400-acre lake emptied in a deluge that swept away bridges for miles, doing a million dollars in damage and taking two lives. Without the caretaker's alarm, more lives might have been lost that August of 1933.

The dam was never rebuilt, and today you can still see the dam ruins and evidence of the flood's scouring downstream. Yet the area is now a beautiful and charming park where visitors picnic, hike, climb rocks, observe wildlife, and cross-country ski amid 873 acres of unique geology. Future plans include trails designated for horses and mountain bikes. Check with park rangers: 688-7505 or 973-3959.

We often think of forests standing above grasslands, but Castlewood turns that notion on its head. North of the Black Forest, the high ground between Denver and Colorado Springs is a high plains environment. Castlewood is a crack in that grassland, a moist corridor where Douglas fir and Ponderosa pine thrive. Through it flows Cherry Creek on its way to Denver. From the bridge on Hwy. 83 south of Franktown you get just a peek of the canyon.

Its steep cliffs are composed of Castle Rock conglomerate, a kind of volcanic cement studded with hard gravel and cobblestones. Where cobblestones fall out, the pockets left behind form

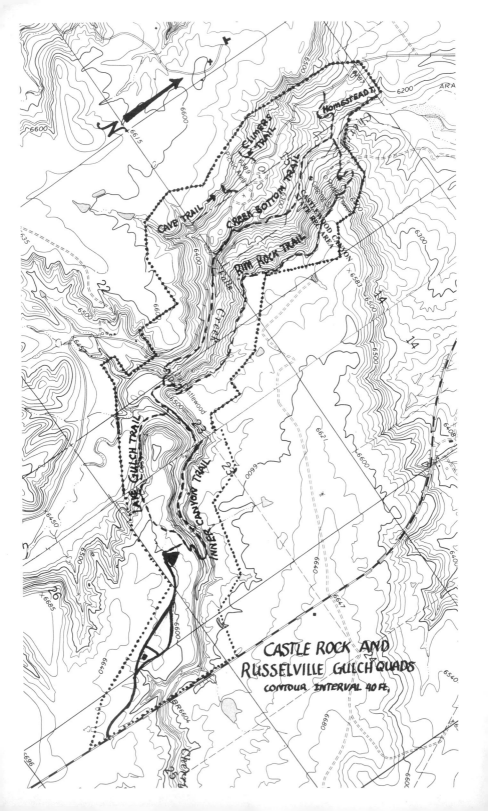

CASTLE ROCK AND
RUSSELVILLE GULCH QUADS
CONTOUR INTERVAL 40 FT.

hand-hold that climbers call Wacos. The cliffs are not gigantic, but are very popular training climbs because of their many interesting situations. Bolting is not allowed. Free climbing is allowed, but beware of letting your children imitate the experts.

Farther down you'll find a fine-grained rock called rhyolite: Denver's brownstones are made of rhyolite. And in the canyon floor you'll see chalky looking faces cut by the stream. This is clay, now blamed for the dam's failure because water seeped through, undermining the dam.

No hunting or firearms are permitted. Dogs must be on a leash no more than six feet long. Visitors are encouraged to stay on trails to help protect delicate plantlife. (Too, there are a few rattlesnakes to watch out for.)

A day pass is required. Vehicles must stay on roads. No camping or ground fires (self-contained grills or camp stoves.are permitted) Only 3.2 alcohol is permitted in the park. Picnic tables are available. Hours are sunrise to sunset. Don't forget this is a low-altitude park enjoyable at all times of the year. Guided nature tours and group presentations can be arranged.

The park is undergoing many improvements, including a new main entrance, parking lots, a group picnic shelter and a Visitors Center complete with nature exhibits. A hard-surface wheelchair accessible trail is also in the works; this new one-mile loop will have 40 picnic sites. Volunteers for Outdoor Colorado continue to improve other trails. The park is located on USGS Castle Rock South and Russellville Gulch quads.

ROAD DIRECTIONS: The original park entrance is located on Hwy. 86 just west of Franktown at the Cherry Creek bridge. Take I-25 to Castle Rock and drive seven miles east to find it. The new main entrance, still under construction, is located on Hwy. 83, five miles south of Franktown, immediately south of the other Cherry Creek bridge. From Colorado Springs, the most scenic route is Hwy. 83, a drive of 30 miles north from its intersection with North Academy. Blvd.

TRAIL DESCRIPTIONS: The system features two loops formed by several trails, plus side branches. We'll begin at the new terminal parking lot northwest of the new main entrance, all of which is under construction at press time.

INNER CANYON TRAIL, one mile one way, elevation loss 200 ft., rated easy to moderate. Features scenic walk down into canyon.

This trail switchbacks down through Douglas fir and Ponderosa to the floor of the canyon, where it crosses the creek and continues downstream on the other side. Rhyolite underfoot occurs in several colors, one almost purple. Watch for watermarks on the rocks showing the level of the old lake. Near the end of this section, you'll see Lake Gulch Trail branching off to your left, crossing the bridge to loop back to your starting point, but we'll describe that one later. Right now continue on Inner Canyon to the next intersection.

RIM ROCK TRAIL, 1.9 miles one way, elevation gain 160 ft., loss 340 ft.; rated easy to moderate. Features great views of the dam and the Front Range from Pikes Peak to Longs Peak.

Close to the dam at the bottom of the basin once filled by the lake, we find a fork. To the left is Creek Bottom Trail and to the right is Rim Rock Trail, which together form a loop. We'll take Rim Rock, a steep climb at first. Because of its sunny rocky terrain, Rim Rock is a good place to watch out for rattlers. As you climb the switchbacks, a full view of the dam construction unfolds. This is a cliff-edge walk, close enough to give great views but not close enough to be scary. Ponderosa and juniper line the rim, as well as many hardy plants that survive in shallow soil. Near the end you'll see a gauging station, which looks like a metal chimney near the creek. Beyond lie the ruins of the Lucas homestead. Descend through trees to the creek, where you'll find a fork in the trail. Downstream is Creek Bottom Trail, continuing our loop, but first let's explore the other fork, Homestead.

HOMESTEAD TRAIL, 0.4 miles, elevation gain 60 ft.,rated easy to moderate. Features link to old county road entrance through Lucas homestead.

Before the new entrance was established, this was the major gateway to park trails, but is now only a short spur connecting the back loop with a county road parking lot. It climbs up from the creek bottom through the stone ruins of the Lucas ranch homestead.

CREEK BOTTOM TRAIL, I.5 miles one way, elevation gain 280 ft., rated easy to moderate. Features stream and forest walk past waterfall.

Current trail work will improve the grade and make this one easier. As you follow the stream, notice the chalky-looking clay layer cut by the 1933 flood. Soon you'll find a 20-foot waterfall. Springs oozing beside the falls form a much higher ice sheet during winter that is enjoyed by ice climbers. Hiking is easy until you get to the base of the dam, where a moderate climb takes you to the top. An overlook position is marked atop the dam, but please do not go out farther on the dam. This has been the scene of sad accidents. You complete this loop by hiking down to the intersection with Inner Canyon Trail, and you complete the next loop (the one we began at the parking lot) by crossing the creek onto Lake Gulch Trail.

LAKE GULCH TRAIL, 0.65 miles one way, elevation gain 200 ft., rated easy to moderate. Features rim trail to main entrance parking.

Beginning at the footbridge, Lake Gulch soon leaves the gulch, but gives you a fine view of the basin once filled by the lake. Notice the cottonwoods that once lined the lake. Now growing in drier soil, they look as if they're trying to become shrubbery. The trail takes you back along the south rim to the main entrance parking.

CLIMBERS TRAIL, 0.9 miles one way, elevation gain 110 ft., rated short but steep. Features access to popular climb.

This shorty starts at a picnic ground on the old entrance road and climbs up to a cliff called the Grocery Store Wall, popular as a top-roping area. Rock climbers are welcome, but visitors without training should think twice. A faint path linking this area with the Cave Trail may be improved in the future.

CAVE TRAIL, less than a mile, elevation gain 120 ft., rated short but steep. Features access to shelter cave.

This one is very much like the Climbers Trail, leaving another picnic area on the old entrance road and climbing steeply to the cliffs, but its destination is the large-looking cave that can be seen from below. Actually the cave is quite shallow, only going back about a dozen feet. The climb to the cave is moderately technical, however, and most climbers require equipment to reach it.

DEVIL'S HEAD AREA

Devil's Head Trail
Zinn Trail

Devil's Head is the last forest fire lookout post in the Pike National Forest, but it's major attraction is the view. On a clear day, you can spot landmarks for a hundred miles around. Denver and Cherry Creek Reservoir almost look close by. Long's Peak stands in the distance to the north, and to the west you can see the Collegiate Peaks--Princeton, Yale, etc.--beyond Buena Vista. To the south you can see beyond Pikes Peak to the Sangre de Cristo Range, west of Pueblo.

The station still operates as a fire spotting lookout, but the other six like it have given way to more modern methods: radar, aircraft and the many radio and phone-linked personnel who populate the region. Fire prevention seems to be working. On average, people account for slightly less than half the forest fires in the Pike National Forest. Lightning causes the majority.

Come equipped for a hike. The trail leading to the lookout may be only 1.37 miles, but it climbs 1,000 feet, and if you add in Zinn Trail , the total round trip is 3.75 miles. Unfortunately, some of its 10,000 visitors per season come unprepared, not bringing water or proper footgear for this steep hike. There is a faucet at the trailhead, but no water at the top, so bring plenty.

Dogs must be on a leash. Bikes and horses are allowed, but are not really appropriate because of the heavy foot traffic. Camping is banned along trails, but three large pay campgrounds have been provided along the road leading to the parking lot.

The name Devil's Head refers to one of the mountain's granite outcrops, which some think looks like a devil's profile. This can only be seen from the Rampart Range Road just to the north, but even with a FS sketch to go by, it takes a large dose of imagination and a little squinting.

The lookout opens about Memorial Day and closes in mid to late September. It is located on the USGS Devil's Head quad.

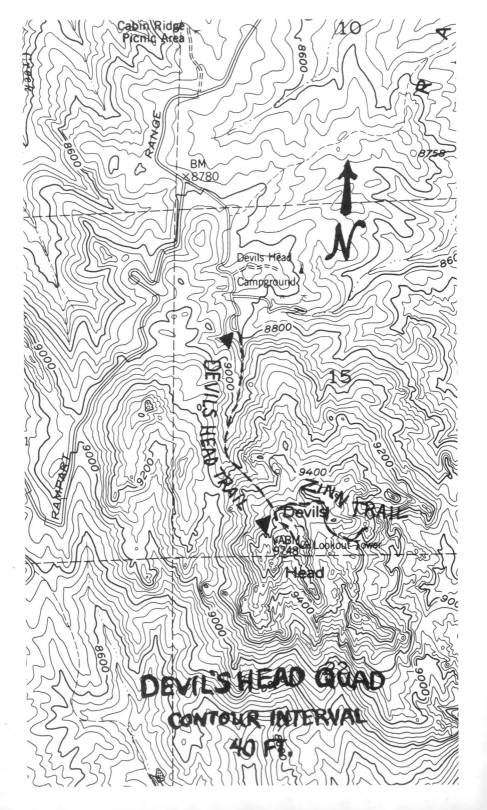

ROAD DIRECTIONS: Devil's Head is located one mile east of the scenic Rampart Range Road, 42 miles from Denver or 52 miles north of Colorado Springs. From Denver, take Santa Fe Drive (Hwy. 85) south to Sedalia, then 67 southwest to. pick up the Rampart Range Road at Indian Creek Campground.

From Colorado Springs, find the main entrance to the Rampart Range Road in the southern part of the Garden of the Gods. Or you can bypass some gravel by taking 67 north of Woodland Park for 10 miles to the gravel road marked for Rainbow Falls, a pay fishing area. From here to the Rampart is 10 miles, but after only a quarter of a mile be sure to turn right onto FS-348, then right again at the next prominent fork (unmarked). When you reach the Rampart, you are seven miles from the Devil's Head turnoff.

DEVIL'S HEAD TRAIL, FS #611, 1.12 miles one way, elevation gain 1,000 ft., rated moderately difficult. Features steep climb to panoramic lookout post.

This well-developed trail has some tables and benches along its climb, as well as informative plaques sponsored by the Colorado Federation of Business and Professional Women's Clubs. The forest is dense, but has occasional lookouts.

Near the top, your trail T-junctions, with Zinn Trail to the left and Devil's Head continuing to the right. Soon you pass through a narrow slot in the granite and curve past some restrooms before finding the clearing where the ranger's cabin lies. At the far edge of the clearing is a long stairway (143 steps) that jogs up huge boulders to the lookout post on top. If you think this looks high from the bottom of the steps, wait until you see the drop off on the other side. No place for acrophobics.

You are welcome to enter the lookout post and visit with the ranger (buy a FS T-shirt; the ranger carried them up on his back along with the rest of his groceries and supplies), but your stay must be limited by the press of other visitors. Notice the glass insulators on the legs of the ranger's seat. This post is often struck by lightning.

ZINN TRAIL, FS #615, 0.5 miles one way, elevation loss 400 ft., rated moderate. Features spur to overlook of Pikes Peak.

Leaving the Devil's Head Trail, Zinn Trail winds down through a cool glade, ending at a cliff-edge overlook where Pikes Peak is framed in a notch of granite. A nearby bronze plaque dedicates the trail to Commander Ralph Theodore Zinn, a conservationist.

ROXBOROUGH STATE PARK

Fountain Valley Trail
Lyons Overlook
Willow Creek Trail
South Rim Trail
Carpenter Peak Trail
Roxborough Link Trail

Snuggled up against the Pike National Forest, Roxborough—"a city of rocks"—is a unique state park dedicated to nature walks and cross-country skiing. Its unusual geology and its position as a transition zone have created microclimates for seven different plant communities, plus an unusual richness and variety of wildlife. (We saw about two dozen deer before reaching the parking lot.) So at Roxborough, even more than at other parks, the watchword is preservation.

This is the kind of special place where naturalists tread very softly. At Roxborough, it is especially important for you to stay on trails as much as possible, to pick up litter, and try not to change anything. That's why no pets are allowed, no horses, no mountain bikes, no rock climbing, no fires, no camping, no firearms, no hunting. Even picnic tables are not provided, though visitors are welcome to bring a meal and eat at one of the benches at the Visitors Center or along the lower park trails. Please don't spread blankets on the wildflowers, however.

This is an especially good place to view wildlife. Apparently, the ban on dogs has made wildlife feel more secure and has prevented the park from being scent-marked as dog territory. Even bear and mountain lion are seen here.

Perhaps the best way to appreciate Roxborough is to arrange for a tour with volunteer naturalists. You'll learn from experts about the plants and animals, birds and mushrooms, history and geology, even a little "belly botany," the close-up study of tiny plants. Call 303-973-3959 to arrange tours or group activities.

A day pass is required. Hours are posted and change with

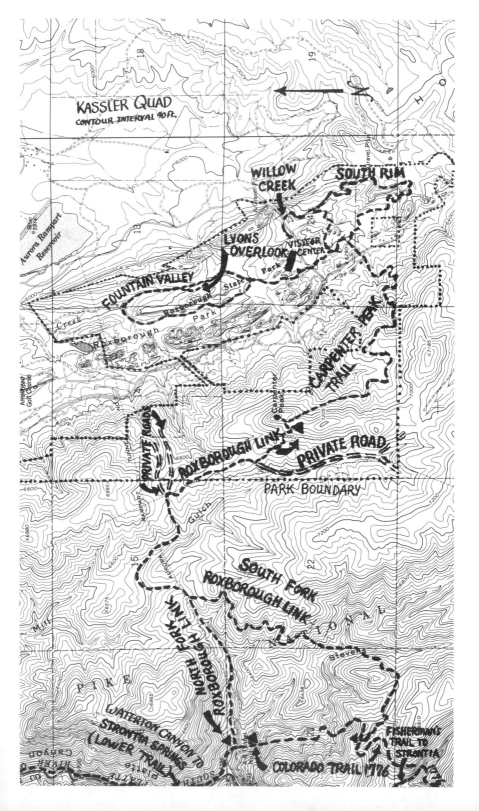

the season. If you return to your car after closing, you may be ticketed, so watch the time. Drinking water and restrooms are available only at the Visitors Center. There arc none along the trails. The Visitors Center also offers exhibits, interpretive signs and educational materials.

Be aware that Roxborough is home to poison ivy and a few prairie rattlesnakes, another good reason to stay on trails.

Because of its low altitude, Roxborough can be enjoyed year round. Each season brings a different beauty. When fall colors fade, for example, elk start moving down into the area, and winter storms only open up the area for cross-country skiing. Ski trails are not groomed, but the park road is plowed.

Park trails have benefited from volunteer work by the Colorado Mountain Club, Martin Marietta Corp. and Volunteers for Outdoor Colorado. All trails located on USGS Kassler quad.

ROAD DIRECTIONS: Roxborough is located south of Chatfield Reservoir. From Denver, take Hwy. 85 (Santa Fe Drive) south to Titan Road. From Colorado Springs, take I-25 north to the Sedalia-Hwy. 85 Exit just north of Castle Rock. Titan Road is located 5.8 miles north of Sedalia on 85. Titan heads west from 85. After three miles, Titan turns south . Go straight. Near the entrance to Roxborough housing estates, you'll see park signs directing you to the left. Follow signs.

FOUNTAIN VALLEY TRAIL, 2.25 mile loop, elevation gain 240 ft., loss 240 ft., rated gentle to moderate. Features unusual geology with fairly easy hiking and cross-country skiing.

This loop begins at the Visitors Center and winds northward through spectacular rock formations. The red rocks studded with gravel are called the Fountain formation (also found in Red Rocks Park and Garden of the Gods). Their color comes from iron compounds, and they were formed from stream sands and gravel eroded from the ancestral Rockies 300 million years ago. The yellow-orange sandstone is the Lyons formation, once a series of sand dunes and stream deposits along the shores of ancient seas. At the far end of the trail is a group of buildings dating to the turn of the century when Henry S. Persse had a summer home here. He planned to develop a resort, but eventually sold the land to a cattle ranching family, the Helmers.

LYONS OVERLOOK TRAIL, 0.5 miles, elevation gain less than 100 ft., rated moderate. Features spectacular views.

This is just a short spur off the Fountain Valley Trail, climbing up to an overlook. From there you have a view of the Fountain and Lyons formations, plus the Dakota Hogback to the east. The hogback is sandstone formed 135 million years ago from beaches and floodplain sands. All of these formations were laid down horizontally, then were tilted up on edge when the Rockies rose from below.

WILLOW CREEK TRAIL, one mile loop, elevation gain nil, rated easy; features easy hiking or cross-country skiing.

Starting at the Visitors Center, this is naturally one of the easiest and most popular routes for hikers and cross-country skiers. It takes you through the streamside environment of Little Willow Creek, with its cottonwoods and box elders and meadows with tall grasses. It also serves as a link to longer trails beyond.

SOUTH RIM TRAIL, 3 mile loop, elevation gain 280 ft., rated moderate. Features scenic overlook.

One of the park's newer trails, South Rim takes off from the Willow Creek trail not far from the Visitor Center. The first part is gentle enough for cross-country skiing. Soon it enters an old hay meadow where a huge cottonwood stands. Nearby Carpenter Peak Trail branches away to your right (west). South Rim then crosses Willow Creek, which is often dry in August. In spring, this is a lush cool spot. The trail rises to open meadow again, then climbs to the top of a ridge (Lyons formation) where you have a good view of the park and its formations to the north. Make sure children stay on trail, there are some dropoffs here. Your path then winds down to drier prairie terrain and and joins Willow Creek Trail at the road.

CARPENTER PEAK TRAIL, 2.8 miles one way, elevation gain 960 ft., rated moderate to difficult. Features hike to mountain summit and to new trailhead for ROXBOROUGH LINK.

This one is steep and long enough that rangers want to remind you about getting back before closing time, especially because it leads to an even longer new trail called Roxborough Link (next). Carpenter Peak Trail branches off the South Rim Trail and soon crosses a dirt road that leads to private property. From here you can see an old stone farmhouse called Sundance Ranch. Skirting the Fountain formation, your trail climbs switchbacks and ducks in and out of ravines. There are many clumps of Douglas fir and Ponderosa along here. Past a meadow with views of the summit, the trail avoids a big ravine to keep elevation and goes through a jungle of large scrub oak. Here the rocks are gneiss (pronounced like the word "nice"), a beautiful metamorphic stone that glistens in the sun and has banded colors. Carpenter Peak has some very nice gneiss! A tenth of a mile below the rocky summit, you find the new Roxborough Link trailhead. From the top you have a grand view of downtown Denver, the plains to the east and the mountains to the west.

ROXBOROUGH LINK TRAIL, Pike National Forest, Colorado Division of Parks and Outdoor Recreation and the Denver Water Board, Y-shaped trail measuring 5.2 miles one way or 8.9 miles round trip if used as a balloon loop with Colorado Trail 1776; elevation gain 360 ft., loss 1,440 ft. on Y; rated moderate to difficult. Features backcountry link with CT 1776. NOTE SPECIAL RULES.

Completed in 1990, Roxborough Link is a long way from anywhere because you can only reach it by starting on other trails. And it has some special rules because it begins in Roxborough Park (where you can't have mountain bikes or horses) and ends in the Pike National Forest, where you can bike, ride horses or even camp and make campfires. So if you want to ride this trail or camp, you'll have to start from the National Forest and turn back when you reach the park boundary. See COLORADO TRAIL 1776, Segment One, for directions.

This brings up some practical problems. If you want to hike from the park and do the entire Roxborough Link as a balloon-shaped loop with 1776, your total distance round trip will be almost 14.5 miles—and if you're not planning an overnighter, that is a very tough day hike, especially considering that you must return to your car before closing.

However, if you start from the National Forest, you have a six-mile trip along Waterton Canyon before you reach a Roxborough Link trailhead, so doing the entire trail from that end would be a round trip of 20 miles, even if you turn around at the park boundary, as horses and bikes are supposed to do. It's a long trip either way, but at least the Waterton Canyon parking area does not close.

Still, the official trailhead is in the park, so we'll begin there. Starting down from the summit of Carpenter Peak, you soon find an old four-wheel track that leads down along a ridge. This takes you over the Aurora Rampart Tunnel and down to a meadow area owned by the Denver Water Board. After leaving the meadow, the trail splits. The right branch heads west down a ravine 0.8 miles to the Waterton Canyon access road, arriving near a DWB caretaker's home. This road is closed to all motor vehicles except those belonging to authorities. If you want to make a balloon loop, turn left on that access road and go 0.4 miles uphill to the trailhead for CT 1776 and climb the switchbacks another 1.1 miles to a saddle ridge where you'll find the other Y trailhead for Roxborough Link. This next branch (2.2 miles) starts out in scrub oaks and pines and wraps around a hillside before starting down into Stevens Gulch (water undependable). Then it heads due north along an old horse trail through the gulch, hugging a hillside on its way back to the Y intersection. From there you return the way you came.

Watch your trail markers because there are a number of unofficial routes in this area that locals have used for years, especially near the park boundary. These spurs soon take you into trespass situations.

The Roxborough Link was built with volunteer labor from the Colorado Trail Foundation, Martin Marietta Corp. and the Boy Scouts.

STRONTIA SPRINGS RESERVOIR

Waterton Canyon Trail
Upper Strontia Trail

Strontia Springs Reservoir, owned by the Denver Water Board, is a deep lake made by damming the South Platte River gorge. Although the lake is 1.7 miles long, its banks are so steep (cliffs mostly) that only two small inlets are really accessible. However, the two trails leading to those inlets offer miles of additional fishing along the South Platte.

The lake itself is stocked with catchable size rainbow trout, some of which grow to large size. The river at each end is famed for its browns, as well as rainbow and brook trout. Because this is Denver drinking water, there are many special regulations. Do not attempt to hike around the lake, which is dangerous, or approach the dam, which is off limits. Also off limits is the entire northwest shore because this is a special habitat for bighorn sheep. No boats, kayaks or floatation devices of any kind are allowed, except on the river above the lake. No dogs are permitted, again because of the bighorns, which often come right down to the trails. No swimming or fireworks are allowed. Firearms and bows are only permitted during hunting season.

Waterton Canyon Trail is located on the USGS Platte Canyon and Kassler quads. Upper Strontia Trail is located on the USGS Platte Canyon quad.

ROAD DIRECTIONS: WATERTON CANYON TRAIL begins at the Waterton Canyon Recreation Area parking lot at Kassler, south of Chatfield Reservoir. See Road Directions for COLORADO TRAIL 1776, Segment One. UPPER STRONTIA TRAIL begins at the South Platte townsite at the confluence of the North and South Forks of the South Platte River. From Denver, take Highway 285 south. Just past Conifer, turn left on Foxton Road (County 97). Past Reynolds Park, take a left on County 96 and follow the river downstream to its confluence. The trail begins immediately downstream and across the street from the boarded-up South Platte Hotel. From Deckers, go north on Hwy 67, follow-

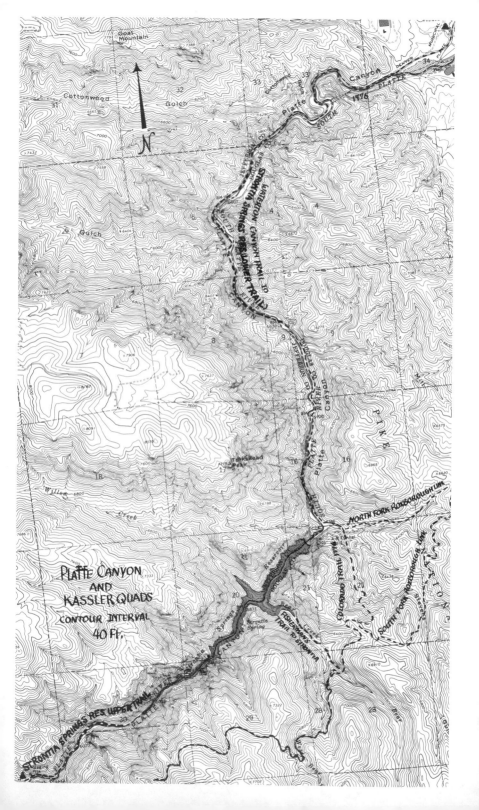

PLATTE CANYON
AND
KASSLER QUADS

CONTOUR INTERVAL
40 Ft.

ing the river downstream to the confluence. Your trail begins on the right, following the canyon downstream.

WATERTON CANYON TRAIL, Denver Water Board and Pike National Forest, about 8.5 miles one way, elevation gain 1040 ft., loss 560 ft., rated easy at first, difficult later on. Features over six miles of river fishing leading to deep lake.

Here's a place where you'll see grandmothers and small children strolling and mountain bikers carrying flyrods. It's a very popular area, though the vast majority of visitors never make it to the lake. Most turn back when they have glimpsed the 243-foot dam and the switchbacks that climb up and around it.

What we're calling the Lower Trail starts as an unpaved access road closed to all but official vehicles. After snowstorms, this first six-mile section is popular with cross-country skiers and snowshoers because it rises only gently as it follows the river. No camping is allowed until you climb into the National Forest along the Colorado Trail 1776.

Bait fishing is allowed for the first couple of miles, as far as the Marston Diversion. The limit is eight trout of any size for that stretch. Upstream from Marston, only flies and artificial lures are allowed, although you can also use any larvae or nymphs that you actually find in that water. Here the limit is two trout over 16 inches. No ice fishing.

Once you see the dam, the road climbs more sharply. Just beyond a caretaker's house on your left is one of the trailheads for the new Y-shaped Roxborough Trail, here looking like a road. Less than half a mile higher begins the CT1776 trailwork. Hike up its switchbacks through dense forest. When you reach a high saddle, another Roxborough trailhead will be on your left. From there, the CT heads down to cross Bear Creek at mile 8.0 from the parking lot. Once you reach Bear Creek, watch for a path leading down the creek to the lake. This was once a logging road built by C.A. Deane, who had a sawmill at the confluence of Bear Creek and the river. Deane supplied the railroad with ties and later added a hotel and whistlestop which was called Deansbury. That site has now been swallowed by an arm of the lake, but that arm is your destination. Happy fishing!

UPPER STRONTIA TRAIL, Pike National Forest and Denver Water Board, 1.5 miles one way, elevation loss 160 ft., rated easy. Features river and lake trout fishing.

At the old South Platte townsite, the two forks of the river converge and pour down a canyon toward Strontia Springs Reservoir. This 1.5-mile section is open to walk-in fishing, biking, horse riding, cross-country skiing and camping, although you'll have a hard time finding a good place to pitch a tent. There is very little room in the canyon for anything but the river and the road.

The main "trail" is an access road closed to all but official vehicles, but near the lake is a footbridge leading to a fisherman's trail on the other side of the river. This unofficial path leads all the way back to South Platte. The footbridge also allows access to the other side of the river's inlet. Because of the cliffs, only the inlet portion of the lake is really fishable here. Do not attempt to explore the northwest side of the lake because this is a special bighorn sheep habitat.

Partially because of the bighorn, a dog leash law is vigorously enforced. DOW officers are legally empowered to shoot dogs chasing wildlife and to arrest their owners. Both criminal and civil penalties apply.

Both the lake and river are stocked with rainbow trout, some of which grow large. The river also has fine browns and a few Snake River cutthroats. Both the river and inlet have a limit of two trout of any size. Bait fishing is allowed. No ice fishing.

Kayakers enjoy this river section, but are banned from the lake. No floatation devices of any kind are allowed on the lake.

COLORADO TRAIL 1776

Segment One (Waterton Canyon)
Through Segment Six (Georgia Pass)
Plus the Lost Creek Wilderness Bike Detour

Extending from Denver to Durango--469 miles--the Colorado Trail 1776 is a continuous non-motorized trail created by thousands of dedicated volunteers. This is not an old historic route, but since it was begun to commemorate Colorado's centennial and the nation's bicentennial, it has a new claim to history of its own.

Most people enjoy this trail by taking it in pieces, for it is cut by roads in many places, providing excellent access. For that reason, our descriptions will offer a lot of road directions to help you enjoy the six segments that cross the Pike National Forest.

Beginning in Waterton Canyon just south of Denver, 1776 wanders 73.7 miles across the Pike National Forest before leaving our area at the Continental Divide just above Georgia Pass. That's the only bite this book can chew, but the entire route is described in an excellent book by Randy Jacobs, *The Colorado Trail.* All proceeds from the Jacobs guide, plus the set of topographic maps which are sold separately, go to the non-profit Colorado Trail Foundation to help maintain and improve 1776.

No other trail is so versatile. Many major trails connect with it, so you can design your own adventures. Mountain bikers now outnumber hikers and horse riders in many areas, and some sections are also very popular with cross-country skiers. In the Pike National Forest, all of 1776 is open to bikes except for the Lost Creek Wilderness, so an alternate route has been created to skirt that area. We describe this detour at the end of Segment Six.

The Colorado Trail Foundation will continue to need public support. You can help in several ways. You can volunteer to work on a trail crew; you can even adopt a section to maintain as your very own. You can contribute a tax-deductible donation to the Foundation, becoming a "Friend of the Colorado Trail," and you can buy the Jacobs book and maps. Our CT maps are based on

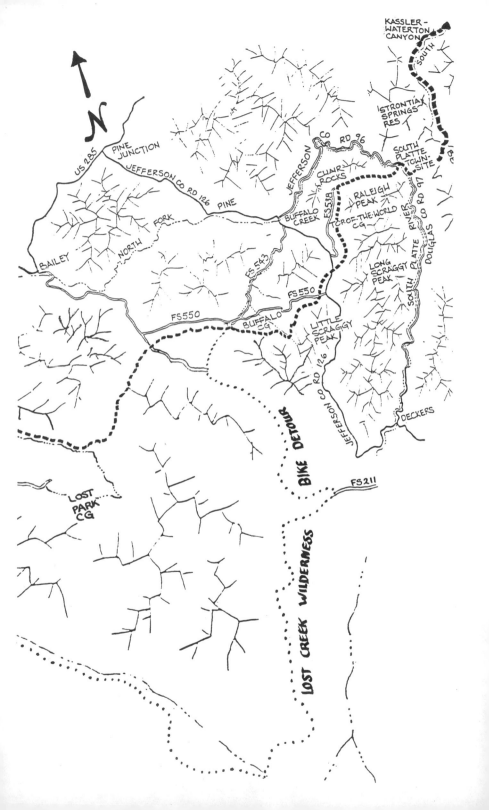

those in the Jacobs book, courtesy of the CTF, but they do not show topography because we want to encourage you to support the foundation by buying the official map series.

SEGMENT ONE, FS 1776, 10 miles one way including 6.2 miles for non-motorized approach through Waterton Canyon (See Strontia Springs Res. Area, Waterton Canyon Trail); elevation gain 1,720 ft., loss 1,500 ft.; rated difficult. Located on USGS Kassler and Platte Canyon quads.

ROAD DIRECTIONS: From Denver take I-25 South to Colorado 470, then west 12.5 miles to Colorado 126 (Wadsworth). Go south on Wadsworth 4.5 miles to its end just before the entrance to Martin Marietta. Turn left onto a side road and continue 0.3 miles, following signs to Waterton Canyon Recreation Area parking lot. From Colorado Springs, take I-25 North past Castle Rock and take the Hwy. 85 exit to Sedalia. Go 5.8 miles past Sedalia and turn left (west) on Titan Road. After three miles this straight road turns left (south). Another 1.7 miles distant, turn right onto Waterton Road. Follow signs for another 2.4 miles to the parking lot.

Trailbuilders could not have picked a more fitting gateway to the Rockies, for the Pike National Forest drains to the plains here at Waterton Canyon. Both forks of the South Platte River meet at your next destination and flow down through Waterton, interrupted only by Strontia Springs Dam, which you'll see just before reaching the trailhead. In 1820 the Long Expedition noticed this gateway, and in 1877 Territorial Governor John Evans built his Denver South Park and Pacific Railroad up this canyon.

Still, you can think about the trailhead two ways. Our measurements begin at the parking lot at the canyon's mouth because that is where you must leave your car and begin hiking or riding, but the Colorado Trail construction begins 6.2 miles higher up. Your exploration begins with a gentle journey up the canyon along a wide gravel service road that is closed to all but official vehicles. This roadway is a popular recreation trail in itself, featuring bighorn sheep and some fine fishing, but there are many special regulations. For example, no dogs. See STRONTIA SPRINGS RESERVOIR AREA, Waterton Canyon Trail for details.

After passing the dam and one trailhead for the new Roxborough Link, you find the official trailhead for 1776. It begins with a series of switchbacks through dense Douglas fir, leading to a saddle where the second Roxborough Link (south fork) joins your trail from the left. (Roxborough Link is a Y-shaped trail. See Roxborough State Park for special rules.)

Now your trail dips into the Bear Creek watershed (your last reliable water). Where it crosses the main creek, notice a fisherman's trail on your right leading down to Strontia Springs Reservoir. Now you cross a tributary called West Bear Creek and climb a mile to a point where 1776 shares its route with Motorcycle Trail #692. After another half a mile, you recross the tributary and leave the motorcycle trail, climbing to your right. The motorcycle trail crosses the CT once more about a half mile higher. At last you are traveling the side of the canyon itself with views of the lake and foothills. After skirting a high valley, you begin switchbacking down to the river again.

At the bottom you have to travel a paved highway (67 from Deckers) for a short distance, following the river to its confluence at the historic South Platte townsite, the end of Segment One.

SEGMENT TWO, FS 1776, 9.4 miles one way, elevation gain 580 ft., loss 80 ft.; rated difficult, then easy. Located on USGS Platte Canyon and Deckers quads.

ROAD DIRECTIONS: No matter which way you go, you'll find some public roadside fishing along the rivers leading to South Platte townsite, but please respect private property. From Denver take Hwy. 285 south. Immediately south of Conifer, turn left on Foxton Road (County 97). Past Reynolds Park, turn left on County 96 and follow the North Fork downstream to South Platte. From Colorado Springs, take Hwy. 24 to Woodland Park, then right on 67. At Deckers, continue on 67 (not 126), following the South Fork downstream to the South Platte townsite. Look for a dirt road beside the hotel with a bridge that crosses the North Fork. Ignore the first uphill route you see closed to motor vehicles. The CT trailhead lies just around the corner, about 180 yards from the bridge.

Not much remains of historic South Platte except a boarded-up hotel, but in the old days a lot of trains passed this way. But before you start out from here, water your horses and fill your canteens because there is no more reliable water for the next 13 miles. At first, it's all uphill, switchbacks through timber. Several miles later, you find a huge chunk of Pikes Peak granite from which you can see Pikes Peak, Devil's Head and the Platte Canyon. Watch your markers because the trail makes use of short sections of old roads before ducking back into the woods as a single track once more. Bikers, watch out for cactus beside the trail. At mile 7.1 a short side trail leads uphill to Top of the World Campground, which has no water, but does have a full panoramic view, including everything from Pikes Peak to the Kenosha Mountains. At present, there is no CT trailhead at Top of the World, but you can reach this campground by taking FS-538 east from 126 near Buffalo Creek.

Beyond this point, the CT rolls through Ponderosa forest so gently that it is used by cross-country skiers. This Segment ends at County. 126, not at a trailhead, but by suddenly crossing the pavement on a blind curve. Careful! See Segment Three for parking.

SEGMENT THREE: I3.4 miles one way, elevation gain 1,320 ft., loss 600; rated easy, then moderate. Located on USGS Deckers, Green Mountain and Windy Peak quads.

ROAD DIRECTIONS: From Denver take Hwy. 285 32 miles south to Pine Junction, then left on 126. From Colorado Springs, take Hwy. 24 West to Woodland Park, then right on 67 to Deckers and left on 126. Two parking areas serve the CT along 126, but neither is located where the trail actually crosses. The northern lot is on the west side of 126, 3.1 miles south of Buffalo Creek or 12.3 miles north of Deckers. To find the southern lot, turn west on FS-550, located 4.1 miles south of Buffalo Creek or 11.3 miles north of Deckers. The CT trailhead is immediately on your right. Note: some maps seem to show the CT crossing 550 at the southern lot, but it actually crosses half a mile farther west. This is only important because there is a false trail marked close to motor vehicles immediately across from the CT lot.

If you make it across 126 without getting squashed, you find yourself on an old double track heading south, paralleling 126, just out of sight of the highway. Within a third of a mile, you'll find a spur on your left which leads to the northern lot. Your track con-

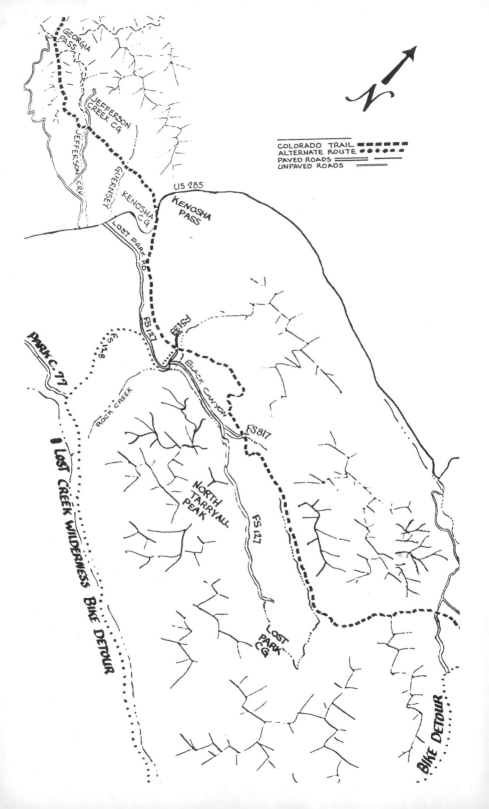

GEORGIA PASS

JEFFERSON CREEK CG

JEFFERSON CRK.

GUERNSEY

KENOSHA CG

US 285

KENOSHA PASS

LOST PARK RD.

N

COLORADO TRAIL
ALTERNATE ROUTE
PAVED ROADS
UNPAVED ROADS

FS 127

FS 133

BLACK CANYON

FS 128

Park C. 77

Rock Creek

FS 817

NORTH TARRYALL PEAK

FS 127

LOST PARK CG

LOST CREEK WILDERNESS BIKE DETOUR

BIKE DETOUR

tinues south toward the second lot on FS-550, which is accessed by another short spur. Near that lot your trail turns west, staying out of sight of 550 for half a mile, then turns to cross 550. On the other side, the CT heads west again, then southwest, all pretty easy until you come to stream crossings. Our rating changes to moderate from now on. Your trail is designed to skirt the Meadows Group Campground (reservation only), but does cross the entrance of the campground. Shortly after, at mile 9.5 you cross the stream called Buffalo Creek and FS-543 (which you will cross again later). Now climb steeply out of the Buffalo Creek watershed to a yucca ridge with views of the granite outcrop called The Castle to the south. At mile 13.4, the CT drops down to cross FS-543 again, where a parking lot marks the end of this segment.

SEGMENT FOUR, 15.3 miles one way, elevation gain 2,800 ft., loss 920; rated more difficult. Located on USGS Windy Peak and Topaz Mountain quads.

ROAD DIRECTIONS: From Denver, take Hwy. 285 south 39 miles to Bailey. Go left on County 68, which becomes FS-543. The CT crosses 543 about eight miles south of Bailey. From Deckers, take 126 11.3 miles to FS-550. Turn left and follow 550 (5.1 mile) to FS-543 and turn left. When you reach Wellington Lake, stay on 543, going northwest. Only 0.7 miles past Sylvania of the Rockies, find parking for ROLLING CREEK TRAIL and the CT.

Bikes are not allowed in the Lost Creek Wilderness, so an alternate route for bikes will be described at the end of this segment. All others get ready for a climb because this segment gains a lot of altitude.

Leaving the parking lot, you climb 0.3 miles up an old road to a gate that closes the road to vehicles. Rolling Creek Trail goes to the left, the CT to the right. Almost a mile later, 1776 joins the old Hooper Trail, a logging road built by W.H. Hooper between 1885 and 1887. His sawmill in Lost Park was eventually shut down by the Department of the Interior for persistent violations, and now the Lost Creek Wilderness is so highly protected that not even the Forest Service can use a chainsaw there.

After a climb of 1.8 miles, pass through a gate to enter the

Lost Creek Wilderness, the last stronghold of wild buffalo in Colorado until they were wiped out in the late 1800s. Turn left where the trail forks at mile 2.3. The Payne Creek Trail (also called Craig Meadow) comes down from your right to join the CT at mile 3.1. You continue straight ahead, climbing southwest through aspen and lodgepole forest. At mile 4.5, you cross a small stream marked by a junked truck, then leave Hooper's road at mile 5.7 to avoid Bluestem Draw, a giant bog where the log corduroy used to run for almost a quarter of a mile. Half a mile later, 1776 returns to Hooper's trail and climbs over a wooded ridge to find the long meadow of the North Fork of Lost Creek. At mile 7.8 a side trail from Lost Park Campground joins 1776 from the south (left). Notice the remains of a sawmill to the south across the creek. Lots of brook trout here. For road directions to Lost Park Campground, see Jefferson Area.

Brookside-McCurdy Trail will branch off to your right at mile 8.0, but 1776 continues straight up the open valley, a steady gentle climb with views of the Kenosha Mountains. At 10,880 ft., you mount the saddle at the head of the valley (mile 13.2), leaving the Hooper Trail and contouring through spruce forest. You glimpse the Continental Divide and then switchback down to cross a tiny stream at mile 15.2. Just past some washed out beaver ponds, you pass an eroded side trail coming up from FS-817 on the Lost Park Road. This is a popular access. For directions see Segment Five.

SEGMENT FIVE, 14 miles one way, elevation gain 960 ft., loss 1,160; rated moderate. Located on USGS Topaz Mountain, Observatory Rock, Mount Logan and Jefferson quads.

ROAD DIRECTIONS: Kenosha Pass is located north of Fairplay and Jefferson on Hwy. 285, about 58 miles from Denver. Just 1.2 miles north of Jefferson and 3.2 miles south of the pass, turn east onto Lost Park Road (FS-127). Your first CT access is not the beginning of Segment Five. Go 7.3 miles and turn left onto FS-133, marked for the Ben Tyler Trail. The CT crosses this route 1.3 miles farther up; this is where mountain bikes pick up the CT once more, after detouring around the wilderness. Segment Five begins at the next access along Lost Park Road, 11 miles from the highway. Turn left onto tiny FS-

817, which is only about 0.2 miles long. Park and climb up this rutted road to where the CT crosses it at right angles.

Trails through grassy meadows can be obscure, especially where cattle are busy making their own paths in other directions, but as more people use the CT, its path becomes clearer. See our advice about meeting cattle in the early part of this book.

Continuing through aspens above FS-817, the CT turns north and crosses the head of Black Canyon, then makes a slow descent to Rock Creek at mile 7.1. This is the point that can be accessed via the Ben Tyler trailhead as mentioned earlier. Find your way through brush to cross the creek's footbridge. Follow an old road downstream for only a tenth of a mile and watch for the CT suddenly ducking into the spruce forest to your right. After passing through a gate, turn right onto another old road and look for the CT on your left a third of a mile higher. At mile 7.7 you'll cross Ben Tyler, here a road, then descend through a meadow to Johnson Gulch (seasonal flow) and cross at mile 8.2. Posts mark your way through the grass for more than a mile until you reach timber at the head of the valley. A clearing up ahead offers views of the Black Canyon behind and the CT as it crosses the Continental Divide far ahead. Many faint roads complicate the route, so watch your markers. The last leg is through aspen forest, leading down to the saddle of Kenosha Pass, which is popular with cross-country skiers.

SEGMENT SIX, 11.6 miles one way to Pike National Forest boundary, elevation gain 2,600 ft., loss 620; rated moderate to difficult. Located on USGS Jefferson and Boreas Pass quads.

ROAD DIRECTIONS: For directions to Kenosha Pass, see Segment Five. The CT crosses at the Kenosha Pass Campground, but there is more parking across Hwy. 285 (east side). To find the Jefferson Lake Road Access, go 4.4 miles south to Jefferson and turn west on Jefferson Lake Road. Drive 2.1 miles and turn right toward the lake. Find the CT crossing the road 3.1 miles farther. Parking is available a tenth of a mile farther at Beaver Ponds Picnic Ground, and overnight parking is available 0.6 miles farther, near the entrance to Jefferson Creek Campground.

Passing through the edge of Kenosha Campground, find the CT exiting through a fence amid aspens and lodgepole. This early section is popular for cross-country skiing. The trail washboards through meadow and forest, then across Guernsey Gulch, Deadman Gulch, and past Jefferson Hill before dropping down to the Jefferson Lake Road. There are great views of South Park and distant mountains. From there 1776 switchbacks uphill again, sometimes adopting old roads, climbing through forest that changes from bristlecone to spruce closer to timberline. At 11,400 feet (mile 10.5), you find the krummholz transitional zone, where forest gives way to tundra. Here runted trees barely grow at all, their branches shaped by prevailing winds. Please stay on trail going across tundra because this delicate vegetation takes many years to regrow. At mile 11.6 (11,880) you reach the Continental Divide just east and above Georgia Pass. This is the boundary of the Pike National Forest, the end of our area, but the Segment Six continues down to Hwy. 9 north of Breckenridge.

LOST CREEK WILDERNESS BIKE DETOUR, 72 miles one way, elevation gain 3,560 ft., loss 1,240; rated moderate.

There is only one mile of pavement along this 72-mile detour around the Lost Creek Wilderness. It passes several campgrounds and goes through the old mining town of Tarryall, known as Puma City when it was founded in 1896. If you don't mind pavement and the danger of traffic, there is a more direct route not described in detail here. Go northwest on FS-550 and FS-543 to Bailey, then take busy Hwy. 285 to Kenosha Pass.

Our detour begins about halfway through Segment Three, where 1776 first crosses FS-543 at mile 8.9. Our mileage figures now start over. Follow 543 southwest 2.7 miles to Wellington Lake, then turn left onto FS-560 and climb Stony Pass (8560). About seven miles past the summit, go right onto FS-211 at mile 13.6, then right again 5.4 miles later, following signs to Goose Creek Campground. Turn right onto Park County Road 77 at mile 35.8, which is paved for about a mile. Continue through the town of Tarryall and pass the Spruce Grove Campground. Go past the Tarryall Reservoir to mile 63.0 and turn right onto Park County

Road 39, also called FS-128 and Rock Creek Hills Road. Go north to Lost Park Road (FS-127) and turn right (east) at mile 68.6. About two miles farther, turn left onto FS-133 where the sign points toward Ben Tyler Trail. Travel another 1.3 miles and find the CT crossing your road. This point is called mile 7.7 in the description of Segment 5 (9720). Now you're back on 1776, heading west toward Kenosha Pass.

Another popular biking route starts at the end of Segment Five at Kenosha Pass. Since bikes are allowed on the last 6.5 miles of Segment Five, some like to make a loop by starting at Kenosha Pass, pedaling east on the CT to Rock Creek, then down to Lost Park Road, returning to Hwy. 285 and then up to Kenosha Pass once more. Only the last 3.2 miles is on pavement.

MORRISON TRAILHEAD

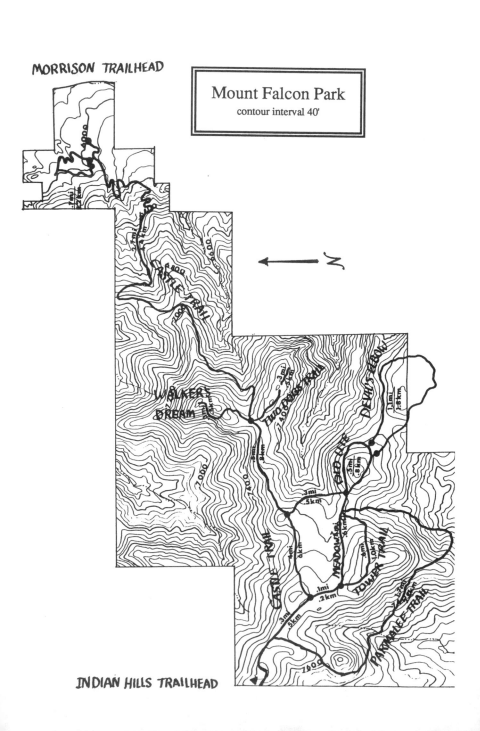

Mount Falcon Park
contour interval 40'

INDIAN HILLS TRAILHEAD

MOUNT FALCON PARK

Parmalee Trail
Castle Trail
Walker's Dream
Two Dogs Trail
Meadow Trail
Tower Trail
Old Ute Trail
Devil's Elbow

Surely a millionaire conservationist would select a majestic spot for his dream castle in the mountains--and that's exactly what John Brisben Walker did. Unfortunately, the castle was struck by lightning and burned in 1918, but all the natural wonders still remain, and now this scenic estate belongs to everyone.

If you start at the lower trailhead on Hwy. 8, just south of Red Rocks Park, you have a long climb up through grasslands, then through brush, then forest. But we'll start at the top, where the scenery is best and the grades are easiest. This is where you'll want to go cross-country skiing or take the family for leisurely outings. The high trailhead boasts a beautiful picnic area, potable water, clean restrooms and even a pay phone to report fires or other emergencies. Yet all trails lead downhill from here, so save a little energy for the return trip. Horses can be rented just outside the park's high entrance.

The usual rules apply: no hunting, no firearms, no fireworks, no camping, no open fires (grills only), no collecting of wildflowers, rocks or other souvenirs. Dogs must be on a leash. Park hours are one our before sunrise to one hour after sunset. The park is located on the USGS Morrison and Indian Hills quads.

ROAD DIRECTIONS: To reach the upper trailhead, take the Parmalee Gulch Road exit off Hwy. 285 (also marked Indian Hills).

This exit is located 2.5 miles west of the Evergreen-Hwy. 8 exit off 285 or northwest of Conifer. Go three miles to Indian Hills and turn right at the Mount Falcon Park sign. Follow this winding road past the stables to the trailhead.
The lower trailhead can be reached from Hwy. 8, which connects Morrison with 285. From Hwy. 8 turn west onto Forest St., about a mile from Morrison, then right onto Vine, which leads to the parking area. Picnic and restroom facilities are available at this area also.

PARMALEE TRAIL, 1.7 miles, elevation gain 700 ft., loss 820; rated moderate to difficult. Features fun bike and equestrian route.

This is one of the more difficult and less traveled trails, diving downhill and washboarding over two drainages before climbing back up to Meadow Trail. Parmalee is a favorite among equestrians because there is less traffic and because there is some water available at stream crossings--at least, early in the year. Fine views to the south.

CASTLE TRAIL, 3.9 miles, elevation loss 1,750 ft. from high trailhead, rated easy at the top, difficult below. Features fabulous scenery, castle ruins, great cross-country skiing.

Described from the top or bottom, this would sound like two entirely different trails because the top is so easy and the bottom so steep. This is the park's longest trail, tracing the top of the ridge, and is the spine to which four other trails connect. Many people use it as a one-way downhill adventure by leaving another car at the bottom. The top also ranks as one of the area's most spectacular cross-country ski trails. The views must be seen to be believed. Clever fencing around the castle ruins allows you to see it all without the danger of climbing around among the crumbling walls and chimneys.

WALKER'S DREAM, 0.3 miles one way, elevation gain 240 ft., loss 120; rated moderate. Features scenic lookout.

Walker dreamed of having the President of the United States as a next door neighbor, so he began to build a presidential summer home near his castle. Thousands of Colorado school children contributed dimes to the project, but construction never went beyond the foundation and laying of a cornerstone carved from Colorado marble. No President ever visited Mt. Falcon, but from this perch you can see another of Walker's dreams that did come true, Red Rocks Park Amphitheater.

TWO DOGS TRAIL, 0.3 miles one way, altitude gain 100 ft, loss 40 feet, rated easy. Features another scenic lookout.

Every promontory in the park offers another fabulous view, so that is the purpose of this short side trail. It leads up a forest path to a meadow overlook with vistas to the north, east and south.

MEADOW TRAIL, 0.8 mile, elevation gain 160 ft., loss 240 ft., rated easy. Features great cross-country skiing, biking.

A favorite with cross-country skiers and bikers, Meadow Trail takes off south from Castle Trail and rounds a lovely meadow, forming connections with three other trails.

TOWER TRAIL, 0.6 miles one way, elevation gain 140 feet, loss 240 feet; rated moderate. Features wonderful views.

This shorty features two remarkable lookout points, a wooden tower reminiscent of fire watch towers and a large pavilion called Eagle Eye Shelter, which can be reserved for group activities. Just keep an eagle eye on small children, however, for the pavilion is a high perch.with views of Pikes Peak and Hwy. 285.

OLD UTE TRAIL, 0.6 miles as a balloon loop, elevation gain 180 ft., loss 180 ft.; rated moderate. Features technical biking.

If it weren't so short, this trail might have to be rated more difficult because of many steep bumps and rocks that don't map out for elevation gain. Bikers will find it far more narrow and technical than most other trails. More great views.

157

DEVIL'S ELBOW, 1.1 miles as a loop, elevation gain-loss 150 ft.; rated moderate. Features loop trail with southern views.

The Devil's Elbow starts down a steep grassy saddle, then circles a ridge that is thinly forested on the south and thickly forested on the north. Your path dips into land owned by Denver Mountain Parks before returning to Mount Falcon. Combined with Old Ute, you can make a 3.4-mile loop from the upper parking lot.

Adult Mountain Lion Track
Actual size

ELK MEADOW PARK

Painter's Pause Trail
Meadow View
Too Long Trail
Elkridge Trail
Sleepy 'S' Trail
Bergen Peak Trail

The best time to see elk at Elk Meadow Park is just after sunrise or just before sunset, with your best chance in fall and winter. In the spring, the herds calve in a state wildlife area next door. Then the herds break up, one herd summering in Genesee and the other on Mount Evans. In daylight hours, elk are pretty crafty at hiding from you, but often you'll find where they bedded down in the grass at night.

Some Elk Meadow Trails are great for cross-country skiing after winter storms. Park rangers sometimes groom the trails with snowmobiles. Call 303-278-5925 for conditions.

Nearly two square miles in itself, this park seems even larger because its trail system wanders into adjacent areas owned by the Denver Mountain Parks and the Division of Wildlife. You can help encourage such inter-governmental cooperation by obeying all rules. For example, keeping your dog on a leash is a very serious matter. Aside from elk, there are also ground-nesting birds.

Of course, no hunting is allowed, no firearms, no fireworks, no open fires (grills only), no camping and no collecting of wildflowers, rocks or any other souvenirs. Hours are from one hour before sunrise to one hour after sunset. The park is located on USGS Squaw Pass and Evergreen quads.

ROAD DIRECTIONS: The northern trailhead is located on Hwy. 74 two miles north of Evergreen or 0.6 miles south of Bergen Park. The southern trailhead, with its scenic picnic area, is located 1.25 miles west of Hwy. 74 on Stagecoach Blvd.

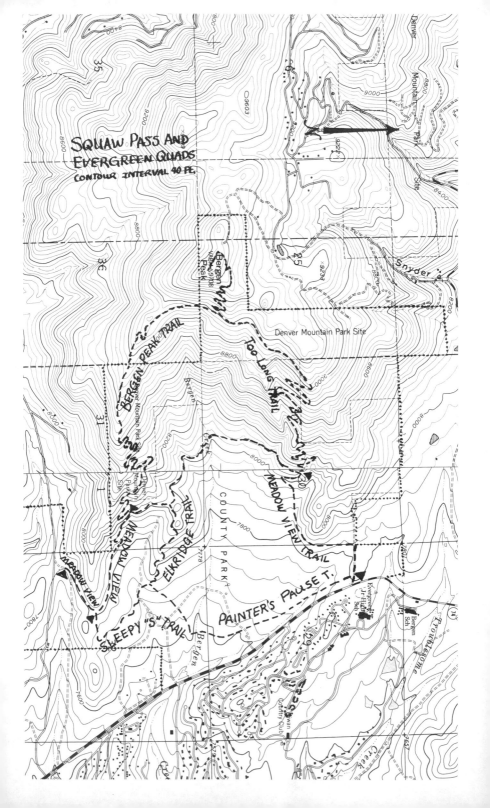

SQUAW PASS AND
EVERGREEN QUADS
CONTOUR INTERVAL 40 FT.

Bergen Peak VABM 9708

Denver Mountain Park Site

BERGEN PEAK TRAIL

Too Long Trail

MEADOW VIEW TRAIL

MEADOW VIEW

ELKRIDGE TRAIL

SLEEPY "S" TRAIL

PAINTER'S PAUSE T.

Denver Mountain Park Site

COUNTY PARK

Evergreen Jr High Sch

Bergen Sch

Country Club

PAINTER'S PAUSE, one mile one way, elevation gain 200 ft.; rated easy. Features easy strolling, cross-country skiing, jogging, etc.

Paralleling the highway, this trail is used by joggers and cross-country skiers because it is so flat. Bikers will enjoy the new rubber flap erosion barriers that fold down when a tire hits them. This trail is most important as a link to other areas of the park.

MEADOW VIEW, three miles one way, elevation gain-loss 350 ft.; rated easy. Features easy meadow link to higher trails and picnic area.

Leaving the highway behind, this lovely trail circles the back edge of the meadow, dodging in and out of the woods. If you're looking for elk, this is your route. Cross-country skiers and bikers will enjoy its gentle roll. Both ends are at the same elevation, but if you start at the north, your climb is more gradual.

ELK RIDGE TRAIL, 0.5 miles one way, elevation gain 240 ft., rated moderate. Features link with other trails to form loops.

This ridge walk allows you to make two different loops, using Meadow View and Sleepy "S" (2.6 miles) or those trails plus Painter's Pause for a loop of four miles.

SLEEPY 'S' TRAIL, 1.1 miles one way, elevation gain 160 ft., rated easy. Features more cross-country skiing amid scattered ponderosa.

Named for its shape, this trail snakes through scattered ponderosa, a marvelous wildflower area. Cross-country skiers and families with small children enjoy this easy route. Ignore the side trail at the northern end; it only leads to the park manager's residence.

TOO LONG TRAIL, 2.4 miles one way, elevation gain 1,120 ft., rated moderate to difficult. Features scenic forest climb to Bergen Peak Trail.

Don't let the name and all the switchbacks worry you. If it weren't so long, this trail would be pretty steep, and all those switchbacks are designed to make it easier. If you're looking for a shorter adventure, try for the scenic overlook about a mile up the trail: Combined with your approach via Mountain View, that will make a four-mile round trip. Farther up, Too Long crosses a stream and eventually leads to the Bergen Peak Trail.

BERGEN PEAK TRAIL, 2.7 miles one way, elevation gain 1,700 ft., rated more difficult. Features climb to mountain summit.

Even horses will want a rest on these switchbacks, and if you can pedal a bike up this route, you're doing very well. Most of the trail climbs through dense ponderosa forest, but there are occasional views of distant mountains. The trail fades on a rocky ridge before reaching the very top, but it is fairly easy to work your way up to the summit. Just watch your backtrail to make sure that you can find your way back the same way.

ALDERFER/THREE SISTERS PARK

Hidden Fawn Trail
Ponderosa Trail
Three Sisters Trail
The Brother Trail

Ever since Evergreen was settled, four rock formations called The Three Sisters and The Brother have been landmarks. Now more than a thousand acres of this beautiful area have become a Jefferson County Open Space Park.

Only one of the park's four trails is downright easy for cross-country skiing, but it links with easy portions of two others to provide a surprising amount of ski trail.

New trails are under construction on the west side of the park. These are meadow trails that will add more ski opportunities. Another expansion south of Buffalo Park Road is also planned.

The usual rules apply: no hunting, no firearms, no fireworks, no camping, no open fires (grills only), no collecting of flowers, rocks or any other souvenirs. Dogs must be on a leash. Park hours are sunrise to sunset. The park is located on the USGS Conifer and Evergreen quads.

ROAD DIRECTIONS: Only 0.6 miles south of downtown Evergreen on Hwy. 73, take Buffalo Park Road west. At mile 0.9 you pass the Wilmot School, where overflow parking is available when school is not in session (weekends and holidays.) The main parking lot is located half a mile farther up on the right. Do not use the church parking lot across from the park.

HIDDEN FAWN TRAIL, one mile one way, elevation gain-loss 160 ft., rated easy. Features cross-country skiing and easy riding and hiking.

Alderfer/Three Sisters Park

Park

contour interval 40'

SCALE

0   500   1000   1500

FEET

Arching through ponderosa forest, this is a very pretty trail enjoyed by cross-country skiers and anyone else looking for a gentle journey. It also connects to an easy portion of Three Sisters and to a fairly easy piece of Ponderosa Trail, forming a loop 0.39 miles longer.

PONDEROSA TRAIL, 1.76 mile loop, elevation gain-loss 400 ft., rated easy to moderate. Features more challenging cross-country skiing and riding.

Our description of this loop begins at its intersection with Hidden Fawn. Skiers will want to turn left and go clockwise because this is the gentlest climb. The trail repeatedly contours, then switchbacks to follow the next contour. On the west side it loses elevation, going down to skirt the edge of a meadow before climbing toward The Brother Trail. Skiers often avoid that area by taking Three Sisters instead.

THREE SISTERS TRAIL, one mile one way, elevation gain 80 ft., loss 260, if done clockwise; rated easy to moderate. Features more skiing and access to landmark rock formations.

Going clockwise, Three Sisters starts out rolling gently through the pines for over a third of a mile before switchbacking up to the saddle between the big rocks. There is no easy way to the top of the rocks themselves, and we urge you not to try. (Do The Brother instead.) Then it switchbacks down to another easy stretch leading to Ponderosa Trail.

THE BROTHER TRAIL, 0.18 miles one way, elevation gain 80 ft., rated moderate. Features fabulous panorama.

Once you see this view, you'll understand why you needn't bother trying to scale The Sisters. The Brother is actually much taller and bigger than its siblings. The path leads to within a few feet of the top and from there it's easy to find a way up. Best of all, the top is quite broad, so you don't have to stand near an edge to enjoy the panorama, which includes Mount Evans, the Alderfer Ranch, Evergreen and a lot more.

Reynolds Park

contour interval 40'

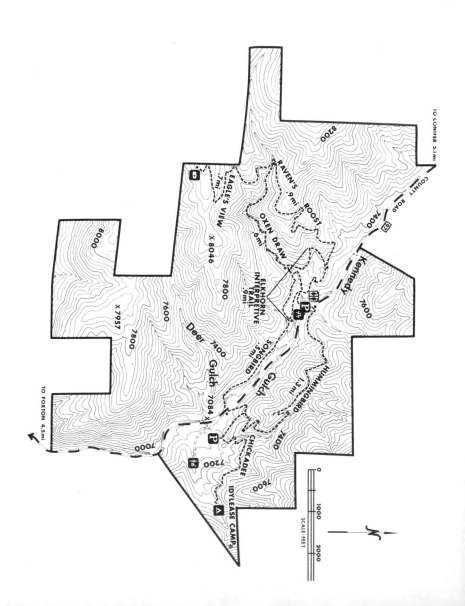

REYNOLDS PARK

Songbird Trail
Elkhorn Interpretive Trail
Oxen Draw
Eagle's View
Raven's Roost
Hummingbird Trail
Chickadee Trail

This was one of the first areas settled in pioneer days. The Reynolds Ranch house, now the park manager's home, once served as a Pony Express station and as a stop for pack trains trekking between Denver and Leadville. Between 1913 and 1942, the park was a dude ranch called Idylease. At one time there were 14 cabins for guests who came from as far away as the East Coast. Later, the Reynolds family switched to cattle ranching. The park is named in memory of John A. Reynolds, whose family gave a large portion of the ranch to Jefferson County.

The main parking area is beside a stream where picnic tables are arranged among the shade trees. There are clean restrooms, but there is no potable water. Camping is allowed by reservation: See Chickadee Trail. Dogs must be on a leash. No hunting, no firearms, no fireworks, no open fires (grills only), no collecting of wildflowers, rocks or other souvenirs. Park hours are one hour before sunrise to one hour after sunset. Reynolds is located on the USGS Platte Canyon quad.

ROAD DIRECTIONS: Just 6.6 miles north of Pine Junction or immediately south of Conifer on Hwy. 285, take the turnoff marked Foxton Road (County 97). Five miles later the pavement ends, and the road cuts through Reynolds Park. Parking is on the right for most trails, but another lot farther down serves Idylease campground.

SONGBIRD TRAIL, 0.5 miles one way, elevation loss 160 ft., rated easy. Features easy hiking or cross-country skiing.

This gentle streamside trail does attract a lot of songbirds, but in winter it attracts cross-country skiers. It connects with Elkhorn, next.

ELKHORN INTERPRETIVE TRAIL, 0.9 mile loop, elevation gain 240 ft., rated easy. Features easy nature study.

This easy nature trail is marked with a series of numbered signposts. Look for the interpretive guide pamphlet available at the trailhead near the restrooms, then follow the numbers. Great place to teach the kids about plants and animals. Gentle enough for cross-country skiing.

OXEN DRAW, 0.6 miles one way, elevation gain 440 ft., rated moderate. Features forest hike to higher trail.

In snowless times, Oxen Draw is the best route up the mountain, easier than Raven's Roost. It climbs through a heavily timbered ravine, but should be avoided in winter or early spring because it can gather up to a foot of ice.

EAGLE'S VIEW TRAIL, 0.7 miles one way, elevation gain 300 ft., rated moderate. Features fine lookout.

Our favorite, this short trail takes off from the intersection of Oxen Draw and Raven's Roost. It climbs up through dense timber to a grassy ridge guarded by ponderosa. From the overlook, you can see Pikes Peak and a lot more. Great picnic spot. No tables.

RAVEN'S ROOST, 0.9 miles one way, elevation gain 240 ft., rated moderate. Features ridge hike to higher trail.

When ice fills Oxen Draw, this is your best route to Eagle's View. It begins as road, then changes to single track as it follows a rocky ridge with a sunny southern exposure. Pretty steep, but short.

HUMMINGBIRD TRAIL, 1.3 miles one way, elevation gain 160 ft., loss 200; rated moderate. Features sunny hillside hike.

This is a good winter trail because its southern exposure helps keep it free of snow and ice. Good for winter conditioning. Bikers, watch out for cactus. Good views of the rest of the park.

CHICKADEE, less than a mile one way, elevation gain 160 ft., rated moderate. Features access to campground.

Like Hummingbird, Chickadee climbs a high dry ridge. After crossing a grassy slope, it leads to Idylease Campground, which is just inside the trees. Clean restrooms, but water provided in steel drums is **not** for drinking. Bring your own. Each of the five sites has a table and grill. Free permits to camp here are available from the office at 18301 W. 10th Ave. in Golden.

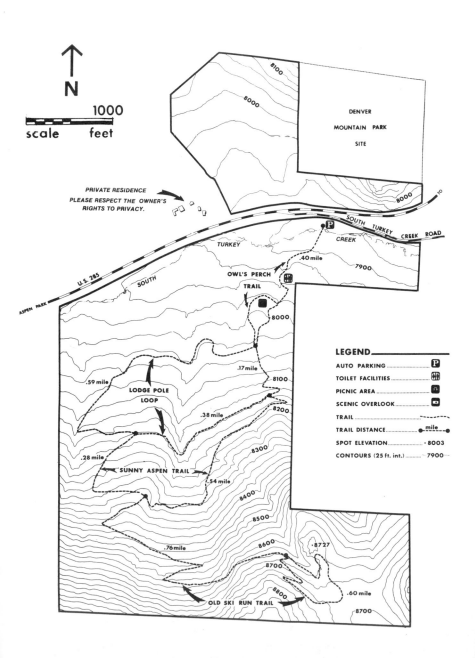

Meyer Ranch Park
contour interval 40'

N

1000
scale   feet

8100

8000

DENVER

MOUNTAIN   PARK

SITE

8000

10

PRIVATE RESIDENCE
PLEASE RESPECT THE OWNER'S
RIGHTS TO PRIVACY.

P

SOUTH   TURKEY   CREEK   ROAD

TURKEY   CREEK

.40 mile

7900

OWL'S PERCH

U.S. 285   SOUTH

TRAIL

ASPEN PARK

8000

.17 mile

8100

LODGE POLE
LOOP

.59 mile

.38 mile   8200

8300

.28 mile

SUNNY ASPEN TRAIL

.54 mile

8400

8500

.76 mile   8600   •8727

8700

.60 mile

8800

OLD SKI RUN TRAIL   8700

LEGEND

AUTO PARKING .... P

TOILET FACILITIES ....

PICNIC AREA ....

SCENIC OVERLOOK ....

TRAIL ....

TRAIL DISTANCE .... ● mile

SPOT ELEVATION .... •8003

CONTOURS (25 ft. int.) 7900

MEYER RANCH PARK

Owl's Perch Trail
Lodge Pole Loop
Sunny Aspen Trail
Old Ski Run Trail

Legend holds that the Meyer Ranch once served as the winter home for animals of the P.T. Barnum Circus for several years during the late 1880s. And in 1915 Norman Meyer discovered an old board on the ranch marked "Circus Town, 1889."

The Meyers still reside in the historic Victorian home on the north side of Hwy. 285; please respect their privacy. Some 397 acres of their ranch now belong to the public as a Jeffco Open Space Park.

Its trail system begins with a meadow often used for cross-country skiing. After big snowstorms, park officials sometimes use snowmobiles to make additional ski trails here. But as you move up into the trees, trails gradually become more difficult, with the steepest trail leading to the top of the mountain.

Picnic tables, grills and clean restrooms are provided, but there is no potable water in the park. Dogs on leash only. No hunting, no firearms, no fireworks, no open fires (grills only), no camping, no collecting of wildflowers, rocks or other souvenirs. Park hours are one hour before sunrise to one hour after sunset. All trails are located on the USGS Conifer quad.

ROAD DIRECTIONS: The community of Aspen Park is located on Hwy. 285 between Conifer and Pine Junction. Just east of Aspen Park turn onto South Turkey Creek Rd. Meyer Ranch Park is immediately on your right.

OWL'S PERCH TRAIL, 0.4 miles, elevation gain 135 ft., loss 50 ft.; rated easy. Features cross-country skiing, easy hiking.

This is just a stroll across the old hay meadow on a wide trail that leads to the trees. Restrooms are located near the end of this trail, where it forms a little balloon loop. Lodge-pole Loop Trail takes off from the upper end of the balloon.

LODGE-POLE LOOP, 1.14 miles, elevation gain-loss 150 ft., rated easy. Features picnicking and cross-country skiing.

Like Owl's Perch, this gentle trail is used by cross-country skiers and families looking for a non-strenuous outing. It winds through scattered ponderosa pines, an area thick with wildflowers after a rain, and has picnic tables.

SUNNY ASPEN TRAIL, 0.82 miles, elevation gain 175 ft., loss 150 ft.; rated moderate. Features forest link to higher trail.

Sunny Aspen is not so sunny because it wanders through a dense forest that really doesn't contain a whole lot of aspens either. Large logs used as erosion barriers form a wide stairway that is perfect for horses, but hard on mountain bikes. Many logs have sprocket marks on them. At the top of this horseshoe loop, where Old Ski Run Trail takes off, there is a tiny clearing with sun and aspens, probably the spot trail-namers had in mind.

OLD SKI RUN TRAIL, 1.36 miles including small balloon loop at summit, elevation gain-loss 375 ft., rated moderately difficult. Features climb to mountain top.

This upper section was used as a ski trail in the 1940s, so there are no level spots. It's pretty much all uphill through dense, mixed forest. Oddly enough, the best views are not from the summit loop, but from a spot just below the loop. A wooden bench marks this overlook where you can see Aspen Park and Mount Evans. Great place to eat your lunch.

LAIR-O-THE-BEAR PARK

Still under construction, Lair-O-The-Bear is a new Jefferson County Open Space Park. It features trout fishing and picnicking, as well as trails for hiking, cross-country skiing and some wheelchair access. The Division of Wildlife is stocking Bear Creek with catchable-sized rainbow trout (Bear Creek is a sizeable stream flowing from Mount Evans, through Evergreen and down Hwy. 74). The park boasts one and a half miles of trout stream, with another four miles downstream along a strip of adjacent undeveloped land owned by Denver Mountain Parks.

You can see much of the park as you drive Hwy. 74. Those areas along the creek and highway were the first to be completed. More trails are planned for the higher portions of the park to the south. The creekside trails are gentle enough for cross-country skiing and are being improved for wheelchair access. Some ramps for wheelchair fishing are also planned.

The usual park rules apply. Hours are from one hour before sunset to one hour after sunset. Dogs on leash only. No hunting, no firearms, no fireworks, no camping, no open fires (grills only), no littering, no collecting of wildflowers, rocks or other souvenirs. Other rules are still being worked out. For example, horses and bicycles may not be allowed.

The park is located on the USGS Evergreen quad. For more information, call 303-278-5925.

ROAD DIRECTIONS: From Denver, drive to Morrison and take Hwy. 74 west. The entrance is about 1.5 miles west of Idledale.

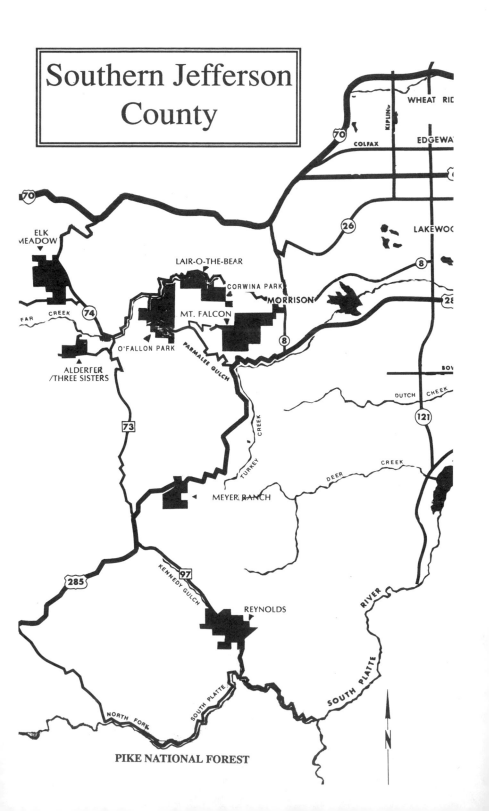

DENVER MOUNTAIN PARKS

Corwina Park
O'Fallon Park

Denver Mountain Parks owns a patchwork of land in Jefferson County, but those lands south of I-70 (our area) have few trails due to lack of funding. Two areas adjacent to Jefferson County Open Space Parks share in those county trail systems, but the only Denver Mountain Park in our area with a mountain trail of its own is Upper Corwina Park near O'Fallon Park. Both are located on the USGS Morrison quad.

ROAD DIRECTIONS: Beginning at Morrison, take Hwy. 74 west. At mile 6.2, pass Lower Corwina Park, with picnic areas on both sides of highway. Only 0.8 miles later, find Upper Corwina Park on your left. O'Fallon Park is another quarter of a mile west, again on the left, only half a mile from Kittredge.

UPPER CORWINA PARK TRAIL, 0.8 miles one way, elevation gain 300 ft., rated moderate. Features forest trail to aspen meadow.

Like Lower Corwina Park downstream, Upper Corwina is generally considered a roadside picnic area with a trout stream (stocked by the Division of Wildlife with catchable size rainbows). Yet near the restrooms there is a trail leading up the draw. This straight-forward path climbs through a timbered ravine, steep at first, then more gentle, as it finds an open meadow with aspens. For those willing to pack their picnic, this is a good choice.

O'FALLON PARK, trails destroyed, but features mazed of logging roads amid beautiful forest.

Ringrose and Rathbun, authors of *Foothills to Mountain Evans,* have dropped O'Fallon from their excellent guidebook because its trail system does not really exist any more. Over a decade ago, foresters cut a lacework of logging roads to remove beetle-infested trees. The cure saved the forest, but destroyed the trails, making the area so confusing that we cannot map it. Still, this is a charming and beautiful area, a flourishing habitat with great potential. Obviously, funding and volunteer work will be necessary to restore this beautiful park.

We cannot recommend O'Fallon for the average family looking for a place to hike or ride horseback or mountain bikes. It should only be attempted by experienced explorers who are accustomed to bushwhacking with map and compass. Fortunately, the park is bounded by highway on the north and west and is not a vast wilderness (860 acres), but it is no place to go for a stroll late in the day or you might have trouble finding your way back before dark.

O'Fallon has streamside picnic areas with shade trees, a trout stream stocked with rainbows, level areas for games, and a giant four-place stone barbecue that is often mistaken for a chimney ruin when seen from the highway.

Unfortunately, a forest fire in March of 1991 damaged about 55 acres of this 860-acre park.

Volunteers interested in improving O'Fallon should call Denver Parks and Recreation Dept. at 303-640-1046.

BUFFALO CREEK HANDICAP ACCESSIBLE FISHING TRAIL AND CAMPING AREA

Stocked with rainbow trout, Buffalo Creek is a popular fishing stream, the backbone of the Buffalo Creek Recreation Area. And right in the middle lies this special area, located at Baldy Campground, designed to allow handicapped persons the opportunity of fishing and camping in the National Forest.

ROAD DIRECTIONS: From Denver take Hwy. 285 south for 32 miles to Pine Junction, then go left on County 126 to the community of Buffalo Creek. FS-543 turns west from Buffalo Creek, following the stream about four miles to Baldy Campground. From Colorado Springs, take Hwy. 24 to Woodland Park, then 67 north to Deckers and 126 north to Buffalo Creek, where FS-543 will be on your left.

BUFFALO CREEK HANDICAP ACCESSIBLE FISHING TRAIL, 0.25 miles one way, elevation gain nil, rated easy.

Winding through blue spruce and ponderosa pines, this trail leads for a quarter of a mile along the creek, with specially designed turnouts and a bridge to allow wheelchair anglers to work the stream from a variety of vantage points. The hard surface has been treated to make it look more natural and has an average slope of 3% or less.

The trail leads from Baldy Campground, where restrooms and two of the eight campsites have been modified for handicapped visitors. Picnic tables feature an overhang that allows wheelchairs to roll right up to them, and grills have also been designed for easy use.

There is no fee, but donations are requested. The facility is operated on a first-come basis.

All this was accomplished by cooperative efforts of the Forest Service, National Park Service, Volunteers for Outdoor Colorado, Jefferson County Road Dept., Trout Unlimited, Colorado Division of Wildlife and the Boy Scouts.

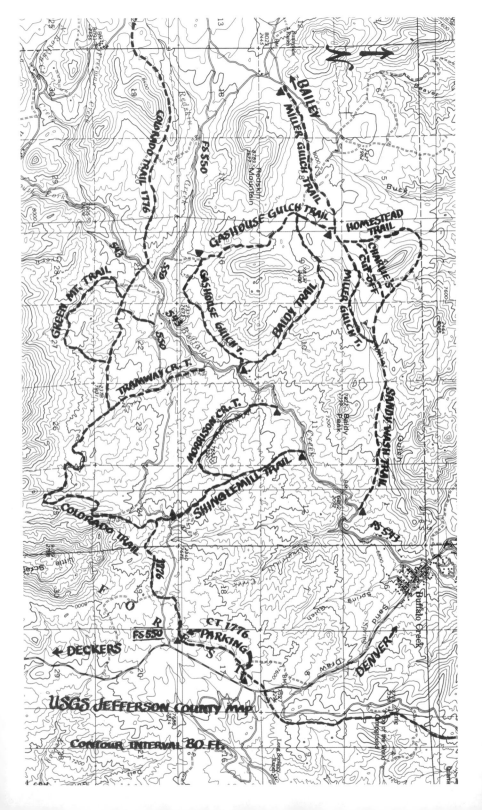

BUFFALO CREEK MOUNTAIN BIKE AREA

Miller Gulch Trail
Sandy Wash Trail
Gashouse Gulch
Baldy Trail
Homestead Trail
Charlie's Cutoff
Shinglemill Trail
Morrison Creek Trail
Tramway Trail
Green Mountain Trail

In 1990 the Forest Service created the Buffalo Creek Mountain Bike Area to complement the Colorado Trail. Utilizing old logging roads with single-track connections, the system is a versatile 40-mile maze, allowing you to design loop adventures of any length that suits you. The area is only about an hour's drive from Denver and an hour and a half from Colorado Springs. Mild winters at this altitude (7,000-8,000) mean that trails remain clear eight to 10 months a year. The routes are well marked with a bike symbol, unless vandalized. But since this is a maze, it's hard to know just where to begin. Our road directions are complicated, but if you follow them on our map, you should get the grand tour.

The Buffalo Creek Mountain Bike Area is located around the Buffalo Creek Recreation Area, which includes several campgrounds, a wheelchair access facility and, of course, Buffalo Creek itself, a popular fishing stream stocked with rainbows. Roadside parking is restricted by law, so watch the signs.

Trails are located on USGS Green Mountain and Pine quads.

ROAD DIRECTIONS: *The community of Buffalo Creek is located on Jefferson County 126 between Deckers and Pine Junction. From*

Denver take Hwy. 285 south 32 miles to Pine Junction and turn south on 126. From Colorado Springs, take Hwy. 24 west to Woodland Park, then 67 north to Deckers, then 126 to Buffalo Creek. Two gravel roads heading west of 126 in this area provide access to bike trails.

Starting at the community of Buffalo Creek, FS-543 heads west. At mile 1.7, SANDY WASH TRAIL is on your right and at mile 3.0, SHINGLEMILL TRAIL is on your left, but both are considered one-way downhillers, so these are destinations, not starting points. At mile 3.6, you find MORRISON CREEK TRAIL on your left. At mile 4.4, the trailhead serving both BALDY and GASHOUSE GULCH is on your right. At mile 4.9, TRAMWAY'S trailhead is at Tramway Campground. At mile 6.3, your road (FS-543) intersects with FS-550, coming from the left. (The sign saying Buffalo Creek is five miles back is wrong.) To describe how trails link with FS-550, we should start back at the pavement at Jefferson County 126.

FS-550 begins on a ridge 4.1 miles south of Buffalo Creek or 11.3 miles north of Deckers. Immediately on your right on 550 is a trailhead for the COLORADO TRAIL 1776. The CT parallels 550 for half a mile, then crosses 550 and parallels the road on the south to intersect with bike trails ahead. At mile 1.6, SHINGLEMILL TRAIL crosses 550 to join the CT. Trailhead parking is on the right, even though this is not the end of the trail. At mile 4.2, TRAMWAY TRAIL crosses 550. Ignore the apparent trailhead at mile 4.8. GREEN MOUNTAIN TRAIL joins 550 from the left at mile 4.9, but there is no good parking here. (GREEN MOUNTAIN has no trailhead parking of its own, being just a detour off the CT.) At mile five, 550 T-junctions against FS-543, but does not end here. Instead, it jogs left for half a mile, then takes off west again from 543. Along that jog you'll find Meadows Campground, reserved for groups, but the FS does not recommend parking here. There is a small parking lot farther along that may be used for the COLORADO TRAIL, linking with GREEN MOUNTAIN TRAIL, though neither trail leaves from that lot. The CT crosses 543 just beyond the 550 west turnoff. Head east on the CT to pick up GREEN MOUNTAIN.

To access more bike trails, take 550 west from 543 just beyond the Meadows Campground. To find the midpoint of GASHOUSE GULCH, go only 0.4 miles and turn right onto a dead-end road that leads up half a mile to the trailhead. Back on 550, continue west another 1.8 miles and turn right on FS-553 marked "EOS Mill." Climb 1.4 miles from this intersection and turn right onto FS-554. Here you'll find the trailhead for MILLER GULCH, which leads to GASHOUSE GULCH TRAIL, HOMESTEAD, CHARLIE'S CUTOFF and SANDY WASH.

MILLER GULCH TRAIL, 3.5 miles one way, elevation 240 ft., loss 560 ft.; rated easy. Features gentle route linking four other trails

The easiest trail in the system, Miller Gulch rolls gently through a hilltop forest. New trail markers should clarify this route, but note that recent woodcutting to thin out dead trees has made non-trails more distinct than trails because of vehicle traffic. However, this thinning will enhance the wildflower and wildlife habitat. It is home to a small herd of elk and a flock of wild turkeys. Soon, Gashouse Gulch branches off to your right, and Homestead takes off to your left shortly after.

There is one switchback along the route, then a meadow. Shortly beyond, Miller Gulch reaches a stream where Sandy Wash Trail begins.

SANDY WASH TRAIL, 1.6 miles one way, elevation loss 640 ft., rated moderate downhill. Features great downhill ride.

Sandy Wash is rated moderate only if you take its designer's advice and use it as a one-way downhill from Miller Gulch to FS-543. If you try it from the bottom, you'll find it very tough going because it is exactly what its name implies, a sandy wash. It dives down to the Buffalo Creek drainage, joining FS-543 2.1 miles east of Baldy Campground.

GASHOUSE GULCH TRAIL, 3.2 miles one way, elevation gain 930 ft., rated difficult. Features challenging climb to Miller Gulch.

This one is rated difficult because designers imagined it as an uphill from FS-543, but downhill would be a lot easier, of course, and there is also a middle trailhead that avoids the steepest portion. That steepest portion is the first mile climbing up from the Buffalo Creek drainage. The trail becomes much more gentle as it approaches the middle trailhead (off 550). From there it goes up through aspen meadows with only a couple of steep spots, intersecting with Baldy and ending at Miller Gulch. That sounds easy, but the upper half is sandy, which is tougher on a bike. The name Gashouse Gulch was reportedly coined by local children.

BALDY TRAIL, 2.3 miles one way, elevation gain 930ft., rated difficult. Features challenging climb to Gashouse Gulch.

Baldy is named for the mountain and does not begin at Baldy Campground. It is a tough climb up through the woods from the Buffalo Creek drainage on FS-543, but has good views. If you want to make a loop with Gashouse Gulch, the Forest Service recommends that you start up Baldy and return via Gashouse to avoid the sandy climb along Gashouse.

HOMESTEAD TRAIL, 2.6 miles one way, elevation gain 320 ft., rated moderate. Features interesting ride past overlook rock.

Homestead forms a kind of long detour, leaving Miller Gulch and returning again. Put together with Charlie's Cut-off, there are several loop possibilities. It is mostly old logging road, but changes to single track as it arches over a ridge at its northern end. Watch for a high set of rocks on that ridge. If you're traveling clockwise, they'll be on your right. Leave the trail and climb to the top for an impressive view of Kenosha Pass, Mount Rosalie, Mount Logan, the Valley of the North Fork and much more. Descending the ridge, your trail becomes an old road again, then single track after its intersection with Charlie's Cut-off. From here your trail is an old cow path, following a tiny stream toward its intersection with Miller Gulch.

CHARLIE'S CUT-OFF, 0.7 miles one way, elevation gain 80 ft., loss 240 ft., rated moderate. Features shortcut between sections of Homestead.

This shortcut is mostly single track through rocky forest. It makes the whole system more versatile, making it possible to do loops with Homestead and Miller Gulch.

SHINGLEMILL TRAIL, 2.1 mile one way, elevation loss 820 ft., rated moderate as a dcwnhill. Features downhill run to FS-543.

Shinglemill Trail does not follow Shinglemill Creek, but a

ridge above. It is rated moderate as a downhill ride; the FS does not recommend trying it uphill. In theory, it starts at the Colorado Trail, south of 550, but after a few hundred feet, it crosses 550 and finds its "trailhead parking" on the other side of the road. Then it winds gently through evergreens to its intersection with upper Morrison Creek Trail. From there on it dives toward the Buffalo Creek drainage, ending on FS-543.

MORRISON CREEK TRAIL, 1.7 miles one way, elevation gain 480 ft., loss 80 ft.; rated moderate. Features climb along creek to Shinglemill Trail.

Morrison Creek flows into Buffalo Creek just east of Baldy Campground on FS-543. The trail climbs beside the stream, first as a double track and then as a single track where it leaves the creek to avoid private property. It then climbs a ridge to join Shinglemill. This intersection can be easy to miss if you are zooming down Shinglemill, but is easy to find going up.

TRAMWAY CREEK TRAIL, 1.1 mile one way, elevation gain 480 ft.; rated moderate. Features creekside climb to Colorado Trail.

Tramway is an old name for a yarder, a kind of ski lift contraption used to haul logs out of the woods. The tramway is gone now, and the forest has grown tall again, but the contraption is still remembered in the name of the creek, its trail and the campground where the trail begins. The trail follows the creek upstream, crosses FS-550, and eventually links with the Colorado Trail. The section above 550 is rocky and has several stream crossings.

GREEN MOUNTAIN TRAIL, 1.8 miles one way, elevation gain 400 ft., loss, 560 ft. if ridden east to west; rated difficult. Features scenic alternative along Colorado Trail.

This is a kind of looping detour off the Colorado Trail 1776 and has no trailhead parking at the one place where it meets a road. Still, its scenery makes it worth the effort. Green Mountain

Trail is named after the mountain and does not begin at Green Mountain Campground. Considered most enjoyable ridden east to west, it takes off south of the Colorado Trail, climbing an old logging road west of Tramway Creek. After grunting up this road, look for a big granite outcrop on the ridge. Great views from the top. Your road changes to single track for a downhill leading to a double track above the Meadows Campground. Follow bike trail markers around to the Colorado Trail. A spur of Green Mountain leaves the CT shortly and goes down to join FS-550, but there is no parking.

DECKERS-CHEESMAN AREA

Gill Trail
Shoreline Trail
Cheesman Dam Trail

Glistening water flowing beside the highway near Deckers lures many people to pull over and fly fish those sections of the South Platte River open to the public (limit: two trout over 16", flies and lures only). Yet often visitors don't realize that local trails open up miles of better fishing upstream. Gill Trail offers Gold Medal catch-and-release fishing along the Platte, and Cheesman Reservoir features a variety of lake fishing.

Cheesman is a mountain jewel. As Denver's major water source, this lake was closed to all recreation for many years. Now the Denver Water Board is trying to welcome limited recreation, including fishing, hiking and bird watching on a day-use basis. There are many special rules, of course, and the public's cooperation is necessary to protect the resource. In the fall, many people explore Cheesman just to watch our nation's symbol. Caretaker Ed Christensen reports seeing as many as 16 bald eagles at a time. Young ones look much like goldens, all brown, but goldens don't fish. Bald eagles attain their white plumage with maturity and they live mostly on fish.

The Division of Wildlife stocks Cheesman with rainbow trout, kokanee salmon, smallmouth bass and lake trout. There are also brown trout, pike and yellow perch. Steelhead planted in the river and in Goose Creek are expected to migrate to the lake, returning to the streams to spawn. The trout limit is two over 16". Ordinary limits apply to other fish. Check DOW brochures for changes.

Only one of the lake's 18 miles of shoreline is closed to fishing, that being the first mile from the gate leading east to the far side of the dam. You must **stay off the dam**, but may walk any other section of road in the area.

The problem with fishing Cheesman is access. This is a deep lake amid rocky timber with steep banks. In fall, lower levels create stretches of sandy gravel beach, but even these are interrupted

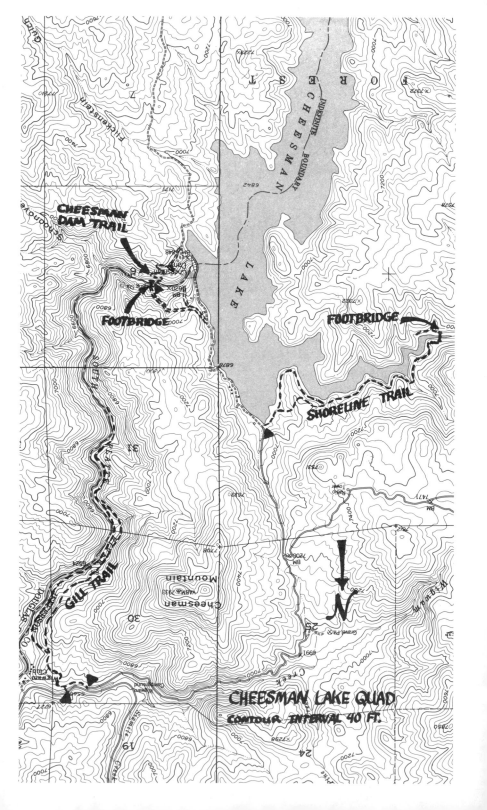

by rock formations. No boats or floatation devices are allowed, so this means scrambling treacherous terrain. For that reason, the Denver Water Board and the Colorado Division of Wildlife have been building trails to help you access more shoreline.

Unlike Gill Trail, Cheesman trails are closed in winter (Jan 1-April 30), but fishermen who want to access the river just below the dam are allowed to enter the gate and walk roads to the footbridge. See Cheesman Dam Trail for directions. Dogs must be on a leash (strictly enforced). No swimming or wading (no waterbody contact at all), no hunting, firearms or fireworks, no fires, no camping, horses or bikes, no ice fishing. Pack your trash. Caretakers vigorously patrol in boats and with trained security dogs to make sure that backpackers don't try to camp along remote shorelines. Remember, you must return to your car within one half hour after sunset. Flies and artificial lures only.

All trails located on USGS Cheesman Lake quad.

ROAD DIRECTIONS: From Denver take Hwy. 285 south to Pine Junction, then head south on 126 to Deckers. From Colorado Springs, take Hwy. 24 west to Woodland Park, then right on 67 to Deckers. To find GILL go 2.6 miles west of Deckers on 126 and park on the right. Cross the highway to find one of the trailheads. The other GILL trailhead is located a tenth of a mile farther west where 211 branches off toward Cheesman. Don't park at that intersection; instead, park at Wigwam Campground another third of a mile west on 126. To find SHORELINE and the CHEESMAN DAM TRAIL, take the Cheesman turnoff (211) 2.7 miles west of Deckers and follow the signs 3.2 miles to the lake. Park outside the fence. As you enter the gate, SHORELINE is immediately on your right. CHEESMAN DAM TRAIL is straight ahead, but you must walk roads to reach it, so see its trail description for directions.

GILL TRAIL, Forest Service #610, over 2 miles one way, elevation gain measures about 300 ft. but is actually larger; rated moderate at first, then very difficult. Features Gold Medal wild trout fishing, catch-and-release only.

Gold Medal fishing means that it's just about as good as fishing can be. If you've ever envied the Wigwam Club's private stretch of the river along 126, take heart: You own an even longer stretch of the same water just upstream. This is a wild trout stream, never stocked, but it is also a catch-and-release area, meaning that fish must be returned immediately to the water. That also means the trout are big and plentiful and highly educated. TV's Curt Gowdy called this one of the finest trout streams in the world, and biologists believe that even the Indians never saw better. This marvelous habitat also happens to be set in one of the most beautiful canyons you'll ever see.

Get an early start because the two parking areas serving the two trailheads both fill up quickly. And bring a flashlight. Often the fish start biting at dusk, and without a flashlight, you might have to leave just when things get lively.

Both topo and FS maps show Gill going all the way to the lake, but it doesn't. It starts out well, but braids and fades and finally vanishes in the cliffs well short of the dam. DOW officers routinely clamber the entire distance to enforce the law, but even though they know all the tricks of the route, they still call it extremely difficult at the far end. Also dangerous. It's an easy place to break a leg, but a hard place to get help. Still, if you want to get away from the crowd, all you have to do is explore a little farther upstream.

Gill also looks flat on maps, rising only a few hundred feet in several miles, but actually it jumps up and down so sharply that its real elevation gain is surely more than a thousand feet.

Because there are two parking areas, two trailheads have developed, but both trails soon join up before starting the climb up and over a wooded ridge. Once you see the river, the trail forks. The left fork goes directly down to the water, and from there you can work your way upstream. Those who want to fish farther up take the right fork, which is a good trail, staying high and offering many scenic views. Trouble is, when waters are clearest, you can see fish from the upper trail, tempting some to shortcut, which always causes erosion damage, if not skin damage.

You'll also notice trails across the river, but those are only pieces, not a continuous route, made by fishermen who wade across. The only public footbridge is just below the dam. Just upstream from the footbridge is a cable marking the no-fishing boundary 1,000 feet below the base of the dam. Another trail from the footbridge leads up to the east side of Cheesman Lake. See Cheesman Dam Trail.

Remember, the fish along Gill are professional entertainers who must be returned to work immediately. Only artificial flies and lures may be used. Spectacular rainbows and browns prove this system works. Report any violators.

Gill is a FS trail, technically open to many activities that are not truly appropriate. It is meant to be a rugged experience, especially upstream. Horsemen, hunters and mountain bikers should consider going elsewhere, and backpackers will have a tough time finding a good place to pitch a tent.

If you want to camp nearby, you have your choice of three FS campgrounds. Wigwam is a free campground with a well but no regular trash pick-up, so please ignore the emergency bin and haul your trash away. Lone Rock, nearer Deckers on the same road, is a pay reservation campground. Call 1-800-283-CAMP. Kelsey is another pay campground eight miles northwest of Deckers on 126.

SHORELINE TRAIL, Denver Water Board, 2 miles one-way, but growing; elevation gain nil, rated easy. Features fishing access.

As you enter the gate, the DWB's Shoreline Trail is immediately on your right. It soon forks. Going left allows you to follow the shoreline around the point. Going right, you find a shortcut over a low ridge. Both meet up beyond the point and then continue along the north shore, leading west toward the Goose Creek inlet. (Goose Creek is known as Lost Creek where it repeatedly dives underground in the Lost Creek Wilderness.)

So far, two miles of this trail have been built, as far as the inlet. But the DOW has completed a footbridge spanning the inlet and is now building more trail to access the lake's west shore.

CHEESMAN DAM TRAIL, Division of Wildlife, less than half mile one way, but access road adds more than a mile to this; elevation gain about 300 feet, rated moderate. Features access to lake's east shore with spectacular view of dam.

This is a short but steep trail, allowing you to reach the east side of the lake without crossing the dam (a major no-no). Since it is only a link, your real hike will be on the access roads leading to and beyond this trail.

Beginning at the gate, walk the road straight ahead toward the dam. This mile is the only shore section closed to fishing. Just before you reach the dam, take the road that branches to your left, climbing uphill. Higher up the road forks, but keep to the left. The right fork leads to another caretaker's residence called the Cave Dwellers, which you'll see later. Then the road pitches downhill and ends at a footbridge that crosses the river just below the dam.

Downstream you'll see a bit of trail used by fishermen, but this does not really connect to Gill, as explained. Hardy souls can scramble the route, just as officers do, but it is dangerous and difficult. During winter, when Cheesman trails are closed, you can still come this way to fish this portion of the river, but you may not climb the Cheesman Dam Trail beyond the bridge and you must return to the gate by sunset.

Upstream you will see a cable marking the no-fishing boundary 1,000 feet below the base of the dam. Your trail begins across the bridge.

It's all up from here, a series of four switchbacks that climb through timber to a road at the top of the canyon. Every switchback gives you a better view of the dam. For us, this was a charming surprise. Instead of being the usual slab of concrete, this dam looks like something the Incas might have built.

Man's first attempt to plug the gorge was rejected by the river itself. An earthen dam, lined with boiler plate, was swept away in the 1800s. So engineers took a lesson from the cliffs forming the gorge and built a dam made of the same granite. Large blocks were cut and artfully pieced together to form a graceful monument that blends in with the surrounding cliffs. Finished in 1905, it has an historical designation.

When you reach the road, notice the Cliff Dwellers cabin perched on the cliffs across canyon. Turn to the left and hike the road until it joins the road coming from the dam. Again turn left and you will be hiking along the east shoreline. Have fun!

TARRYALL AREA

Brookside--McCurdy Trail
Ute Creek Trail
Lizard Rock Trail

The mining town of Tarryall was called Puma City back in 1896. It seems that an unsociable prospector named Rocky Mountain Jim moved to this scenic valley to get away from the hectic life in Cripple Creek, but his dream of solitude ended when his discovery of gold brought a population of a thousand!

ROAD DIRECTIONS: As you drive northwest on Highway 24, the Tarryall Road turnoff is located only 1.2 miles beyond Lake George. Travel about 13 miles on Tarryall Road and find Spruce Grove Campground and the trailhead for LIZARD ROCK. At mile 14.7 find Twin Eagles Campground with the southern trailhead for BROOKSIDE-McCURDY. This is an approach to HANKINS PASS. Restroom facilities, a horse loading chute and ample parking are available at the trailhead. For directions to the new BROOKSIDE-McCURDY northern trailhead, see BAILEY AREA. For directions to the middle of BROOKSIDE-McCURDY, see KENOSHA PASS AREA. To find the trailhead for UTE CREEK, travel another 5.5 miles past Twin Eagles and look for parking and a footbridge on your right.

BROOKSIDE McCURDY, Forest Service #607, about 38 miles one way, elevation gain 5,750 ft., loss 4,180 ft.; rated difficult. Features spectacular and varied scenery

This is the giant. Aside from Colorado Trail 1776, Brookside-McCurdy is the longest trail in the Pike National Forest and is now a little longer, thanks to a new trailhead location at Bailey.

Beginning at Twin Eagles Campground on Tarryall Road, the path climbs up to an old road, turns left onto the road and soon changes into a path once more that snakes through evergreens and aspens. A ranch meadow is spread below. Soon you pass the sign

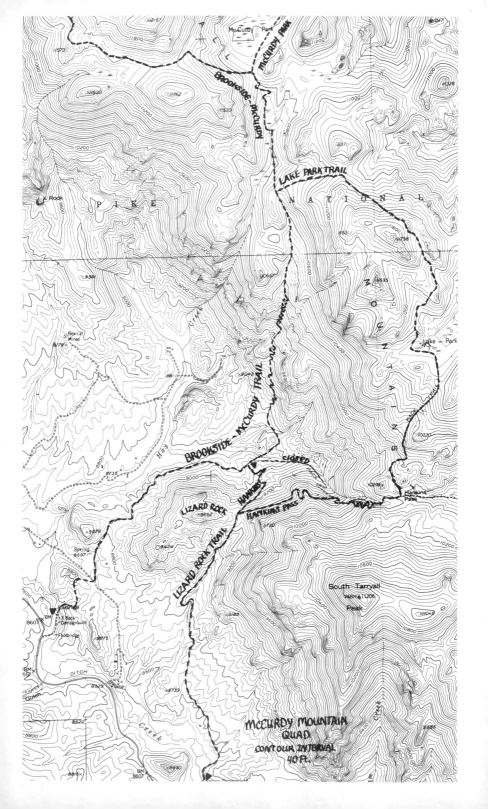

where Hankins Pass Trail branches away to the right. You cross tiny tributaries of Hay Creek and then begin the grueling switchbacks that take you up through red granite crags similar to those in the Lost Creek Wilderness ahead. Two of the crags have holes through them. Each switchback offers a loftier view of Pikes Peak and the Tarryall Valley.

Near 10,700 feet you find the junction where Lake Park Trail heads uphill to your right. Your trail has now become the boundary of the Lost Creek Wilderness. You climb a meadow valley and follow its stream up to the saddle ridge above its headwaters. From here you overlook the broad valley of McCurdy Park (the old Forest Service shelter there burned down some years ago). This overlook is the beginning of McCurdy Park Trail, but your trail turns left and climbs up past McCurdy Mountain toward Bison Pass.

Here you climb through a ghost forest created by a fire around 1868 or 1869. The trees died upright and many remain that way, now weathered to look like driftwood. Erosion of soil after the fire prevented new trees from growing, so you find a grassy timberline environment just below the altitude where timberline usually begins. Your trail continues to climb toward the real timberline into bighorn sheep country. Indeed, the Pikes Peak herd was reestablished with bighorns captured here.

Near Bison Pass you arrive at a grassy knoll at 11,900 feet where you can see across South Park to Antero Reservoir and the mountain ranges beyond. Your trail dives off that western slope, switchbacking down through loose gravel and through bristlecone pines that have reestablished themselves in this part of the forest. You arrive at a ridge saddle where Ute Creek Trail heads southwest toward Tarryall River. Your trail turns north and follows a gentle path through spruce and fir and past long meadows, following Indian creek down to Lost Park Campground.

From here you follow the meadow of the North Fork of Lost Creek north for two miles. Your path curves northwest and finds the remains of an 1890s sawmill. Your trail crosses the creek and joins Colorado Trail #1776. The two trails are one for another two miles as you travel northwest up another meadow valley. A sign marks the point where Brookside-McCurdy heads north again

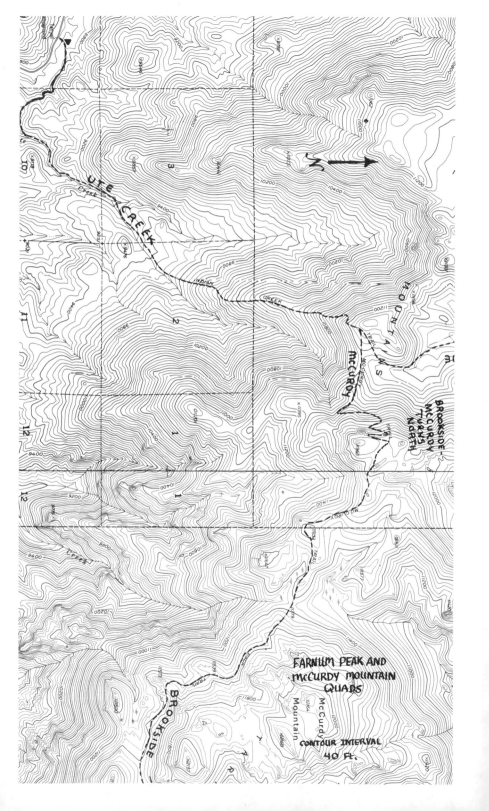

FARNUM PEAK AND
McCURDY MOUNTAIN
QUADS

CONTOUR INTERVAL
40 FT.

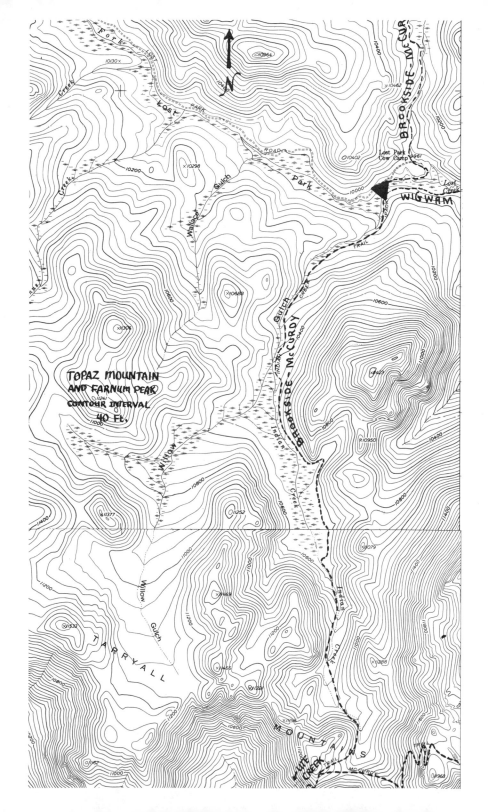

TOPAZ MOUNTAIN
AND FARNUM PEAK
CONTOUR INTERVAL
40 Ft.

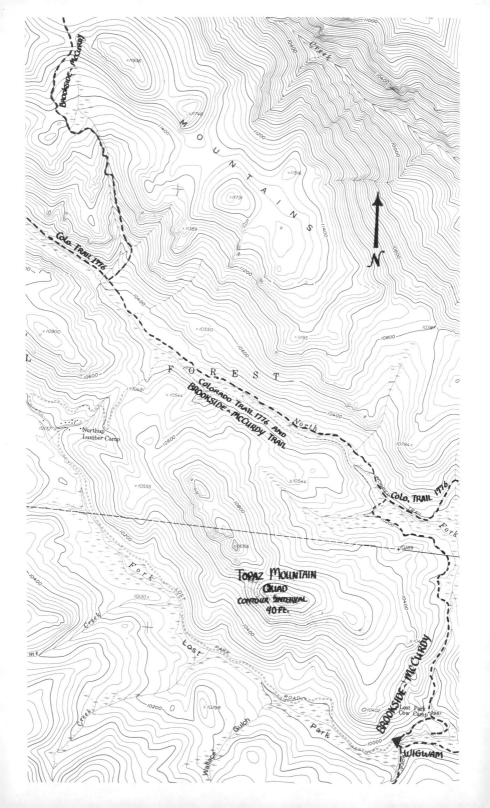

beside a tributary that is hidden in the trees. This steep and rocky path leads up to a ridge saddle, then down the other side to Craig Park, which is similar to the brushy and boggy valley that you just left. After a short stretch going upstream, your trail turns to the right at its junction with Craig Park Trail. See BAILEY AREA.

Again your trail switchbacks uphill, leading north. You arrive at a ridge overlooking McArthur Gulch. Here the old route has been closed and the trail rerouted, switchbacking down to the east and then zig-zagging before joining the newly rerouted Payne Creek (Craig Meadow) Trail. This twin trail then turns north and winds down to end at the Bailey Picnic Ground. See BAILEY AREA for directions.

Brookside-McCurdy is located on the USGS McCurdy Mt., Farnum Peak, Topaz Mt. and Shawnee quads.

UTE CREEK TRAIL, Forest Service #629, about 3 miles one way, elevation gain 2,580 ft., rated difficult. Features forest climb to Brookside-McCurdy.

This one is sometimes used to form a loop with Brookside-McCurdy for it joins that longer trail at the top of Bison Pass. Both trails end at Tarryall Road, but 5.5 miles apart, so a considerable part of the loop will be road travel.

Ute Creek Trail begins at a footbridge crossing Tarryall River, skirts private property where a beaver pond lies then begins climbing beside Ute Creek. It is a long sustained climb with no relief. This area boasts very large ponderosa pines, as well as aspen and blue spruce. After crossing near the fork of tributaries, the trail leaves the creekside and rises steeply on a wooded hillside. There is no more water beyond this point.

The trail ends on a saddle ridge at nearly 11,300 feet, with a grand vista of the Tarryall Valley below. Signs mark its juncture with Brookside-McCurdy. The total distance of the Ute Creek/Brookside-McCurdy loop, including road travel, is estimated at 20.5 miles.

Ute Creek is located on the USGS Farnum Peak quad.

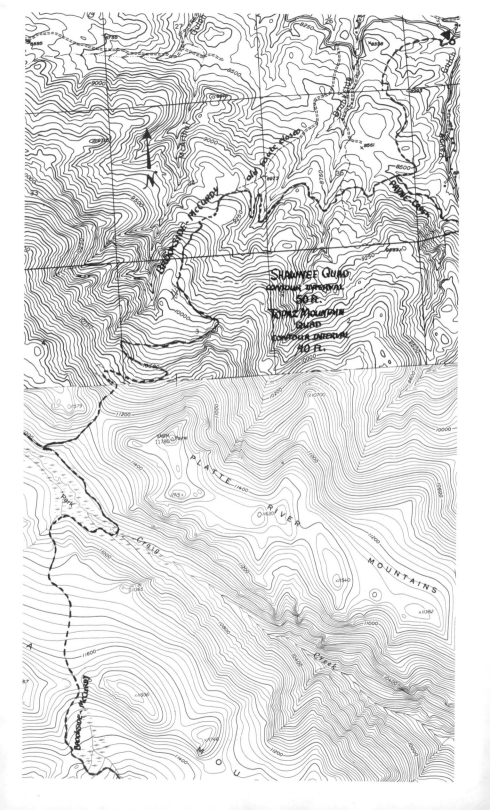

LIZARD ROCK TRAIL, Forest Service #658, 2.5 miles one way, rated easy to moderate. Features easy climb past Lizard Rock to Hankins Pass.

Some rock formations have very imaginative names, but Lizard Rock really looks like an iguana crouching atop a mountain. The trailhead is located at a pay campground, but you can also access it by parking outside the campground. The trail skirts private property, then wanders up a drainage before climbing up toward Lizard Rock, which will be on your left, elevation 9,526. The trail does not climb to the rock itself, but goes past it to link with the new switchbacks of Hankins Pass. The old Hankins Pass route is closed.

Bikers note: Mountain bikes are discouraged on Lizard Rock Trail because it leads into the Lost Creek Wilderness, where bicycles are not permitted.

Located on the USGS McCurdy Mountain quad.

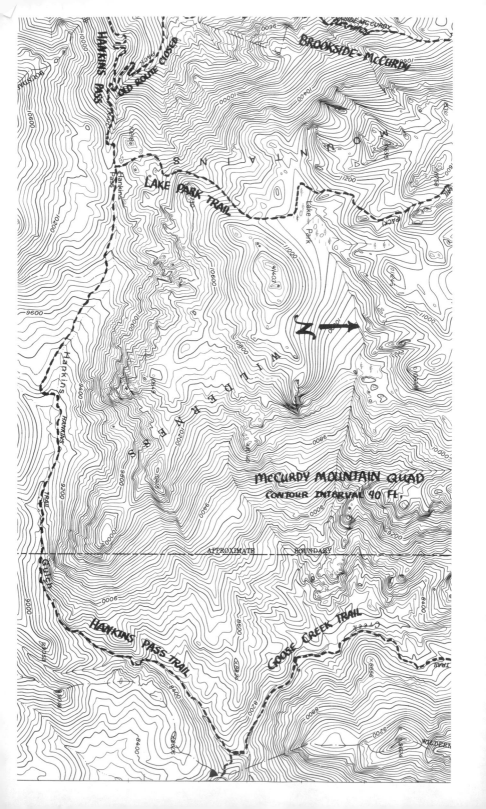

LOST CREEK WILDERNESS

Hankins Pass Trail
Lake Park Trail
McCurdy Park Trail
Goose Creek Trail

The Lost Creek region has been set aside as a Wilderness Area to protect its primitive nature. Mountain bikes are prohibited, so you can only see this wonderland by hiking or riding horseback, a hard journey either way. This was the last refuge of Colorado's wild bison, killed off here in the late 1800s.

Robert Leasure offered this description of the region's strange geology in his novel, *Black Mountain*:: "Jim, I took only a quart of whiskey to help out my breakfast coffee, but I saw whales, teakettles, cowled monks, ships and sheep, frogs, dragons, Indians, colonial squires, kings, clowns, and goblins. It seemed like a city in the sky, its ornaments both noble and grotesque, a strange, secret place where silence in those tortuous corridors and rubbled granite avenues is broken only by the monotone of a crazy river. I call the river 'crazy' because it seems to hate the sunlight. It forms nine separate box canyons and flows as often under the ground as above."

This "lost creek," disappearing under cliffs and reappearing from caves beyond, makes the area a dangerous place to get lost in, so beware. If you want a very long expedition, you can approach the Lost Creek area by two long trails, but the most popular route is the shortest one, a 24-mile loop that begins and ends near Goose Creek Campground. Many parts of this loop are difficult and most hikers take two to four days to complete it, so make sure that you take along what you need. You will be a long way from help.

The loop can be hiked in either direction, of course, but we will describe it from left to right, beginning with Hankins Pass and ending with Goose Creek Trail. All trails are located on USGS McCurdy Mt. quad, plus Windy Peak for Goose Creek.

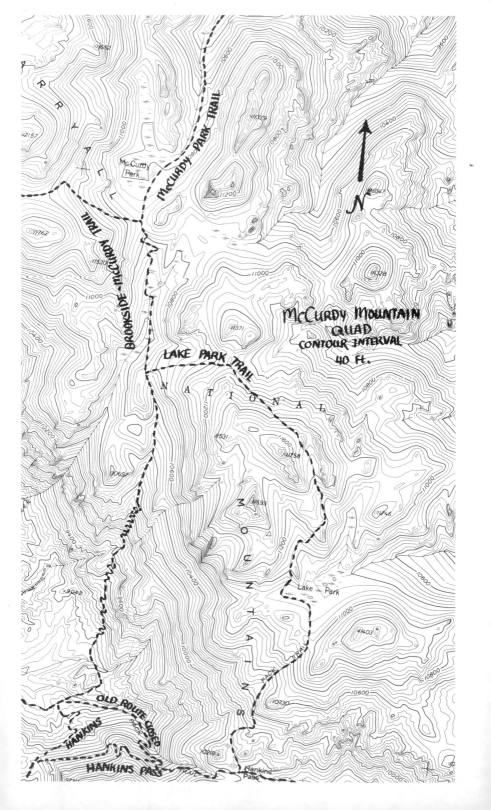

ROAD DIRECTIONS: To find the Goose Creek trailhead, take the gravel road that joins Highway 126 just three miles west of Deckers. Follow the signs to Goose Creek Campground, a distance of 11 miles, then keep heading south past the campground for 3.5 miles, taking Trailhead Road to your right. Horses unload at a special parking area along this road. Both Hankins Pass and Goose Creek share a common trailhead at the auto parking lot.

HANKINS PASS TRAIL, Forest Service #630, 5.9 miles one way, elevation gain 1,820 ft., loss 1,040 ft.; rated moderate to difficult. Features access to Lake Park and Brookside-McCurdy Trails.

Leaving the trailhead, your path dips into Hankins Gulch, crosses a stream at the bottom, then forks. The left fork leads to Hankins Pass and the right fork to Goose Creek. Now you begin following the stream uphill through spruce and large aspens. There are no confusing side trails. About halfway to the pass itself, you find an aspen meadow with active beaver ponds, a nice place to camp and fish for brookies. Above this point, the path crosses the stream and follows the hillside above it. The trail eventually leads above the headwaters to a saddle ridge, and there you find an intersection with Lake Park Trail.

If you continue on Hankins, you will go down a new set of switchbacks on the other side of the ridge and join Brookside-McCurdy Trail. Hankins ends there at the intersection with Brookside-McCurdy. From there you can take Brookside-McCurdy north to McCurdy Park, then McCurdy Park Trail and Goose Creek Trail, making a circuit, but that route is longer and the more difficult because you lose more than 1,000 feet of altitude and must make up that loss by climbing killer switchbacks.

The more popular route is still pretty difficult: Turn right off Hankins Pass onto Lake Park Trail at the saddle ridge. This eventually leads you to Brookside-McCurdy below McCurdy Park.

LAKE PARK Forest Service #639, 3 miles from Hankins Pass to Brookside-McCurdy Trails, 1.25 miles to Lake Park itself; elevation gain 1,480 ft., loss 720 ft.; rated difficult. Features grand vistas and camping at Lake Park.

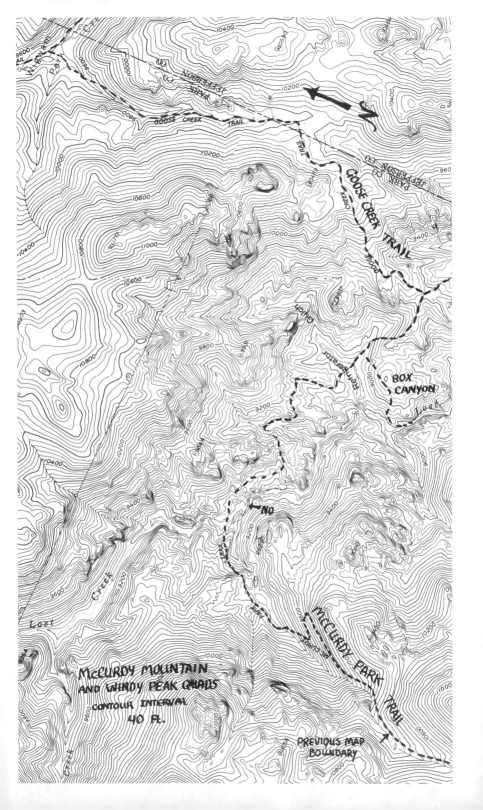

As you stand atop Hankins Pass itself, the sign says "Lake Park Three Miles" and points uphill. Be sure to fill your canteens for the Lake Park Trail is a long, dry march over high country. It begins at 10,000 feet and climbs to almost 11,000 feet before descending to join Brookside-McCurdy.

Lake Park is a high meadow surrounded by majestic rock formations and the silvery snags of a ghost forest, created by fire. All lakes eventually silt up, but the process is quickened if a forest fire denudes the mountainside and increases erosion. Today, the lakes are only shallow puddles in the midst of bog. Campers will find good places on the south side of the meadow, but to reach flowing water, you must bushwhack carefully across the bogs to the streams that come down creases in the north slope. Test the ground with care because some of these bogs are very deep!

The trail climbs out of the park on the west side, very rocky and steep. As you cross the highest portion, watch for alpine columbine, a high-altitude miniature of the State Flower. From here the trail dives down to join Brookside-McCurdy. At this T-junction, signs say that Lake Park is two miles behind, that Tarryall Creek is 4 3/4 miles to the south and McCurdy Park is one mile north. That last mile to McCurdy Park climbs to the headwaters of a creek and up to a saddle ridge that overlooks the park.

McCURDY PARK TRAIL, Forest Service #628, 5.3 miles one way, elevation gain 1,080 ft., loss 400 ft.; rated moderate. Features camping at McCurdy Park, lake fishing north of park.

McCurdy Park is a high valley with a flowing stream. The old A-frame shelter is now gone. Many of the most beautiful rock formations in the Lost Creek area are located along this trail.

Since we are describing the circuit from left to right, we assume that you will be approaching McCurdy Park from the south, along Brookside-McCurdy Trail. Brookside-McCurdy is a long trail that leads to McCurdy Park and branches away to the west. McCurdy Park Trail begins at this intersection on a ridge overlooking McCurdy Park itself.

From this point you hike through the long grassy valley following a stream north. Then you leave the creek and take a long

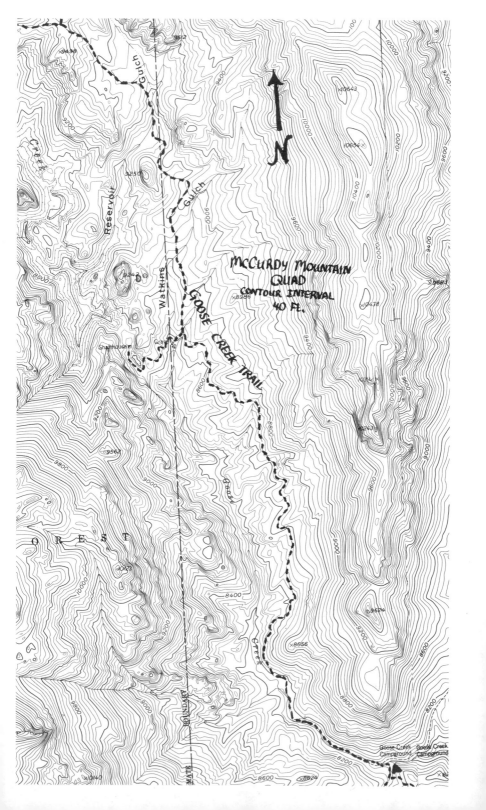

series of steep switchbacks down the side of a canyon. At the bottom you find a deep lake that was built by beaver at a narrow part of the gorge. There are only a couple of campsites, so if you wish to stay here, try to arrive early. This lake has never been surveyed, but should contain nice brookies.

From here the trail climbs up and over ridges and crosses a stream. The USGS topographic map still shows this stream to be the one draining from the beaver lake, which would mean that the water comes from your right as you cross it, but the map is mistaken. The water comes from your left and is another lost piece of Lost Creek. See our map. A few campsites are available here, and many sections of Lost Creek have nice brookies.

Up and over more steep ridges and you find another stream crossing marked Refrigerator Gulch. The USGS map shows you crossing at beaver ponds, but these have now turned to swamp so you would hardly know you were in the right place without the sign.

As soon as you cross this stream, you find that the trail branches left and right. The right branch looks very distinct because it leads to a box canyon used by horse riders as a campsite and corral. Another piece of Lost Creek emerges in the box canyon, so horses have water but limited forage.

The left branch leads up to a saddle ridge where McCurdy Park Trail ends at a junction with Goose Creek Trail. From this point, Goose Creek Trail follows the ridge north toward Wigwam Park or descends the ridge to complete the circuit by winding up at Goose Creek Campground. A sign marks the intersection.

GOOSE CREEK, Forest Service #612, 11.8 miles one way; elevation gain 2,000 ft., loss 780 ft.; rated difficult. Features fishing, camping and majestic rock formations.

If you are hiking the Lost Creek circuit from left to right, you will join Goose Creek Trail at a ridgetop east of Refrigerator Gulch. But there is no use beginning our description in the middle of the trail, so let's start back at the main trailhead near Goose Creek Campground.

The early part of this trail is popular among fishermen who are after the rainbows and brookies, so it is wide and easy and has a fine bridge. (Lost Creek becomes Goose Creek when it stops being lost.)

As you leave the auto parking lot, you descend a trail and cross a fairly small stream that flows from Hankins Gulch. These signs direct you to the left for Hankins Pass or to the right for Goose Creek.

Goose Creek is wide and active, occasionally interrupted by the beaver corps of engineers. The campsites are in the meadow across the stream, so campers can be away from the day traffic. Farther upstream the trail grows narrower and steeper. As you descend a ridge well away from Goose Creek itself, you find a trickle of water crossing your path and a clear trail branching away to the left. This leads to a fascinating and scenic area called the Shafthouse.

Follow this path and you will find several log cabins that you may use on a first-come basis. There is very little firewood close by. At the cabins, the trail goes left and right, left to dead-end at Goose Creek itself and right to the Shafthouse area.

Many years ago engineers tried to dam Reservoir Gulch by sinking a shaft and pumping concrete underground in an attempt to stop the flow of Lost Creek. Yet the creek only found new channels underground. You will not find a shaft or a house at the "Shafthouse," but you will find some rusting equipment on a concrete slab and some very pretty scenery. Just a few yards before you reach the machinery, there is a opening in the rock on the left side of the trail where giant boulders have tumbled together to form a cave-like room. Yet the room has a concrete floor!

Return to the main trail and follow it north to find another charming area, the upper end of Reservoir Gulch. This area offers more campsites with a convenient stream. It's a steep climb out of this area to the saddle ridge where Goose Creek Trail joins McCurdy Park Trail, and from there Goose Creek Trail leads north, crossing over into another watershed and following a stream downhill past a balanced rock pinnacle toward Wigwam Trail. That's where Goose Creek Trail ends.

WELLINGTON LAKE AREA

Rolling Creek Trail
Wigwam Trail

Wellington Lake is located on a gravel road between Bailey and Buffalo Creek. The lake itself is private, but since all the small roads in this area have signs pointing toward Wellington Lake, that's a good place to start our directions.

Rolling Creek Trail no longer begins at the Bancroft Ranch near Wellington Lake, but now has a trailhead a couple of miles north that allows you to bypass private property. Because of the Lost Creek Wilderness, mountain bikes are prohibited from these trails.

ROAD DIRECTIONS: Proceed northwest on the gravel road #543 that leads from Wellington Lake to Bailey. Soon you pass the little community of Sylvania of the Rockies, and only 0.7 mile later you find a turnoff to the left. This dirt road leads to trailheads for the Rolling Creek and Colorado Trail 0.3 mile later.

To find Wigwam, take FS-560 five miles south toward Deckers from Wellington Lake. The turnoff to Wigwam trailhead will be on your right after you cross Stoney Pass. Since this can be a rather round-about way of getting there, however, we will describe a shorter but more complex route from Deckers: Take Highway 126 west of Deckers for three miles and turn left onto the gravel road marked for Lost Valley Ranch, Cheesman Lake, etc. Travel 1.1 miles and turn right at fork marked JVL and Lost Valley Ranch. Travel another 1.1 miles and turn right at the fork marked Wellington Lake. Two and one-half miles later you will turn right again following a sign toward Wellington Lake. Only 2.6 miles later you find the Wigwam Trail road marked on your left. This is a dirt road that gets worse as you travel the 1.4 miles to the parking area. The last section may be very poor, so explore ahead on foot before attempting it with a passenger car.

ROLLING CREEK, Forest Service #663, 9 miles one way, elevation gain 2,650 ft., loss 1,200 ft.; rated moderate to difficult. Features forest trail, then steep climb through canyon.

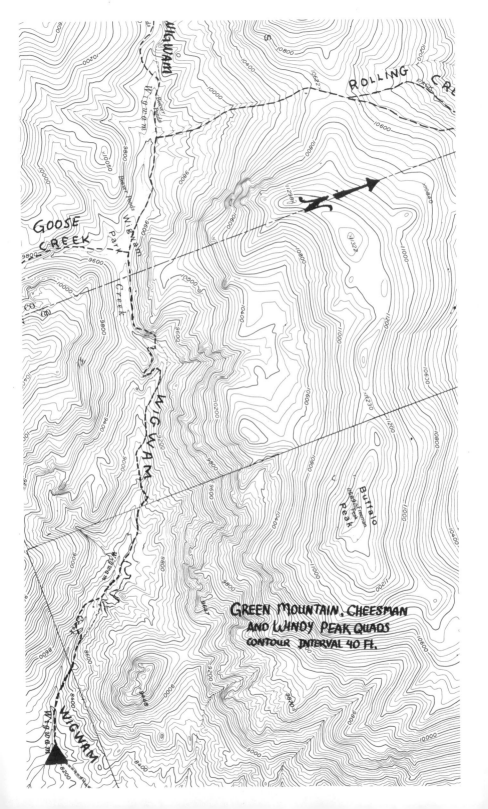

GOOSE CREEK

ROLLING CREEK

WIGWAM

Wigwam Creek

WIGWAM

Buffalo Peak

GREEN MOUNTAIN, CHEESMAN
AND WINDY PEAK QUADS
CONTOUR INTERVAL 40 Ft.

WIGWAM

This trail begins with a pleasant forest walk with no exceptionally steep parts. You cross small ridges and intermittent streams, heading toward the rock formation known as The Castle, where you cross Rolling Creek itself. At first you leave the creek and hike up into the woods to a place where the old route from Bancroft Ranch has been closed off. Turn right and climb a little farther and you return to the creek once more.

Now you begin the most beautiful part of the climb, a steep section that takes you up through a narrow canyon where boulders have tumbled together in interesting ways. The forest is cool and mossy here, a charming place. (Some brookies, but small.)

Finally, you leave the creek as you start up the ridge that separates this watershed from the Wigwam watershed beyond. Old maps show two routes here, both converging higher up, but one of the routes is entirely gone and the other is fading among rocks and roots and fallen timber. Then you go up and over the ridge and down to Wigwam Park, where a sign marks the southern intersection with Wigwam Trail. Located on USGS Windy Peak quad.

WIGWAM TRAIL, Forest Service #609, 13.3 miles one way; elevation gain 2,220 ft., loss 500 ft.: rated moderate to difficult. Features meadows and forest with fishing at creeks and beaver ponds.

Wigwam is a long and varied trail with only a few steep sections. Much of the trail skirts long valleys rich in wildlife such as grouse, beaver and deer. The DOW rates Wigwam's brook trout fishing as "good, but needs fishing" to improve size.

Beginning at the eastern trailhead, start down a washed out four-wheel track to a glade where you find Wigwam Creek and a small pond. Your trail follows Wigwam upstream, crossing and recrossing on log bridges. You pass through a rolling forest, then climb more steeply. The creek beside you forms small waterfalls.

At Wigwam Park itself, the creek meanders through a grassland, often interrupted by beaver dams. Your trail stays on the northern edge of this valley, finally coming to a sign indicating that Goose Creek Trail is to your left, across the valley. From

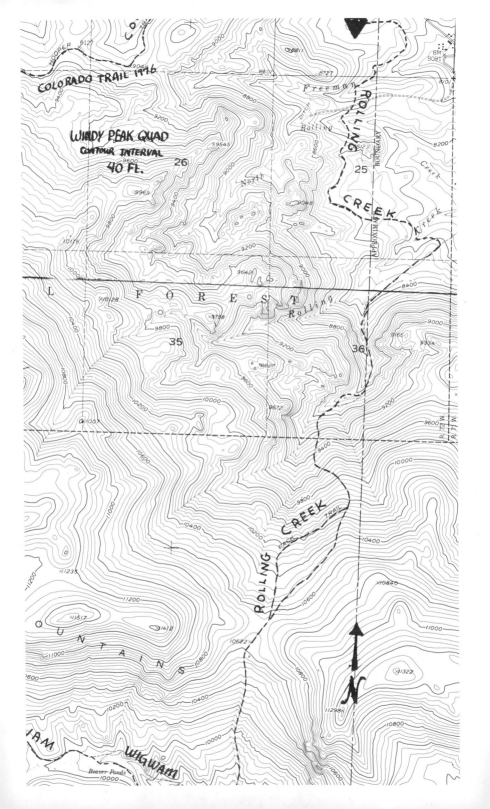

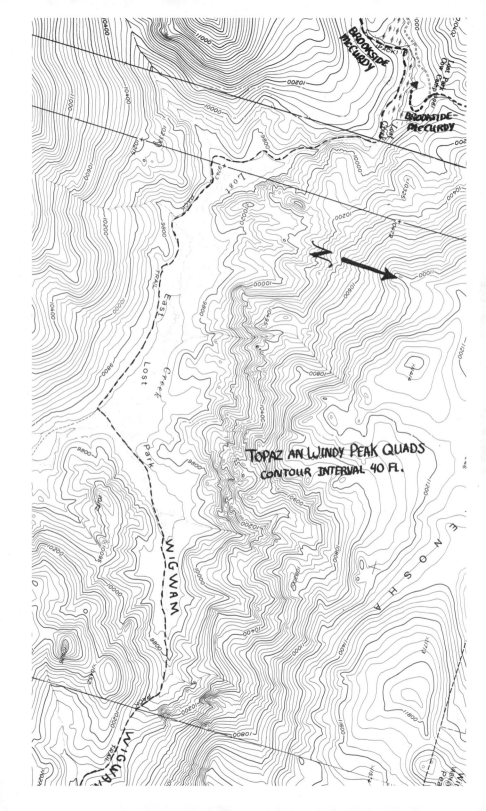

TOPAZ AN WINDY PEAK QUADS
CONTOUR INTERVAL 40 FT.

there you can see the tributary ravine that Goose Creek Trail follows, and framed within this notch is a rock formation with a thumblike projection that has a balanced rock on its tip.

The largest beaver pond marked on your old topographic maps is now a flat field of grass that makes comfortable camping. You can still see remains of the huge dam which stood about six feet tall and over 200 feet long. This kind of beaver activity built much of the flatland seen in Wigwam Park.

As you follow the valley higher, you find a sign for Rolling Creek Trail on your right. At the time of our exploration, the sign itself was about all that remained of this half of Rolling Creek Trail. The sign mentioned Wellington Lake, but Rolling Creek's trailhead is now located several miles north of Wellington Lake.

Farther up the valley, you find a place where the original trail becomes faint and where a newer trail crosses Wigwam Creek. Take the new trail, cross the creek, and follow it up through the woods to a higher park.

At the entrance of this park, your trail is covered with water from a spring that flows from beneath a huge rock. That is the clearest source of water in this park, but it still needs treatment because the pool itself may be contaminated.

The trail grows more faint as you climb up to the low saddle ridge (only 10,150 feet) that separates Wigwam from the East Lost Creek watershed. Wigwam Trail continues down into East Lost Park, across Lost Creek and along an even wider valley to end at Lost Park Campground. (See KENOSHA PASS AREA).

Wigwam is located on the USGS Cheesman Lake, Green Mountain, Windy Peak and Topaz quads.

BAILEY AREA

Payne Creek Trail (Craig Meadow)
Ben Tyler Trail
Craig Park Trail

Bailey is located beside the North Fork of the South Platte in northeastern Park County on Hwy. 285. This scenic area has few services, but it is a jumping off point for some long and lovely pack trails. Aside from the Colorado Trail 1776, Brookside-McCurdy is the longest trail in the Pike National Forest and has recently been rerouted in this area, making it even longer. Craig Park is another long trail made even longer by the fact that it has no road access and can only be reached via Brookside-McCurdy or Ben Tyler. Bikers Note: These trails lie within the Lost Creek Wilderness, where no mountain bicycles are permitted.

ROAD DIRECTIONS: Turn south off Hwy. 285 at Moore Lumber and Hardware in Bailey and follow a paved road until it curves back toward the highway. At the beginning of this curve is a gravel road that leads straight ahead. Proceed 1.5 miles on gravel to Bailey Picnic Ground, where you'll find the new trailhead serving PAYNE CREEK (CRAIG MEADOW), BROOKSIDE-McCURDY and CRAIG PARK. For directions to the southern trailhead for BROOKSIDE-McCURDY, see TARRYALL AREA. For directions to the middle, see KENOSHA PASS AREA.
The trailhead for BEN TYLER is located on Hwy. 285, 6.4 miles west of Bailey. Parking for about half a dozen vehicles is on the north side of the highway, and the trailhead is on the south side.

PAYNE CREEK TRAIL (CRAIG MEADOW), Forest Service #637, about 6 miles one way; elevation gain 1,030 ft., loss 1,200 ft. Rated moderate. Features scenic meadow with beaver ponds and good fishing.

Craig Meadow is a grassy park with beaver ponds, a great place to catch brookies up to eight inches long. The trail leading there is called Payne Creek, but it does not really follow Payne

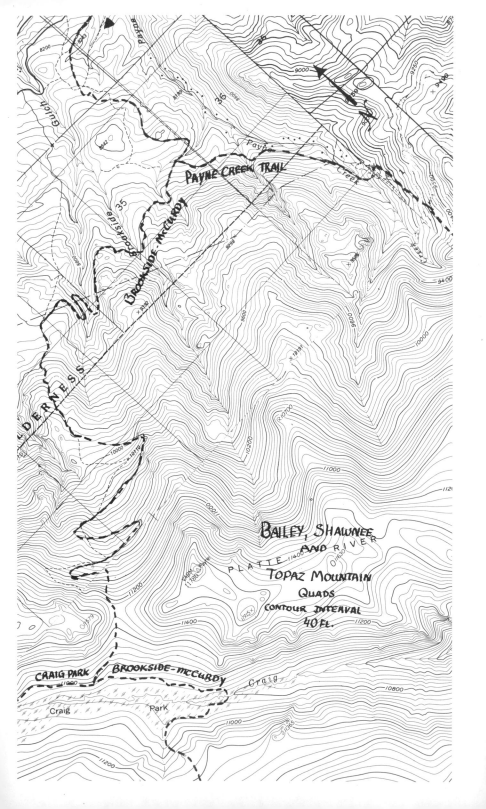

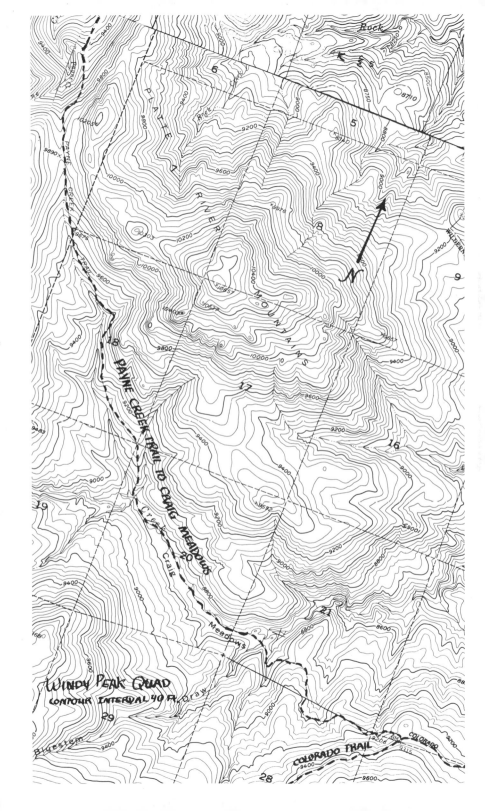

WINDY PEAK QUAD
CONTOUR INTERVAL 40 FT.

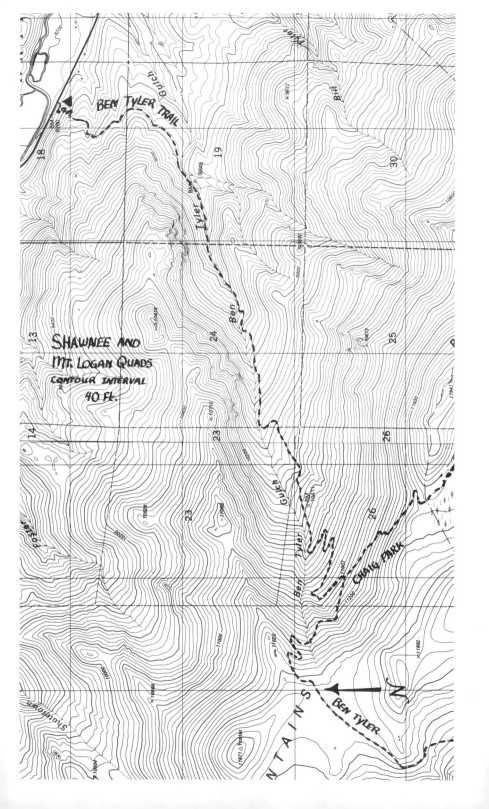

Creek very far. But at least this name helps keep it from being confused with Craig Park Trail.

Starting at the new trailhead, you climb the ridge between Brookside Gulch and Payne Creek, going up through the woods to the T-junction where Brookside-McCurdy heads west and Payne Creek Trail heads southwest along the ridge above Payne Creek. Eventually, it picks up a tributary of Craig Creek and follows that down to the meadow. Your trail makes a bog crossing at Craig Creek and follows the stream where the beavers are at work. Large blue spruce grow widely spaced in the meadow.

Beyond the meadow, the trail crosses Bluestem Creek and then you will find an old road known as Pine Ridge joining the trail from the right. This is now closed to vehicles.

From here you begin climbing a trail uphill through the trees to join Colorado Trail #1776 two miles from the meadow. This is where Payne Creek Trail ends.

One warning: there is no trail between Craig Meadow and Craig Park upstream because this creek plunges through a rock gorge where hikers have become lost and injured. Payne Creek Trail is located on the USGS Shawnee and Windy Peak quads.

BEN TYLER TRAIL, Forest Service #606, 9 miles one way, elevation gain 3,460 ft., loss 2,040 ft., rated moderate to difficult. Features streamside and high mountain hiking.

The way we heard it, Ben Tyler lived with is family near the mouth of the gulch that bears his name and there he had a lumber operation in the early days. He sawed up timber and shipped it by rail to mining towns. As you hike this spectacular trail, you can thank Ben for showing the way.

Starting at Hwy. 285, climb a series of switchbacks, go through a gate that keeps cattle in, and then head down a path on a grassy hillside that overlooks Ben Tyler Creek. Your trail follows this creek up through the woods, crosses it and continues to follow it past ancient beaver doings toward the place where loggers' cabins used to be. Only the foundation and some trash remain now. They are located on the west side of the creek.

Your trail continues up the east side, leaves the water and then

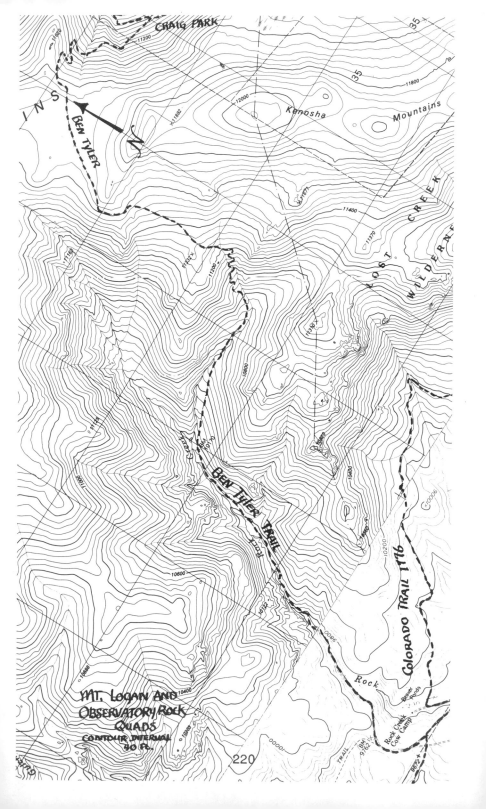

CRAIG PARK

Kenosha Mountains

Ben Tyler

N

LOST CREEK WILDERNESS

Ben Tyler Trail

Rock Creek

COLORADO TRAIL 1776

Rock

Rock Creek Cow Camp

MT. LOGAN AND
OBSERVATORY ROCK
QUADS
CONTOUR INTERVAL
40 FT.

220

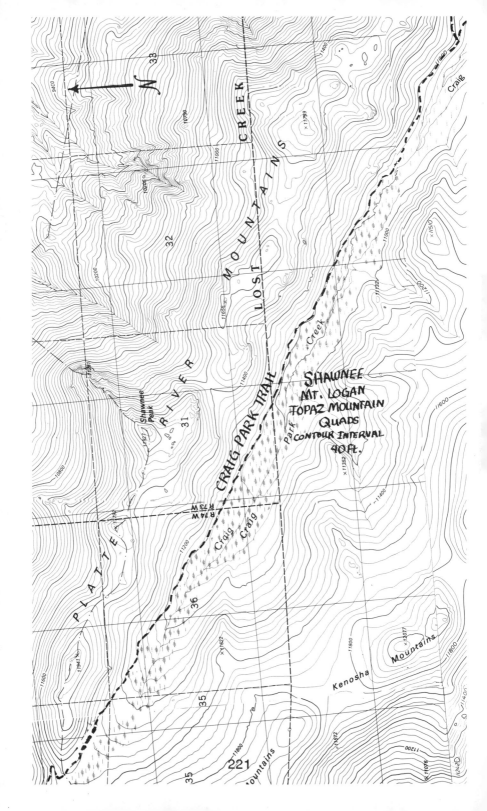

N

33

CREEK

× 11,759

Craig

LOST

MOUNTAINS

32

RIVER

Shawnee
Peak

31

Creek

SHAWNEE
MT. LOGAN
TOPAZ MOUNTAIN
QUADS
CONTOUR INTERVAL
40 FT.

CRAIG PARK TRAIL

Park

× 11,352

R.7.W. R.7.W.

Craig Craig

36

× 11,623

35

PLATTE

× 11,941

× 2,007

Mountains

Kenosha

× 11,672

221

35

Mountains

begins rising very steeply. A short side path returns to the creek higher up, and from there you have a view of the gulch laid out below. The hillsides are practically nothing but aspens, a golden vista in late September. Brook trout fishing along the creek is rated above average by the Division of Wildlife.

Now your path becomes a little less distinct (and less popular) because it switchbacks up past its junction with Craig Park Trail and on up to a high ridge. Then it angles down the other side, where you'll find an outstanding view of distant mountain ranges. Heading down, your trail joins Rock Creek and follows that down to a road access off East Lost Park Road (see KENOSHA PASS AREA). Ben Tyler is located on USGS Shawnee, Mt. Logan and Observatory Rock quads.

CRAIG PARK TRAIL, Forest Service #608, 7 miles one way; elevation gain 660 ft., loss 630 ft., rated moderately easy. Features mountain hiking and timberline scenery with brook trout fishing

Few trails in our area are so little traveled as this one. That's because Craig Park has no road access of its own. To reach it, you must hike to it from Ben Tyler or Brookside-McCurdy, which adds many miles to the trail length given above.

But once you get there, you find a long grassy meadow area surrounded by wooded hills and rock outcroppings. The lower part of the trail is very easy going and is interrupted only by several bogs that you must get around. The only steep section is at the west end where the trail climbs up above the headwaters of Craig Creek to a high ridge, where it joins Ben Tyler.

Craig Park is normally explored as part of a long excursion, but if your purpose is to reach Craig Park itself, the most popular route seems to be from the north end of Brookside-McCurdy, a distance of 5.5 miles. Brook trout fishing is rated excellent.

Notice that no trail links Craig Park with Craig Meadow downstream. That is because Craig Creek plunges through a steep gorge where hikers have become lost and injured. Craig Park Trail is located on USGS Mt. Logan, Shawnee and Topaz quads.

DEER CREEK AREA

Meridian Trail
Rosalie Trail
Tanglewood Trail

In the northeast corner of Park County, on Highway 285 between Pine Junction and Bailey, you find a prominent turnoff marked Deer Creek. This leads to some wonderful trails, but our directions are going to sound strange because Meridian does not begin at Meridian Campground and Rosalie does not begin at Rosalie Campground. Follow this paved road 6.5 miles west to a fork. The right fork, marked "Camp Rosalie," leads to Meridian trailhead. The left fork, marked "Deer Creek Campground," leads to the Rosalie-Tanglewood trailhead. Sounds backwards, but that's the way it is.

Bikers Note: These trails lie within the Mount Evans Wilderness, where mountain bicycles are prohibited.

ROAD DIRECTIONS: To find MERIDIAN follow the cross-markers toward Camp Rosalie. Soon the pavement ends and you are following a gravel road that leads to a gate with a National Forest sign. Instead of entering here, turn right on another good gravel road and follow it around to an intersection marked by a sign saying "Elk Creek Highlands." Turn left here and right at the next T-junction. From here on, the road is dirt but passable. You cross a stream with a pond on the right and drive around the edge of Camp Rosalie. At the Y marked Church Fork, turn right and soon you will spot a small bridge over the stream on your right and a horse corral on the left. Park here. Forest Service maps show the road dead-ending here, but it does continue for quite a ways, so watch for the trailhead signs.

For ROSALIE-TANGLEWOOD take the left fork on Deer Creek Road marked "Deer Creek Campground". The pavement ends a mile later and the road becomes gravel. Then you come to a Y with the Deer Creek Campground on the left. The right fork may not be marked, but dead-ends shortly at the Rosalie-Tanglewood trailhead. The last half mile of the road is very rocky and rough but passable for passenger

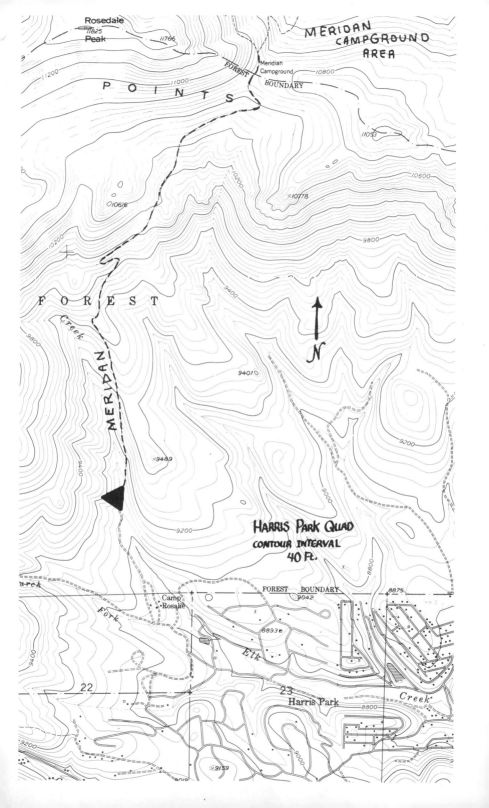

cars. Only one path leaves the parking area: Rosalie and Tanglewood divide several hundred yards higher up.

MERIDIAN, Forest Service #604, 3 miles one way, elevation gain 1,600 ft., rated moderate. Features forest climb to campground where other trails connect.

Meridian connects to a larger system of trails in Arapahoe National Forest. It is a very clear and well-marked trail, but there is one point of confusion: It does not leave Meridian Campground, but it arrives at a place that is called Meridian Trail Campground.

Since the other two trails in the Deer Creek area carry warnings about safety for horses, it would be well to point out that Meridian is a good trail for inexperienced trailhorses. It begins on a gentle gravel path, growing rocky only at the top.

From the trailhead bridge, the path climbs a long ridge high above Elk Creek. There are no real creeks along this route, but small springs that cross the path higher up provide water. As you angle northeast, you hike through a grove of aspen that are unusually tall and straight.

At the top there is a small spring, an outhouse, and a pair of signs on the northern edge of the saddle. The sign pointing northwest says "Lost Creek 4, Truesdell Creek 6, Beartrack Lakes 7," and the one pointing northeast says "Lost Creek 6, Indian Creek Park 7, Brook Forest 12," so get a good rest. These trails are not in our area, and Lost Creek does not refer to the wilderness area in the Pike National Forest.

Meridian is located on the USGS Harris Park quad.

ROSALIE, Forest Service #603, 12 miles one way; elevation gain 3,560 ft., loss 1,120 ft.; rated difficult. Features high altitude trek to Guanella Pass.

Rosalie is a long and rough trail that twice climbs to timberline, yet even at its highest points you find yourself surrounded by bald giants, including Mount Evans. Our description begins at the bottom because the lower section is the most popular.

Trailriders will find convenient corrals at the parking area, but

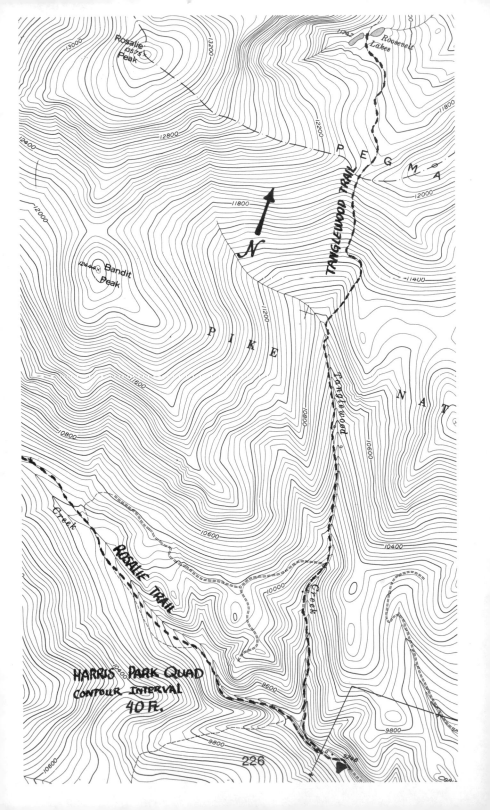

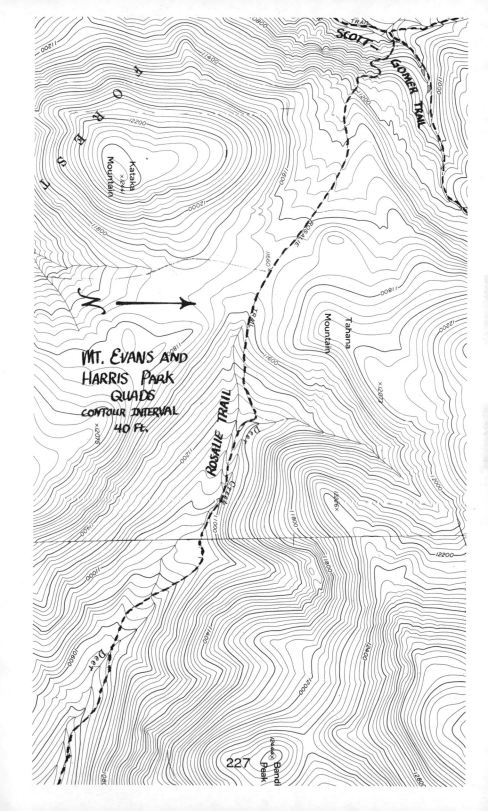

MT. EVANS AND
HARRIS PARK
QUADS
CONTOUR INTERVAL
40 Ft.

Kataka
Mountain

Tahana
Mountain

ROSALIE TRAIL

SCOTT GOMER TRAIL

Deer

Bandit
Peak

227

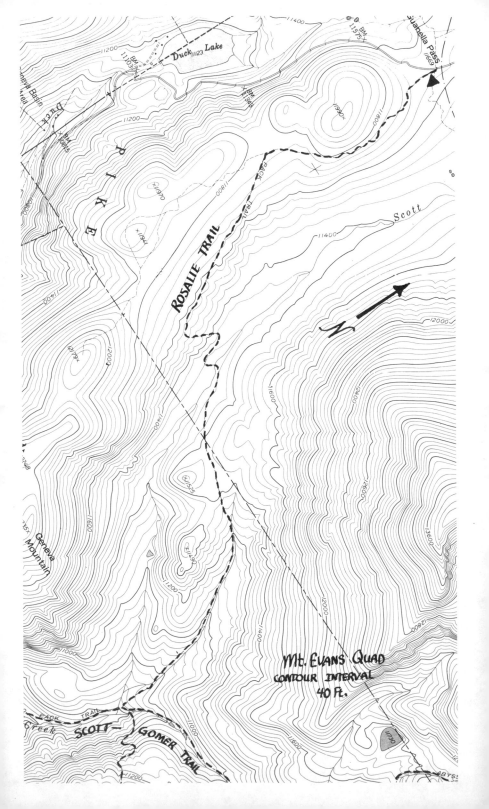

Rosalie is so rocky and rugged that it can only be recommended for the most experienced trailhorses. This is not a good training ground for inexperienced mounts. About a hundred yards from the trailhead, the Rosalie-Tanglewood path splits and Rosalie takes the high road to the left that climbs along and across Deer Creek. This path snakes up through forest and clearings where grouse, deer and beaver are often seen. There are campsites all along the route.

As you can see by the map, you take the left or southern fork at the headwaters of Deer Creek, but since the right fork is by far the larger stream, the left may appear as only a minor tributary or marshy ravine in late summer. The right fork swerves hard to the north at this point, so a compass can help make sure that you have found the right place. The trail grows more indistinct in this area.

Keep heading west up the green ravine. You are headed for a bald saddle ridge between two bald peaks known as Tahana on the north and Kataka on the south. At the top of the saddle there is another road-like trail coming from Kataka Mountain and joining your own. This is the destination of Threemile Creek Trail.

The ridge saddle is that kind of timberline margin where trees grow only in scattered spots, all stunted and windswept. To the north you can see Mount Evans with its building on top and cars going up the switchbacks. Due west is Geneva Mountain, and to its right you see two green ravines where streams angle down to join Scott-Gomer Creek, which runs north-south below you at this point. Rosalie will follow that wide ravine on the right up to tim berline and then beyond to Guanella Pass.

A wooden post marks the place where your faint path starts switchbacking down the mountainside to cross Scott-Gomer. This narrow path angles down through a ghost forest created by a fire long ago. At the bottom you cross Scott-Gomer, then link with Scott-Gomer Trail to Abyss Lake in the manner shown on the map. This creek area is a popular campground, but has no fish. A Forest Service shelter that used to serve Rosalie higher up is now gone.

Now your trail begins to make up the altitude lost in descending to Scott-Gomer. It's a long and steady climb to timberline and above, eventually intersecting a path that used to be a road. A post marks this intersection so that explorers coming downhill won't miss Rosalie and wind up going south along the wrong route. This closed road leads to a dead-end on the shoulder of Geneva Mountain at 12,179 feet.

Rosalie itself climbs to 11,800 feet before winding down to the trailhead at Guanella Pass. To find the upper trailhead by road, see Guanella Pass Area. Rosalie is located on the USGS Harris Park and Mount Evans quad.

TANGLEWOOD, Forest Service #636, 5 miles one way; elevation gain 2,680 ft., loss 160 ft., rated difficult. Features charming streamside hike, rugged climb above timberline to lakes.

If you want to fish Roosevelt Lakes, you'll certainly have to earn the opportunity, for Tanglewood is a high and rocky route. The lower section is gentle and popular among dayhikers, but the higher you go, the rougher it gets.

There are convenient horse corrals at the trailhead and along Tanglewood itself, but trailriders are warned that it is not suitable for training horses unaccustomed to climbing in the rocks. (Meridian Trail would be better.)

As you leave the trailhead, Tanglewood shares its route with Rosalie, but the two soon divide. You take the right fork, cross the creek on a culvert bridge, then follow up along a path that used to be a road. You cross and recross this tumbling creek, climbing through forest and small clearings. High up, the trail leaves the creek and climbs up above timberline. Here the trail fades in the rocks, so head toward a wooden post erected on the ridge saddle. There's not much of a trail there, either, but this marks the place where you're supposed to cross over.

From here you have a spectacular view and can see for miles, but oddly enough, you cannot see Roosevelt Lakes which lie directly below. The lakes are in the bottom of a glacial depression, and you must hike some distance on this gentle incline before you see them. The DOW stocks them with cutthroat trout by air.

A trail from Beartrack Lakes connects with Tanglewood at Roosevelt Lakes, but that's out of our area.

GUANELLA PASS AREA

Threemile Trail
Burning Bear
Scott-Gomer Trail To Abyss Lake
Shelf Lake
South Park

For those coming from I-70 at Georgetown, Guanella Pass is a gateway to the Pike National Forest and its Mount Evans Wilderness. It is best known for Geneva Basin Ski Area, but six major Pike National Forest trailheads are also located along this pass. At its foot on the southern side lies the small town of Grant, 10.5 miles west of Bailey on Hwy. 285, and Grant is the best place to set our odometer and begin our road directions. Bikers Note: These trails lie within the Mount Evans Wilderness, where no mountain bicycles are permitted.

ROAD DIRECTIONS: The trailhead for THREEMILE is exactly three miles up this road from Grant. Watch for it on your right. Drive another 2.1 miles and you find BURNING BEAR on you left. SCOTT-GOMER is located on your right only 0.2 mile farther. Drive another 1.9 miles and watch for a pair of gravel roads that cut away to the left. Take the second of those two roads and travel 3.2 miles to SHELF LAKE trailhead, which is on your right.
Going higher on the Guanella Pass road, you find a pair of trailheads at the very top. SOUTH PARK strikes out to the west and ROSALIE heads east. For a description of ROSALIE, see DEER CREEK AREA.

THREEMILE CREEK, Forest Service #635, 6 miles one way; elevation gain 2,600 ft., loss 200 ft., rated moderate. Features streamside link to timberline and intersection with Rosalie.

Threemile Creek Trail is six miles long, and even Threemile Creek is longer than three miles. It just happens to be the creek you find three miles up from Highway 285.

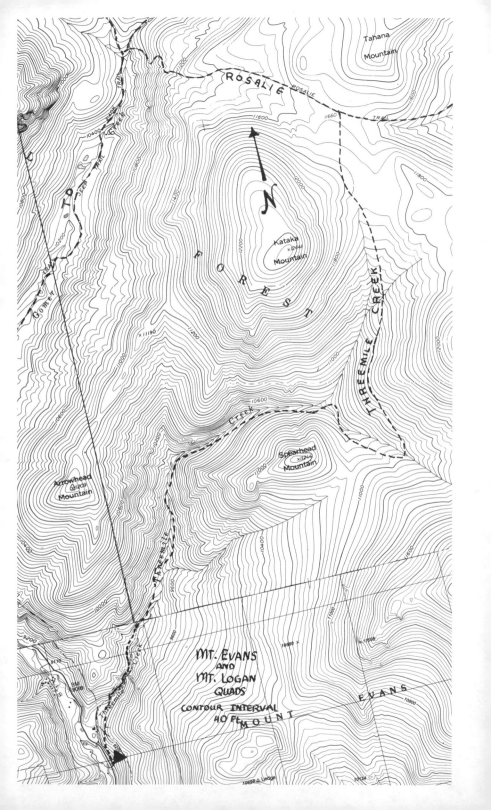

This trail is a popular link to the very middle of two other long trails, Rosalie and Scott-Gomer Trail to Abyss Lake, making the whole system more complex. As the path leaves the parking lot, it climbs steadily to avoid private property where Threemile Creek crosses the road. The creek is somewhat hidden from view and your trail won't find it for half a mile.

Then you join and cross the creek and begin weaving up it as it passes through small grassy areas and cool forest with rock formations on either side. It's a steady and somewhat rocky climb. The brook trout fishing is rated above average on this section of the creek. Steeper sections high up are not as good.

After passing Spearhead Mountain, the main creek and trail swing sharply to the east and grow steeper. The path turns again at a fork of tributaries, following the northern one up to timberline. Here your trail looks like a fading road as it skirts Kataka Mountain to find the saddle between Kataka and Tahana Mountains.

There on the saddle, Threemile Trail ends at a junction with Rosalie. The altitude is 11,660 and you may have to look for a wooden post to make sure you've found Rosalie. The Forest Service shelter that used to be located on Rosalie Trail past its intersection with Scott-Gomer is now gone. (For a description of Rosalie, see DEER CREEK AREA.) Threemile is located on the USGS Mt. Logan and Mt. Evans quads.

BURNING BEAR, Forest Service #601, 5 miles one way; elevation gain 1,160 ft., loss 1,120 ft. Features popular stroll beside valley and through forest, excellent for cross-country skiing.

This is a good trail for easy strolling or cross-country skiing because it is very gentle for a long way. The trailhead is located beside Geneva Creek on the road to Geneva Ski Basin, so skiers should always find the road open, though parking may be limited by snowbanks. Here, Geneva Creek winds through a long valley where cattle graze. Enter the fence near the stream and follow Geneva upstream to a wooden bridge. The DOW considers brook trout fishing here about average, owing to overpopulation.

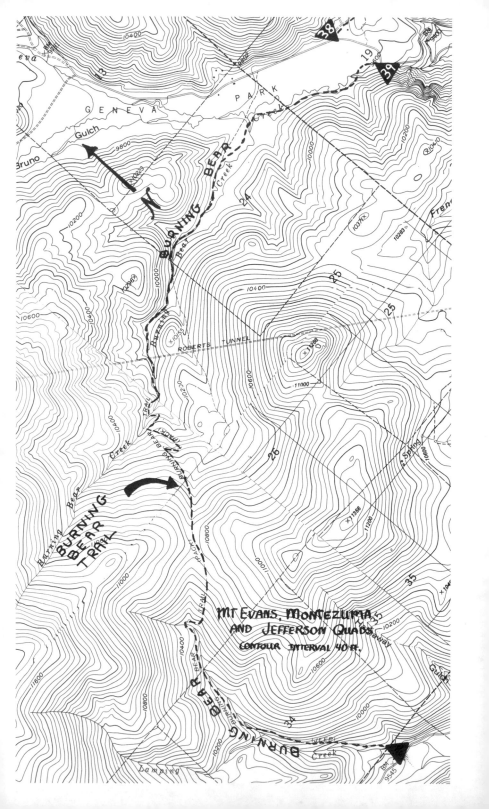

After crossing the bridge, continue upstream on a trail that stays just inside the trees. This area is used for judging snowpack depth, so please stay on the trail when snow is on the ground.

Eventually your trail turns up the tributary that flows from Burning Bear Gulch, a stream too small for fishing. Even here the trail is fairly gentle as it climbs slowly through the forest. You pass the remains of a log cabin, and finally cross to the south (or left) side of the stream, where you find a mild set of switchbacks that lead up and over a wooded ridge into another watershed.

From here it is downhill all the way. You follow a tributary to Lamping Creek, then down Lamping Creek itself to a rough gravel road. This is Park County 60, which joins Hwy. 285 at Webster, about 14 miles west of Bailey.

Burning Bear is located on the USGS Jefferson, Montezuma and Mt. Evans quads.

SCOTT-GOMER TRAIL TO ABYSS LAKE, Forest Service #602, 8 miles one-way; elevation gain 3,050 ft. Features high mountain fishing lakes and link to other long trails.

First of all, we have to warn you about the apparent shortcut shown on many maps. You can actually see Abyss Lake from one of the switchbacks on the side of Mount Evans, but in order to reach the lake from there, you would have to scramble down a rockslide area for a long way. This is very dangerous because the rocks are loose and you may easily start a slide toward one of your companions below, or you may be struck by rocks dislodged (or thrown) by visitors on the overlook above. This route appears on official maps, but is closed.

So our description will begin at the main trailhead on the Guanella Pass road. You climb up through the forest on a trail that resembles an old road. The forest is very young and you don't find the creek for quite a ways.

When you do, you may be surprised at how little you see of Scott-Gomer Creek for the trail gives only a glimpse of it through the brush and only crosses in two places. After the first stream crossing, the real scenery begins with high mountains crowning the trees ahead.

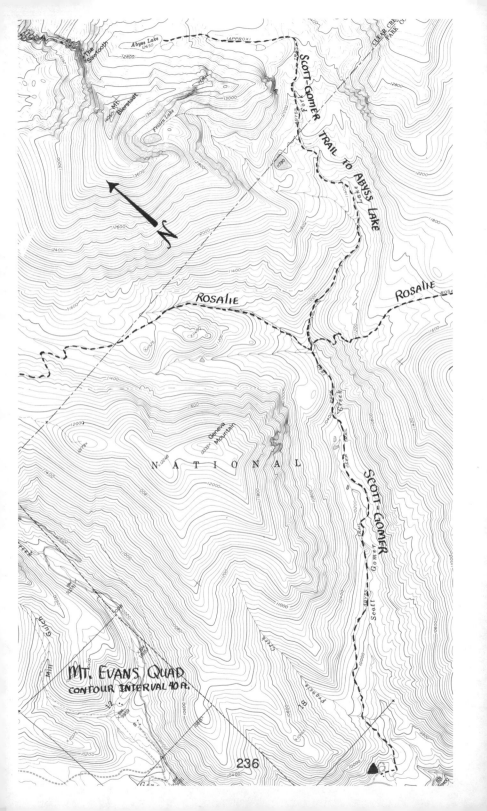

Abyss Lake
12650

The
Sawtooth

Mt.
Bierstadt

Frozen Lake

SCOTT-GOMER TRAIL TO ABYSS LAKE

ROSALIE

ROSALIE

N

NATIONAL

Geneva Mountain

Scott Trail

Gomer Creek

SCOTT-GOMER

MT. EVANS QUAD
CONTOUR INTERVAL 40 Ft.

236

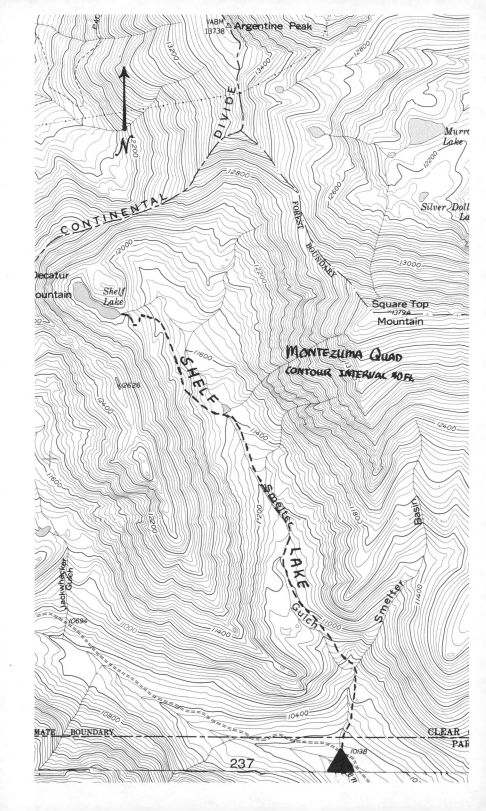

VABM 13738 △ Argentine Peak

DIVIDE

CONTINENTAL

N

Murr Lake

Silver Doll La

13200

13400

12800

12800

12600

12200

12200

13000

12000

12200

12200

Decatur Mountain

Shelf Lake

Square Top Mountain
13794

MONTEZUMA QUAD
CONTOUR INTERVAL 40 Ft.

FOREST BOUNDARY

11600

12626

12400

11400

11600

12200

12400

SHELF

Shelf Lake Gulch

LAKE Gulch

11200

11800

12400

11800

Basin

Smelter

11400

11600

Jackwhacker Gulch

10694

11000

11400

11000

10000

11400

10800

10400

MATE BOUNDARY

237

10138

CLEAR PAR

10

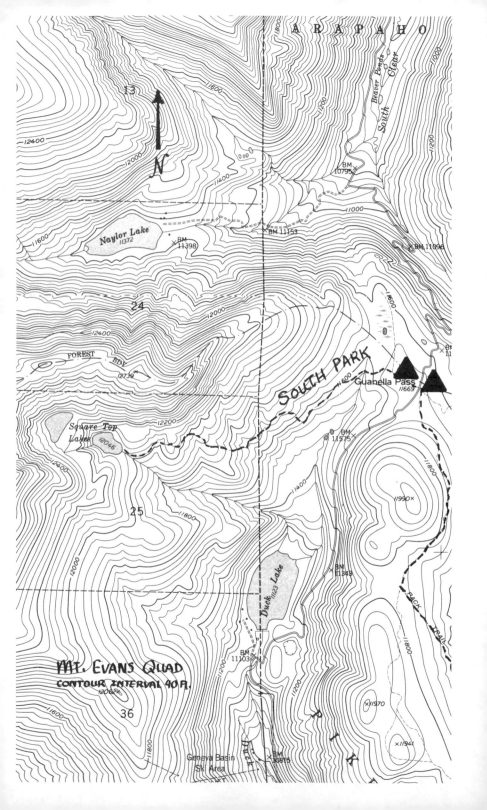

This is a wide stream often used by fly fishermen who wade up its middle, but DOW researchers discovered an amazing problem--no fish. The place is so beautiful, so full of other wildlife, that no one ever guessed it could have an environmental problem. There are a few fish near the bottom, where tributaries dilute higher water, but there are no fish higher up because of heavy metals naturally occurring in the geology. This is not a man-made problem, and the levels are quite low, but trout are especially sensitive and have a hard time during the winter, when there is no runoff to dilute the problem.

After the second crossing, you begin climbing an old road again through aspen. You arrive at a place where tributaries join the creek from the left. An unmarked trail leads up the first tributary, and Rosalie Trail leads up the second toward a Forest Service shelter that is open on a first-come basis.

Your trail stays to the left of the main creek, climbing in the trees to avoid bogs in the grassy areas above. There were fresh bear tracks in this area at the time of our visit. The higher you go, the more faint the trail becomes, yet the ground is very open at this altitude and is surrounded by high landmarks such as Mount Evans ahead.

There is no trail at all once you are near either Frozen Lake or Abyss Lake. Simply follow their drainage. Abyss Lake is stocked with rainbow trout by air, and Frozen Lake is stocked with Pikes Peak native cutthroat. Scott-Gomer is located on the USGS Mt. Evans quad.

SHELF LAKE, Forest Service #634, 3.5 miles one way; elevation gain 1,880 ft. Features high fishing lake.

The State of Colorado uses airplanes to stock this lake with native cutthroat trout, but the only way you can get there is by climbing a very steep and rocky trail to the 12,000 foot level. The trail begins next to a large heap of smelter's slag that looks like coal, and it climbs through aspens, heading up Smelter Gulch. Some of the toughest going is in the first half mile.

Your trail becomes a little less rugged as you hike a meadow area there, but most of your trail stays just inside the trees.

Finally you cross the creek near some beaver workings. All the fishing is above at the lake; the creek is poor, and the large pond shown on topo maps has become a marsh. Follow the water as it curves to the left above timberline and find the big green bowl known as Smelter Basin. Here the trail becomes faint, but to your left the main stream tumbles down a steep ridge. Shelf Lake is up above that ridge, surrounded by tundra and vistas, so get ready for some steep climbing.

If you sit quietly near the shore, pika may come out and feed on the grass. These high altitude members of the rabbit family look something like guinea pigs with round ears. They store grass by making little haystacks under the protection of rocks. There are quite a few at Shelf Lake.

Shelf Lake is located on the USGS Montezuma quad.

SOUTH PARK TRAIL TO SQUARE TOP LAKES, Forest Service #600, 2 miles one-way; elevation gain 375 ft. Features tundra trek to high fishing lakes.

South Park Trail is very old and used to be about 26 miles long, but after decades of neglect, only the top two miles exist in slow-growing tundra. Actually you are following the ruts made by trucks that were once used to stock the lakes with fish. The DOW has used airplanes now for years to stock the lakes with native cut-throat trout, but ruts made on tundra last a long time.

The trailhead is located at the very top of Guanella Pass, well above timberline. Park on the west side of the road and proceed west downhill to the boggy region that feeds Duck Lake below. Duck Lake is private property and can be seen from the road.

After crossing the boggy stream, you climb again and incline to the left. It's a strange hike, in that you can go for a long ways and still look back to see your car. At last you climb up to the far pocket where the lower lake hides. A small glacier on the far side feeds the lake, and the water is deepest over there. The other lake is located just above.

The altitude of the lower lake is 12,046 feet, so take it easy. Please stay on the trail to avoid damaging delicate tundra. Located on the USGS Mt. Evans quad.

KENOSHA PASS AREA

Gibson Lake Trail
Jefferson Lake Trail
West Jefferson Creek Trail
Wilderness On Wheels Model
Mountain Access Facility

Closer to Denver than to Colorado Springs, Kenosha Pass sees a lot of visitors, especially now that Colorado Trail 1776 crosses Hwy. 285 at the top of the pass. This gentle place is especially beautiful when the aspens are in their glory, for Kenosha Pass is covered with them.

ROAD DIRECTIONS: The turnoff toward GIBSON LAKE and the lower trailhead for BURNING BEAR is located 13.7 miles west of Bailey on Highway 285 and is called Park County 62. Signs warn that the road is not suitable for passenger cars, but passenger cars can reach BURNING BEAR trailhead, which is almost three miles from the highway, where Lamping Creek crosses the road. The creek is small and hidden by trees, so watch the lay of the land to predict where it will cross. Park to the right just after passing a house. There is only enough room for one or two vehicles, and the only sign marking the trail is located on a fence gate well back from the road. The road grows worse as you travel toward GIBSON LAKE trailhead, which is located 6.4 miles from the highway, just past Hall Valley Campground.
The turnoff for JEFFERSON LAKE is located at Jefferson on Highway 285 and is well marked all the way. The road is good. Distance: 8 miles. On the way, you'll pass Lodgepole and Jefferson Campgrounds, trailheads for WEST JEFFERSON CREEK TRAIL. Park outside the Jefferson Campground.
Slightly more than a mile north of Jefferson is a turnoff for Lost Park Road. Travel southeast for 7.3 miles and you will see a turnoff to BEN TYLER'S southern trailhead, which is also an approach to CRAIG PARK TRAIL #608, and COLORADO TRAIL 1776. The Lost Park Campground, with its western trailhead for WIGWAM and access to the center of BROOKSIDE-MCCURDY, is located 19.1 miles from Hwy. 285. Horse trailers often park along the road near the campground.

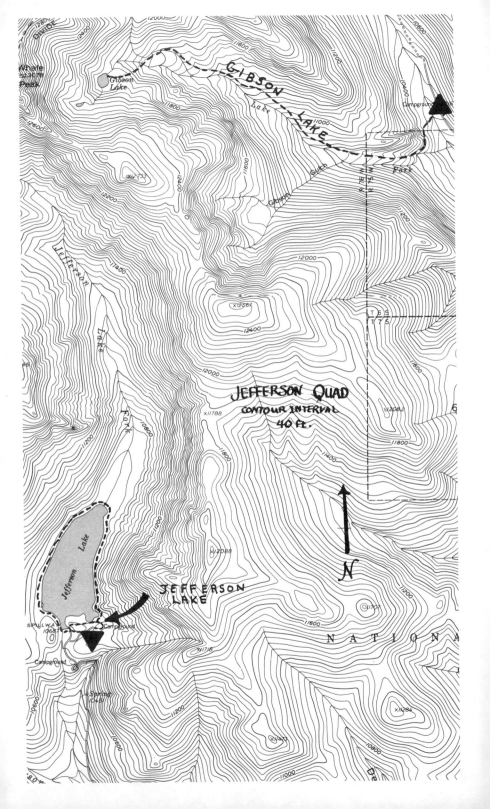

To find the WILDERNESS ON WHEELS MODEL MOUNTAIN ACCESS FACILITY from Denver, take Hwy. 285 south for 60 miles. The W.O.W. facility is on your left 3.8 miles west of Grant. From Colorado Springs, take Hwy. 24 west to Woodland Park, then 67 to Deckers, 126 to Pine Junction, then Hwy. 285 past Bailey and Grant.

GIBSON LAKE, Forest Service #633, 2.5 miles one way; elevation gain 1,760 ft., rated difficult. Features alpine fishing lake.

This may seem like one of the longest 2.5 mile hikes in our area because Gibson Lake Trail is a constant climb over rocky ground at high altitude. The actual length of this trail depends on the kind of vehicle you bring. If you have a passenger car, you won't be able to get near the actual trailhead, so you'll have to walk extra miles. If you drive a vehicle with high ground clearance, you may be able to drive to the trailhead.

Oddly enough, this primitive track leads to a rather elaborate trailhead with good parking, notice board, outhouses, picnic tables and a loading chute for horses. You cross the North Fork of the South Platte on a fine wooden bridge, and there the improvements end. You're in backcountry once more.

The trail itself is wide and rocky, a ghost of an old mining road. It follows the Lake Fork closely so you have frequent glimpses of the noisy waterfalls and fast water. Indeed, the water is fast enough to discourage fish in the creek.

Follow this water up above timberline toward a pocket at the base of granite walls. The trail grows more faint above timberline, but stacked rocks mark the way. The creek splits up at this high level, but you curve to the left. You cannot see the lake until you are very close.

On the day of our exploration, a mountain lion scampered away from a ledge overlooking the lake, and this is one of the few places where we have seen beaver activity above timberline. This is unusual because beaver literally eat trees, but at Gibson Lake they eat shrubs and use marsh willow and mud to dam the water coming from a tiny lake located above Gibson Lake.

Gibson Lake has a self-sustaining brook trout population. If you've never seen a really good-sized brook trout, this is the place. Located on the USGS Jefferson quad.

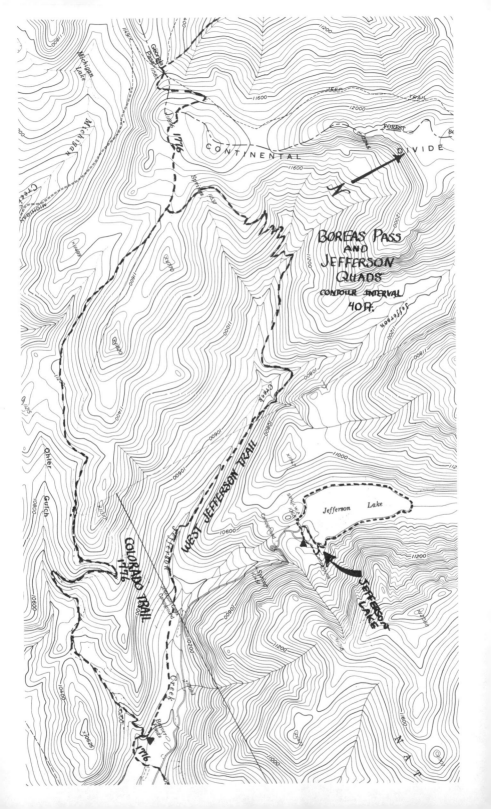

JEFFERSON LAKE, Forest Service #642, 1.5 miles in loop trail; elevation gain 40 ft. Features access to shores of stocked fishing lake.

The State of Colorado stocks Jefferson Lake with rainbow and lake trout and the road extends all the way to the lake, so this is a very popular spot with picnic tables and restrooms and quite a bit of parking. Because of this heavy use, no camping is allowed near the lake itself, but you will pass auto campgrounds on the way to the lake.

This lake is surrounded by scenic mountains, and the only way to see this scenery from every angle is to hike the 1.5 mile trail that circles the lake. A stream and a smaller brook enter the lake on the far side. The trail is best on the eastern shore and makes a nice stroll for persons who do not ordinarily hike.

We cannot exclude Jefferson Lake because of mere popularity, but this area is already considered over-used by the Forest Service and cannot be recommended as a place to "get away from it all."

The lake is open to boating and to ice fishing, but the special limit of one lake trout over 20" is being strictly enforced because some anglers may be spoiling reproduction by taking smaller lakers, perhaps confusing them with other trout. Watch for the deeply notched tail fin that characterizes the laker.

Jefferson Lake is located on the USGS Jefferson quad.

WEST JEFFERSON TRAIL, Forest Service #643, about five miles one way, elevation gain 1,640 ft., rated moderate. Features fishing access to West Jefferson Creek and forms loop with Colorado Trail 1776.

The Forest Service does not consider this trail suitable for horses or mountain bicycles because of a tough stream crossing and stepping stones across high boggy ground, but its easy grades make it a great hike. Sometimes called the Jefferson Creek Loop Trail, it can be used to form a loop with Colorado Trail 1776.

You may start at either the Lodgepole or Jefferson Campgrounds, which are both pay campgrounds, but there is a free parking lot just outside of Jefferson Campground. When hiked as a loop, people often start up the Colorado Trail from where it crosses the Jefferson Lake Road just south of Beaver Ponds Picnic Ground (no place to park there). Go 5.3 miles northwest on the CT and look for West Jefferson Creek Trail when you reach timberline. It takes off through the tundra to your right (northeast), descending into a bowl below the Continental Divide. Snow drifts beside the trail often last until mid-summer here, so it is best to explore this trail later in the season. There are stepping stones across the soggy ground formed by the drifts, so this is not an appropriate area for mountain bikes.

Then your trail enters the trees 0.6 miles after leaving the CT and makes at least 14 switchbacks down to the headwaters of Jefferson Creek. Now you travel southeast for several miles, staying just above the marshy creek bottom. Jefferson Creek and its beaver ponds have a lot of brook trout, and there are primitive campsites along some of its tributaries. Finally you cross the creek and continue down an old road to the Jefferson Creek Campground.

Located on the USGS Jefferson and Boreas Pass quads.

WILDERNESS ON WHEELS
MODEL MOUNTAIN ACCESS FACILITY

Working with a special permit from the Pike National Forest, the Wilderness on Wheels Foundation has built a model disabled-accessible facility near Kenosha Pass. This area features a boardwalk that meanders through one of Colorado's lush forests. It offers both stream and pond fishing and accessible sites for camping out.

W.O.W. BOARDWALK TRAIL, eventually 7 miles, elevation gain eventually 3,300 ft., rated very easy at streamside, easy climbing mountain. (Rise ratio: 1 ft. up for 12 ft. out.)

Under continuing volunteer construction, this boardwalk is eight feet wide and is planned to reach the summit of North Twin Cone Peak (12,300 ft.). There are level rest areas every 50 to 80 feet and picnic sites along the way. With one mile complete in 1991, the elevation gain on the first mile is 200 feet.

The trail begins in an area featuring elevated tent decks, fire rings, boardwalks built around trees and wheelchair accessible restrooms. It follows Kenosha Creek for 1,000 feet of accessible brook-trout fishing. The Colorado Division of Wildlife stocks an adjacent pond with catchable size rainbow trout. No dogs are allowed. As in any wilderness environment, trash must be packed out. Potable water is available. The facility is open from mid April through mid October. There is no fee, but donations are requested. For reservations call 303-988-2212.

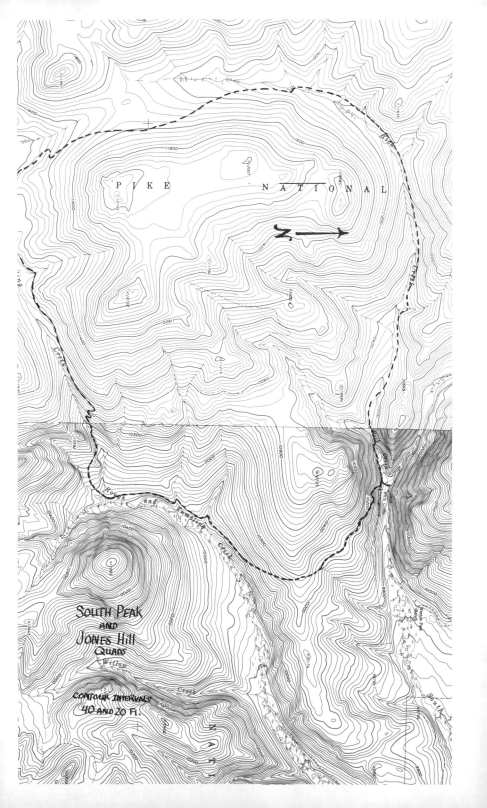

BUFFALO PEAKS WILDERNESS STUDY AREA

Rich Creek Trail
Tumble Creek Trail
Salt Creek

Rich and Tumble Creek Trails share a common trailhead, so they can be hiked as a circuit. They both offer good brook trout fishing and scenery, and future improvements to Salt Creek Trail will make another loop possible with Tumble Creek Trail. Bikers note: Trails in this area are closed to mountain bikes because of the Buffalo Peaks Wilderness Study Area.

Rich and Tumble are located on the USGS Jones Hill and South Peak quads. Salt Creek is located on Jones Hill, Marmot Peak and Harvard Lakes quads.

ROAD DIRECTIONS: Take Hwy. 285 between Antero Junction and Fairplay. Two country roads lead away from this highway toward Weston Pass: Take either one, depending, on which direction you are coming from. Both Park County 22 and Park County 5 head west for about 7 miles, then join. Three miles west of this union, look for a parking area beside the stream. The USGS topo marks this spot as Rich Creek Campground, but there is no campground.

TUMBLE and SALT CREEK TRAILS can also be approached from the Buffalo Peaks Road (FS-431), which leaves Hwy. 285 about 13 miles south of Fairplay. To find SALT CREEK TRAILHEAD, go about five miles to a big sagebrush park and watch for a road on your left (FS-431.2D), which leads less than a quarter mile to a closure. Walk up the closed road to hit SALT CREEK TRAIL.

To find TUMBLE, stay on FS-431. Just over 8.5 miles from the highway, the road enters a clearing where a sawmill once stood. The road then becomes primitive. Passenger cars may proceed about 1/2 mile farther to park at the road closure above Lynch Creek. After crossing Lynch Creek, the road leads about 3/4 mile down to a point where a southwestern tributary joins TUMBLE CREEK and the main trail. Turn left to climb the main trail toward Buffalo Meadows.

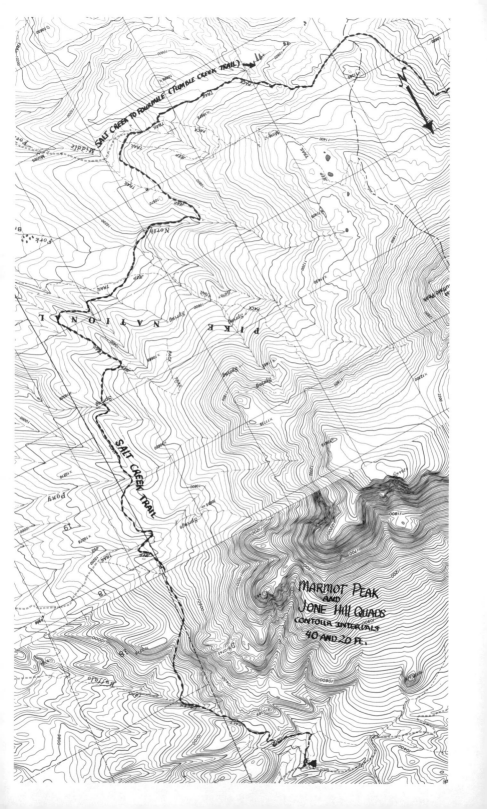

To access other parts of SALT CREEK TRAIL, take Salt Creek Road (FS-435) off Hwy. 285 less than two miles north of Antero Junction. About five miles from the highway, the road forks. To the left is FS-436, a rough road requiring power and high ground clearance. To the right is Salt Creek Road, suitable for passenger cars. Both access the trail.

RICH CREEK, Forest Service #616, 6 miles one way, but can be hiked as an 11.5 mile circuit with Tumble Creek; elevation gain 1,890 ft., loss 520 ft. Features mountain meadow fishing with grand vista of South Park region.

Cross Rich Creek on a footbridge constructed by South Park High School students, follow the path upstream for a few yards and you come to a fork marked "Tumble Creek" to the left and "Rich Creek" to the right. Turning right, the trail crosses and recrosses Rich Creek, then grows steeper before breaking out of the timber into a high valley. From the edge of the valley you can see the mountains and flats of the South Park region. A weathered snag has toppled beside the trail, adding itself to the vista.

Ahead lies a long, curving valley, wide open and grassy, with Rich Creek often hidden in the boggy brush at the valley center. DOW research shows that brook trout fishing is very good here,but your trail turns into a cattle path, for this valley is grazed under permit from the Forest Service.

As you start up the headwaters basin, the trail used to be nothing but a cattle path that faded into brush, but now the trail is better defined. The beaver corps of engineers is constantly shifting their works, however, so be aware that the stream crossing might be flooded.

You are headed for the low wooded saddle that separates the Rich Creek headwaters from the watershed beyond. To complete the circuit, climb over this wooded saddle and follow the trail down to Tumble Creek, another good brookie stream.

TUMBLE CREEK, Forest Service #617, about 6 miles one way to Buffalo Meadows and the junction that links this trail with Rich Creek; elevation gain 1,670 ft. Features many beaver ponds and stream fishing.

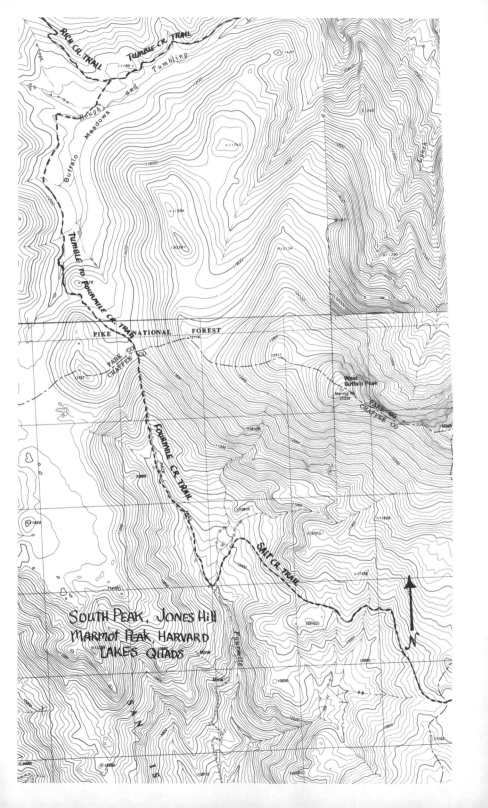

The National Forest Visitor Map shows this trail to be very long, but parts of the upper end are a little indistinct. We have told you how to use Rich Creek to join this trail high up to make a long circuit, but we will describe Tumble Creek from the bottom trailhead for the benefit of those not making the circuit.

Cross the footbridge at the Rich-Tumble Trailhead and take the left fork that is marked "Tumble Creek, 2 miles." That means it is two miles to the creek itself. Hike up and over a high ridge, then drop down into the watershed known on topo maps as Rough and Tumbling Creek. As soon as you arrive, you will see beaver ponds extending up and down the valley. Some will be abandoned, others active, a good brook trout area.

Your trail has been rerouted in this area, now staying on the northwest side of Tumble Creek until it crosses just above the junction with Lynch Creek. Cross on a large timber at a popular campsite above the mouth of Lynch Creek.

A few yards farther up, another tributary enters Tumble Creek from the southwest. At this point the trail veers away from Tumble and follows the tributary a short distance before continuing up the ridge that separates the two streams. For awhile you are away from both creeks, then the path takes you to a log crossing Tumble. Here the creek earns its name, tumbling down rocks in a narrow gorge. And here you start up switchbacks beside that stream. This is the most difficult part of the trail, but perhaps the most beautiful.

Above lies a wide-open valley where Tumble Creek snakes along, growing slower as you follow it up. Soon the trail is only a cattle path that may wander anywhere, so you simply follow the valley as far as you please. Theoretically, Tumble Creek Trail extends up the valley to its head, then changes its name (but not its number) to Fourmile Creek Trail as it slides into the San Isabel National Forest and joins Salt Creek Trail farther down. Careful.

If you want to hike the Rich Creek circuit, the third tributary on your right is the one that leads to the saddle ridge connecting to Rich Creek, but the number of active tributaries may change in wet or dry times, so watch for a signpost that marks the route.

SALT CREEK TRAIL, Forest Service #618, 11.6 miles one way, elevation gain 2,270 ft., loss 2,230 ft.; rated easy to moderate. Features access to Buffalo Peaks Wilderness Study Area.

This long trail begins in the Pike National Forest, then wanders into the San Isabel National Forest, where it finally joins an extension of Tumble Trail, which is called Fourmile Trail in that area. Our description is tentative because more trail work is being done, and part of the Tumble-Fourmile extension is somewhat indistinct.

The first half mile is single track, then becomes primitive road for another half mile, then changes to single track again. It skirts the lower slopes of Buffalo Peak, with views to the east and southeast across South Park. This is bighorn country, though the terrain is gentle aspen and evergreen forest with only a few steep spots. Eventually your trail hits Salt Creek Road (FS-435), a passenger car access. From here the trail drops down to cross Brush Park and a branch of Salt Creek, then goes up over a ridge crowned with bristlecone pines. At the Middle Fork of Salt Creek the trail crosses FS-436, a rough road. About a quarter of a mile farther, you'll find the remains of an old sawmill.

From here the trail wanders up between the Middle and South forks of Salt Creek, up through country that still shows the effects of heavy logging in the early part of the century. Eventually your path finds a flat area where trees are sparse, then crosses a saddle, dropping down into the San Isabel National Forest to join Fourmile Creek and its trail. Though the route is not always distinct, it is possible to hike up the Fourmile Trail to a saddle and over into Buffalo Meadows, where the trail is known as Tumble Creek. Parts of this route are faint, so watch for posts in Buffalo Meadows that will help you find Tumble Trail lower down.

The Forest Service also plans to reestablish an extension of Salt Creek Trail leading from the FS-431 trailhead to Lynch Creek, thus making still another loop with Tumble Creek.

End

GIFT IDEA

Our Guide Makes a Great Gift for Any Outdoor Person. Now you can have an author-signed copy sent directly to a friend anywhere in the United States. Just complete this form (please print neatly; this is your mailing label) and return with your check or money order for $18.95 plus $4.50 shipping and handling. Colorado residents add $1.23 sales tax. Allow three to four weeks for delivery.

Squeezy Press
P.O. Box 60412
Colorado Springs, CO
80906-2455

To:

Name: _____

Address: _____

_____

City: _____ State: _____ Zip: _____